Beleaguered Tower: The Dilemma of Political Catholicism in Wilhelmine Germany. Ronald J. Ross.

Communal Families in the Balkans: The Zadruga. Robert F. Byrnes, ed.

Understanding World Politics. Kenneth W. Thompson.

Diplomacy and Revolution: The Soviet Mission to Switzerland, 1918. Alfred Erich Senn.

The New Corporatism: Social-Political Structures in the Iberian World. Fredrick B. Pike and Thomas Stritch, eds.

America in Change: Reflections on the 60's and 70's. Ronald Weber, ed.

Social Change in the Soviet Union. Boris Meissner, ed.

Foreign Assistance: A View from the Private Sector. Kenneth W. Thompson.

Hispanismo, 1898–1936: Spanish Conservatives and Liberals and Their Relations with Spanish America. Fredrick B. Pike.

Democracy in Crisis: New Challenges to Constitutional Democracy in the Atlantic Area. E.A. Goerner, ed.

The Task of Universities in a Changing World. Stephen D. Kertesz, ed.

The Church and Social Change in Latin America. Henry A. Landsberger, ed.

Revolution and Church: The Early History of Christian Democracy, 1798–1901. Hans Maier.

The Overall Development of Chile. Mario Zañartu, S.J., and John J. Kennedy, eds.

The Catholic Church Today: Western Europe. M.A. Fitzsimons, ed.

Contemporary Catholicism in the United States. Philip Gleason, ed.

The Major Works of Peter Chaadaev. Raymond T. McNally.

A Russian European: Paul Miliukov in Russian Politics. Thomas Riha.

INTERNATIONAL STUDIES OF THE
COMMITTEE ON INTERNATIONAL RELATIONS
UNIVERSITY OF NOTRE DAME

A Search for Stability: U.S. Diplomacy Toward Nicaragua, 1925–1933. William Kamman.

Freedom and Authority in the West. George N. Shuster, ed.

Theory and Practice: History of a Concept from Aristotle to Marx. Nicholas Lobkowicz.

Coexistence: Communism and Its Practice in Bologna, 1945–1965. Robert H. Evans.

Marx and the Western World. Nicholas Lobkowicz, ed.

Argentina's Foreign Policy 1930–1962. Alberto A. Conil Paz and Gustavo E. Ferrari.

Italy after Fascism, A Political History, 1943–1965. Giuseppe Mammerella.

The Volunteer Army and Allied Intervention in South Russia, 1917–1921. George A. Brinkley.

Peru and the United States, 1900–1962. James C. Carey.

Empire by Treaty: Britain and the Middle East in the Twentieth Century. M.A. Fitzsimons.

The USSR and the UN's Economic and Social Activities. Harold Karan Jacobson.

Death in the Forest: The Story of the Katyn Forest Massacre. J.K. Zawodny.

Bolshevism: An Introduction to Soviet Communism, 2nd ed. Waldemar Gurian.

German Protestants Face the Social Question. William O. Shanahan.

Soviet Policy Toward International Control of Atomic Energy. Joseph L Nogee.

The Russian Revolution and Religion, 1917–1925. Edited and translated by Boleslaw Szczesniak.

Freedom and Reform in Latin America. Fredrick B. Pike, ed.

Catholicism, Nationalism, and Democracy in Argentina. John J. Kennedy.

Life and Politics in a Venetian Community

Santa Maria in the fifteenth century

Life and Politics in a Venetian Community

Robert H. Evans

University of Notre Dame Press
Notre Dame & London

Pages xxiv-xxv: An aerial view of Santa Maria

Library of Congress Cataloging in Publication Data

Evans, Robert H
Life and politics in a Venetian village.

Bibliography: p.
1. Italy—Social conditions—Case studies.
2. Villages—Italy—Case studies. 3. Italy—Economic conditions—Case studies. I. Title.
HN475.E82 309.1′45′32 76–21256
ISBN 0–268–01256–3
ISBN 0–268–01257–1 pbk.

Manufactured in the United States of America.

En mémoire de Charles Antoine Micaud,
maître insigne

Contents

Preface

MOST AUTHORS WHO HAVE WRITTEN ABOUT ITALIAN communities, mainly sociologists, anthropologists and economists, have studied the South.[1] I propose to discuss life and politics in Santa Maria, a village in the Veneto, in the northeastern part of the country. I emphasize change in the community, particularly in the area of politics, but include many nonpolitical factors that have an impact on the village's political development and that contribute to an overall appreciation of Marian society. Rather than being a theoretical model open to many pitfalls,[2] this monograph is descriptive. It indicates that in a united community change and progress can be self-generated to a large extent. Many of the social and political situations described also point to the fact that the differences between the Mediterranean and European sections of Italy may not be as strong as has often been assumed.[3]

The study spans a century (1866–1969), from Santa Maria's formal integration into the modern Italian state to the end of my sojourn. I focus on the village's entire social system, emphasizing the changes in the centers of effective power, tracing the community's evolution from a system of equilibrium in the nineteenth century to its present configuration. Undoubtedly every community is unique, but uniqueness and distinctiveness are clearly different. While communities are cells of a larger organization, each village is different, and the distinctive characteristics of this difference are susceptible to comparison in terms of culture, socialization, power, authority, participation and decision-making, the essential ingredients in the world of politics.

Chapter 1 offers a brief physical description of the community, a summary of its history prior to 1866 and an analysis of its position in the Veneto, all of which have a bearing on the Mariani's attitudes towards change. The next chapter studies political development prior to 1951, when emigration reached its peak, emphasizing the population's attitudes towards governmental administration, economic change and politics. These factors contribute substantially to the political milieu that shapes the socialization process, which is dealt with in Chapter 4. Chapter 3 examines the demographic and economic situation of the community that constitutes the base for Santa Maria's future growth. The final chapters address the political developments of the last twenty years, the competing groups and parties, elections and political participation, and the decision-making processes. In spite of the artificial divisions of the schema and the relative neglect of certain themes (manifestations of religious practice, kinship links), I hope this study will give the reader a picture of life in Santa Maria, its particular and unique flavor, and still allow him to compare the community to others.

From the outset my choice of communities was limited. Since other studies had focused upon the South I felt a northern community should be examined. Prior work in communist-dominated Bologna induced me to seek a city that would lean politically more toward the Christian Democrats. Also to truly get to know the people I believed that a village would be more appropriate than a town. Language injected an extra dimension: in villages everybody understands and speaks Italian, but dialects remain very popular. I felt my acceptance in the community would be facilitated if I could learn the vernacular, relying on Italian for only the first few months of my stay. The difficulties of the Emilian and Ligurian dialects limited my choice to Lombardy, Piedmont and the Veneto. These areas had the advantage of being closely connected to the bulk of Europe, physically and historically, while their dialects did not present insurmountable obstacles.

Size was a critical factor in choosing a suitable village. I wanted a community that would be "manageable," with a population not greater than three thousand inhabitants, a village with all the organs of local government (a *comune*), and run by Christian Democrats. Since a potential for change was also required, I searched for a village with a school system extending beyond the primary grades and an economically active population where the secondary and tertiary sectors would have outdistanced the primary groups, in brief a rapidly changing economy. Finally, the community was to be neither too near a major center, nor cut off from the outside world.

The data bank of the Carlo Cattaneo Institute in Bologna was of considerable help in my preliminary investigation to locate a community during the summer of 1967. From the extensive holdings of ecological and political data on Italian municipalities I was able to identify those communities that met the criteria I had selected. The latter part of the summer was spent visiting these villages, interviewing mayors, priests and municipal secretaries on the feasibility of my study, gauging attitudes, considering housing facilities and building up a general impression of the communities. Professor Sabino S. Acquaviva of the University of Padua was kind enough to indicate, among the villages of the Veneto I had chosen, which fell into what he has termed "sociological zones of tension";[4] and I devoted particular care to these. After much deliberation, I chose Santa Maria in the province of Padua. It met the criteria I had set: I believed I could establish a good working relationship with the local authorities as well as with members of the University of Padua, housing did not appear to be a major obstacle, the village was congenial, and the memory of Petrarch, who died there, added an extra attraction.

Traditionally, students of local communities have sought to hide the names of the villages they study. After considerable thought and discussion with the villagers, in spite of the desires of many who urged me to use real names, I concluded that it would be in the interest of all if the village's anonymity was insured. Sooner or later I doubt not that the actual name of the community will come to the fore and the identity of the characters will easily be recognized by the locals. This is all the more true since partial findings have been published in Italian[5] and commented upon in the village. However, this book emphasizes more personal dimensions and, with the "real people" in mind, I have sought to temper my judgments; at least I have tried to be no more severe—some might say uncharitable—than the locals tend to be with each other.

To fulfill the aims I set for myself, total immersion in village life was necessary. During 1967 and 1968 I accumulated as much general and background material on the community as was feasible from a distance, to facilitate my acceptance by the villagers the following year. In June and early July of 1968 I completed my bibliographical research in the libraries of Milan. While I could trace the decline in the size of the goat herds, I knew little about the actual life and politics of Santa Maria! The local archives provided a modicum of information: most of the material had been destroyed in the fire of 1943 and what was available beyond that date was essentially administrative in nature. Though it provided some clues I had to wait until the mayor and his predecessor opened their private files to get at "touchy" matters. A good deal of information for the years 1918–1921 and 1937–1945 was in the city library of Este, the repository of the private files of Carlo Marastoni, a deceased village notable. My major source of information turned out to be the State Archives in Padua. I encountered few difficulties in surveying the period 1866–1918, but it took considerable persuasion to obtain the documents for 1918–1944. The progress of my research made people more willing to talk about events of the past because they were convinced I knew what had occurred. The facts were seldom new; but the narration helped to re-create the atmosphere, characterize the personalities in the community and point out resentments that still cloud the daily relationships of certain families.

The present constituted the major, and the most delicate, focus of my study, since the enterprise could succeed only if I managed to build a relationship of confidence with extremely cautious, at times diffident, people and forge a network of trustworthy informants. The credibility of the participant observer can easily be shattered; and I proceeded with as much caution as I felt was possible after I had made the purpose of my sojourn in the community clear to all. The town hall and the parish were informed before my arrival and through the good offices of a friend in Padua I was interviewed by the local newspaper. It reported that my aim was to see how people lived, acted and governed. My assertions did not allay all suspicions. A few people remained convinced I was on the CIA payroll, and others thought I had to be studying Petrarch because nothing else was worthwhile in the village.

The children in school, my family lodged in a splendid sixteenth-century house, and my promotion to the rank of village photographer, all helped my relations with the various groups and notables. The parish priest was willing to entertain my questions and I learned much from the caution with which he supplied answers. His young assistant was more straightforward in keeping me informed on parish affairs, and his removal in February was a serious loss for me since he also provided a direct link to the youth groups. In the town hall I could not have asked for more as my acquaintance with the mayor and his predecessor grew deeper. A few of my ideas became theirs and I was invited to observe many a meeting, formal and informal, of the local government. Other contacts in the town hall, such as the secretary and the clerks, came while I worked with the municipal records. Through my acquaintance with the village youth (gained while I was lodged at the inn they patronized), I got to know the members of the opposition reasonably well, though with two exceptions I was never considered part of this group. However, my informants kept me posted on what was going on. I encountered no difficulties in maintaining good relationships with another group, which I labelled the anarchist opposition: unfortunately, the quality of their information deteriorated as their consumption of wine increased during the day.

Generally speaking, once a contact was made and renewed once or twice, people were willing to answer my questions. However, I gathered much of my material informally through social conversation around the table or at the café. My information was limited and fragmented whatever the piecing together of material I was able to accomplish. Attempting to create social situations as natural as possible, I did not use a tape recorder after a few experiences I considered disastrous, but committed information to memory and brief notes that I transcribed in the evening while bringing my journal up to date.

What I had gathered from my conversations with the village inhabitants needed to be verified and completed by more reliable data to present a less impressionistic view of the community. The town records provided the basic information on the dead, the living and the emigrants (name, age, sex, origin, marital status, address), and for each I compiled a form. For the 2,040 official residents I added several other items of information: place of residence (Did they effectively live in the territory of Santa Maria?); location (village, hills or plains); type of employment; location of employment; full-time employment or not; property ownership; size of holdings, financial situation; education; religious practice; health; political opinions. I shied away from a direct sample of the population considering the small number of inhabitants that would constitute the statistical universe, and fearing that an inquiry into such personal matters as those indicated above would not elicit accurate responses. Instead I relied heavily upon three trusted informants. All categories but health and religion were completed by the town clerk, who has always lived in the village and is familiar with every detail of his fellow citizens' lives. Religion was completed by the parish priest who has been in Santa Maria since 1937, and he also checked the other categories. Finally, the doctor reviewed the preceding information before filling in the column which concerned him directly. This task accomplished, I checked the data myself, informally whenever possible, and formally with twenty people whom I knew best. In nearly all cases and categories the information proved accurate.

I gathered further data in the spring of 1969 during the elaboration of the town plan when I was given access to all information. The material related to 345 family heads and covered the size and condition of habitations, hygienic facilities, heating, electricity, water, aesthetic qualities, population density, and possibilities and desires to move and where. Finally to verify my own perception of the power situation I asked twenty-five residents to name and rank the ten people they thought were the most important and influential in the village. In this way I obtained a reputational scale that was helpful in my study.

As can be seen, the monograph would have never been written without the help of the many people in Santa Maria who submitted themselves with good graces to my questions, many of which were clearly impertinent. I am grateful that so many of them extended their friendship to me. Most will remain anonymous but they are often in my thoughts.

Though he cannot be named, the archpriest greatly facilitated my insertion in the local society and shared with me much of his knowledge and time. The same is true of the present and past mayors of Santa Maria, the town clerks and the local physician. I am greatly indebted to them.

Dottore Enrico Parisotto of Padua made it possible for us to live in Santa Maria's Taverna di Laura, owned by the provincial tourist office (EPT) of which he is the director. We often reminisce about the splendor of these accommodations. . . . Professor Letterio Briguglio, Director of the Archivio di Stato, was most cooperative in helping me secure documents which otherwise I might have ignored. A special word is due to Professor Enzo Bandelloni of the Faculty of Engineering in Padua who shared his knowledge, ideas, *carissimi amici,* table and wine cellar, and above all his friendship with me and my family.

In Bologna, Mrs. Vittoria Polacchini of the Carlo Cattaneo Institute provided me with great assistance in searching out the community in the computerized wealth of her files.

In the United States, the Committee on International Relations of the University of Notre Dame headed by Professor Stephen Kertesz provided me with the financial resources necessary for my stay in Italy. The University of Virginia's Committee on Summer Grants afforded me the means to write up this study. My research assistants over the years, Richard Linquanti, Thomas Chadwick, Mary Stevens and Michael Yavorsky, contributed skills, ideas and editorial assistance that are gratefully acknowledged.

My wife and children deserve more credit that can be said, not only for the information they provided me with while we lived in Santa Maria, but also for the patience with which they have supported this enterprise.

To all who have been mentioned, and to all in Santa Maria, go my deepest thanks.

And the soft quiet hamlet where he dwelt . . .
. . . shows a distant prospect far away
Of busy cities, now in vain displayed,
For they can lure no further; and the ray
Of a bright Sun can make sufficient holiday,

Developing the mountains, leaves and flowers,
And shining in the brawling brook, where-by
Clear as its current, glide the sauntering hours
With a calm languor, which, though to the eye
Idlesse it seem, hath its morality–
If from society we learn to live

Lord Byron
Childe Harold's Pilgrimage

PROVINCE OF PADUA
MILAN
VENICE
SANTA MARIA
BOLOGNA
FLORENCE
ROME
NAPLES

1. The Community in Times of Change

SANTA MARIA, A COMMUNITY OF SLIGHTLY OVER TWO thousand inhabitants, rests on the slopes of the Euganean Hills in the Veneto. This village, one that I would come to consider "my own," leaves the visitor with an impression of harmony, of near perfect blending with the surroundings, of unity with nature. The image hardly changes as the seasons go by: in summer the haze produced by the heat, in spring the dazzling sun, in fall and winter the colors and the mists of the plains, all seem to push the village into the slope on which it is built, and hide it from the approaching tourist's eye until he is practically at the first houses and then the town emerges.

Neither the isolated island-village floating on the plains nor the more stereotyped Italian hilltop town, Santa Maria is located on an arch from which it derives its name.[1] From north to south the hills descend abruptly from Monte Venton (407 meters) to Monte Castello (108 meters), while they extend rather lazily from east to west, from Monte Calata (135 meters) to the Sasso and the Marlunghe (161 meters). The village rests on the conch, somewhat like a cornucopia, limited by the east-south encounter of the hills, occasionally overflowing to the west. The altitude in the town varies from 42 meters on the lower square, Piazza Roma, to 80 meters on the upper square, Piazza San Marco, while a distance of 200 meters separates the two, providing quite a climb. Approaching the village from the south or the southeast by either of the two main roads, the visitor's view is obstructed by Monte Bignago, Monte Ricco, and Monte Bevilacqua until suddenly he discovers the village, literally unchanged from what it was four centuries ago.

The town developed around the two churches on the squares; and the irregularities of the terrain prevented building along continuous lines, thus avoiding the massiveness of fortifications or the dreariness of parallel rows. The houses remain connected by low walls of containment which line the two meandering streets, via Guido di Santa Maria and via Roma, the village's main arteries of communication. The use of local building stone (limestone or *scaglia*) helps the edifices harmonize with their surroundings, while a fortunate yet accidental disposition of the volumes and use of colors attenuates the impression that the larger palazzi might produce if they stood in isolation. These are generally built against the slopes, and when not, have taken on or been given hues which make them less obtrusive: the church, imposing as it is, hardly stands out from a distance and blends into the village texture. A careful use of empty spaces links the houses, the village and the countryside. The incline is steep enough and space sufficiently limited that gardens are mainly clumps of trees, jujubes, figs, cypress, laurels, pomegranates, acacias. Strewn over the side of the hill and occasionally interspersed with olive trees to the southeast and west, they form a green mantle for the buildings, a cover which blends almost without interruption into the vineyards and olive groves that constitute the community's main source of wealth.

Recently a few unfortunate efforts have been made to modify this picture: one house, built in a false moorish style, has sprung up on the hill and can be singled out for its ugliness. A few deep red houses with multicolor balconies and split level roofs "alla Americana" have appeared on the outskirts, more often than not built against the opinion and orders of the Fine Arts commission: but all told (and not considering 152 minor violations which, according to the mayor, existed in 1969), there are no more than seven houses in the village that detract from the overall harmony. All attempts to ignore the building codes were brought to an abrupt end in December 1968, when a four-story house in an advanced stage of construction was ordered by the local authorities to be razed to the ground to preserve the fundamental unity and harmony of the village and insure the enforcement of the law. It is as if a very peculiar and certainly not modern sense of civility had survived in this small community that views itself as "the summation of such things [as] its trees, flowers, water and sculpture, of its . . . air, of its . . . sun, of the color of its sky, of its terrain, of a way of life, and a history."[2] And this is what constitutes the overall beauty of Santa Maria: ". . . it possesses an architecture which has understood and loved all these non-architectural considerations."[3] One is tempted to say, discovering such a community, that it has an inbred sense of aesthetics.

This pleasant impression, however, is essentially a product of the village's past, its isolation and poverty. Today the inhabitants are torn between the lures of the city—its multi-family dwellings and the conveniences commonly associated with modernity—and the unalienating pace of life and sense of community that are characteristic of a village. But it is not only chauvinism or pride that inspire the peasant who asked me: "Honestly, have you ever before seen anything more harmonious, more pure?" Tilling the hills with the last team of oxen in the village he had time to contemplate it, and was not too far from the truth.

The famous and the humble come to visit and pay their tribute to the memory of Petrarch, the Prince of Poets, who spent the last four years of his life in Santa Maria and is buried there. Poets and travelers who have written about the village naturally do so in reference to the Tuscan poet.[4] "Yesterday I was in [Santa Maria] to see Petrarch's house and his tomb: clouds, the earth without shadows, a perfect view, the Euganean Hills designed, engraved, trees, hedges, roads maybe, a few cypress, many olive trees: pure Tuscany. For this he came to die here, to enjoy his land without the Tuscans."[5] Visitors are struck by the beauty of the surroundings, ". . . warm and welcoming, disposing themselves naturally in beautiful forms, in the manner of Italian landscapes."[6] A new Arcadia seems to be reinvented, where time flows slowly, and where values are preserved and change is imperceptible, as Byron noted.[7]

To the litterati the village is an object of pilgrimage, as foretold by Boccacio, ". . . hitherto obscure, [it] will become famous among the nations. The sailor returning from distant shores will gaze with emotion at the Euganean Hills, and say to his companions: 'At the foot of those hills, Petrarch is sleeping.' "[8] All that is not Petrarch is neglected. "[The community] is immobile through the centuries on the top of the hill. For centuries it has been the same, like when Petrarch. . . ."[9]

In reality the poverty of the village over the centuries leads one to take a more melancholy view, when seeking to go beyond the few monuments that commemorate the great man's sojourn in his "Helicon in the Hills." The first student of the local mores, describing the conditions of life in 1830, declared, ". . . this village, so beautiful because of the nature of its surroundings, could not be more squalid in itself."[10] A century later, a resident, usually sympathetic to the community of which he had been mayor, could trace no different picture and could only lament the state of decay of what was supposedly a national shrine.[11]

But Santa Maria has gone through a total change since World War II, particularly during the 1960s. The streets which were no more than dusty earth-beaten tracks in summer and quagmires in winter have been paved, the more prominent houses restored, and the more modest ones are rapidly undergoing a process of rehabilitation. The community has been reborn and squalor eliminated. The old "villae dominicae" have been rejuvenated and adapted tastefully to the twentieth century. Attempts are being made to return the decaying thirteenth-century dwellings to their original function; the poet's house and the two major churches have either been restored to their original condition or, when that has been impossible, the original elements still extant have been emphasized.[12]

In this process the main foci of village life have regained their decorum, reinforcing the identity and pride of the villagers who are divided according to the proximity of their dwellings to either the lower or upper squares, being classified as either from "up there" or "down there." As the visitor ascends from the tomb towards the house, following the steep road encased between the *scaglia* walls and overhanging gardens, he can sense two coexisting worlds, one near the church and one near the town hall, united by their reverence for the poet.

A Historical Overview Prior to 1866

Archeological findings indicate that a lake-dwelling community had settled on the present site of Santa Maria some two thousand years before Christ.[13] These Euganeans, "well born and noble,"[14] the remnants of Hercules' mythical army, were displaced by the

Veneti who were also of Greek origin, according to Livy.[15] Ateste, which they founded, was conquered by Rome; and in 90 A.D. Domitian granted Roman citizenship to the Veneti of the tenth region's Atestinian colony, which included Santa Maria.

The earliest written material referring explicitly to Santa Maria dates from 985, when it changed from "locus et fundus" to "castrum."[16] In 1040 it belonged to the Este family and was given to their vassal, the Count of Abano, in 1077. The castle is mentioned in documents of 1171. In general the feudal system prevailed,[17] though on the farms that had been granted to the Church at the beginning of the eleventh century by Litolfo di Carrara and Rodolfo of Normandy, "of French race and inhabitant of Santa Maria," the tenants were free men, "*liberi homines*."[18]

From 1257 to 1310 Santa Maria was part of the Paduan Republic and a seat of importance governed by a special magistrate, a Paduan of at least twenty-five years of age, who received exactly the same salary as his counterpart in Fantolon (who traditionally had been far more important). The location of the castle which dominated the plains put Santa Maria in a position that proved costly for the village while under Carrara rule, between 1310 and 1405. The first years of that family's reign brought hardships and the community was ravaged twice in ten years, by Can Grande della Scala in 1312 and Corrado di Vigonza in 1322.[19] However, Santa Maria's eminence was confirmed by its elevation to the rank of *Vicaria*, which gave it control of twenty villages, jurisdiction over 15,000 inhabitants, and, in 1397, a force of 1,200 armed men, 600 of them on horseback.[20]

It was then, in the troubled times of the war between Carrara and Venice, that Petrarch sought peace and retirement in Santa Maria. During the last years of his life, between 1370 and 1374, he described to his protector the plains "denied the fruits of Ceres by the stagnant waters" and the hills "rich in the fruits of Minerva and Bacchus,"[21] but subject to tremendous rain and hail storms.[22] By 1405, when control of Santa Maria passed on to Venice, if we are to believe the proverbs of the times, its population must have been crying for justice, exasperated by bitter misery, conscious of its nothingness.

Venice was known for its wise administration and upheld its

reputation in Santa Maria. The territory was considered to be one of the marches of the Laguna city and it was important that it be reliable and prosperous in order to furnish the city with agricultural products and serve as its first line of defense. Little was changed administratively except that the position of Vicar became elective with a one-year term.[23] To signify its change in status Santa Maria modified its coat of arms to a shield on a red background with a silver hill under a cross and a green garland. The shield symbolized its position in the defense of Venice; the red represented Petrarch, canon of Padua; the garland his elevation to Prince of Poets; the silver hill the fertility of the hills; the cross fidelity to the Church. For a century Santa Maria lived in peace. In 1509 it proved its attachment to Venice by spontaneously joining with it against the League of Cambrai and taking several offensive actions. Rallying to the battle cry of "Marco! Marco!" the Mariani besieged the Duke of Ferrara in Fantolon, forcing him to surrender,[24] while in 1513 "Galeazzo di Pii, condottiere under papal orders, with his company and one hundred imperial soldiers . . . was killed and many of his men carved to pieces by the peasants of Santa Maria . . . who took twenty horses and sixty soldiers prisoners."[25]

The patterns of land ownership that were established during this period remained unchanged for centuries, and the hills, "not only covered with vineyards but also olive groves and orchards, . . . provided the city with delicate oil and grapes."[26] Monasteries (S. Benedetto, S. Sofia, etc.) and Paduan nobility (Zabarella, Beolco)[27] shared the land with the ancestors of the present owners: De Perezolis (Perazol), Fortunius (Fortuna), Brizante (Brizzante), Siverius (Sivieri), Bardino (Bardini), Tosi (Tosi).[28] By 1559 the plains, originally communal property, had passed with the Vicar's connivance into the hands of three families, the Lanzoni, the Franciosi and the Andreoli, though only the Lanzoni appear to have successfully developed their share, south of Monte Bignago, where the large farm they built still stands.[29] One may surmise that the Lanzoni and the other owners provided some work for the local labor force, but that some resentment must have existed among the small landowners in the hills who lost their free pasture rights in the plains to the wealthier Venetian families.

In 1612 the village, with about six hundred inhabitants, was given full Venetian citizenship and granted the privilege of erecting a statue of the Lion of Saint Mark on a column which stood in the center of the upper square facing the Loggia of the Vicars.[30] This was a period of prosperity: the churches were restored and embellished, while painters of some fame such as Palma the Young, Damiani di Castelfranco, and Pellizzari decorated the buildings.[31] However, Santa Maria declined with Venice: by 1700 the Vicar's residence was in ruins, and by 1747 the population had grown to only 647 inhabitants.[32] Misery was once again returning; as before, "the laborer, like the dog, licks the hand that beats him."[33] The Mariani felt no regret when the treaty of Campo Formio in 1797 submitted them to Austrian administration: their first act was to destroy the column that had supported the Lion of Saint Mark. Until 1815 the community was administered alternatively by the French and the Austrians.[34] After that the Austrians took control for fifty-one years, whereupon Santa Maria returned to the Italian fold.

Santa Maria and the Veneto

Throughout its history Santa Maria has always gravitated towards the Italian peninsula and in spite of all its virtues the Austrian administration was but a parenthesis. In 1866 the Veneto was the last province to join the Kingdom of Italy, bringing with it a long tradition of independence and pride, of republican government and a strong *Italianità*. Its history explains many of its peculiar traits.

The Veneto is known as "White Italy," because it did not have to live under the domination of the popes, and never hesitated to fight them when necessary. Not having known the iniquities of papal administration, it has acquired a very strong tradition of conservative Catholicism, making it a bastion of orthodoxy. The region has the highest ratio of clergy to population in Italy and provides the greatest number of priests to the Church. It is the only Italian region that is not yet clerically understaffed. This background is clearly felt in politics, with the exception of the large urban centers, foremost among which is the new Venice, the industrial Marghera. However, to say that rural Venetians are essentially and only conservative is a misstatement. Possibly because of the past glories of the Serenissima they are far from hostile toward development and look to the future more than to the past—but for them progress cannot be dissociated from order; in fact, order is the key to progress. One is tempted to speak of conservatism à la Francis Joseph, under whose scepter they lived, and who is remembered quite vividly by the present-day inhabitants. Austrian domination has gone, but the efficiency of its administration is often recalled. One got speedier service from the bureaucracy in Vienna than from present-day "monkeys" in Rome. The town clerk in Santa Maria is still ready to argue that perhaps the Veneto made a mistake in joining the Italian Kingdom, and that the error became all the more costly when "misguided Italians" opted for the Republic because "like a family needs a father, people in a nation need a king to obey." This basic conservatism coupled with high religiosity means that over 65 percent of the electorate gives its preference to the Christian Democrats and very few seem concerned with that party's meanderings from right to left and then to right again. In fact, the politicians have been able to change their basic orientations and still retain rural voters' support.

One-fifth of the net income of the Veneto is derived from agriculture, placing the region third in agricultural production in Italy. Although industry has developed considerably since World War II, the province still projects the image of an agricultural land.[35] Venice was always oriented towards international trade and its hinterland was never meant to be more than a granary for the Republic.

Lastly, one of the most delightful traits is the Venetian dialect; and one might even call it a language when it boasts such masters as Ruzzante and Goldoni. A romance dialect, with many words borrowed from Spanish and Arabic, it is softer than Italian, more musical, but also more down to earth and more concrete, one is tempted to say Rabelaisian, in its daily parlance. For some ten centuries it was the official language and has survived in the towns and in the provinces, with its local variations, coexisting with official Italian. At all social levels, and in all age groups, Venetian is still understood and spoken, though unfortunately no longer written but only read. In fact, it gives this province a very strong identity

The village of Santa Maria seen from the north (lime quarries in the background)

The village seen from the south

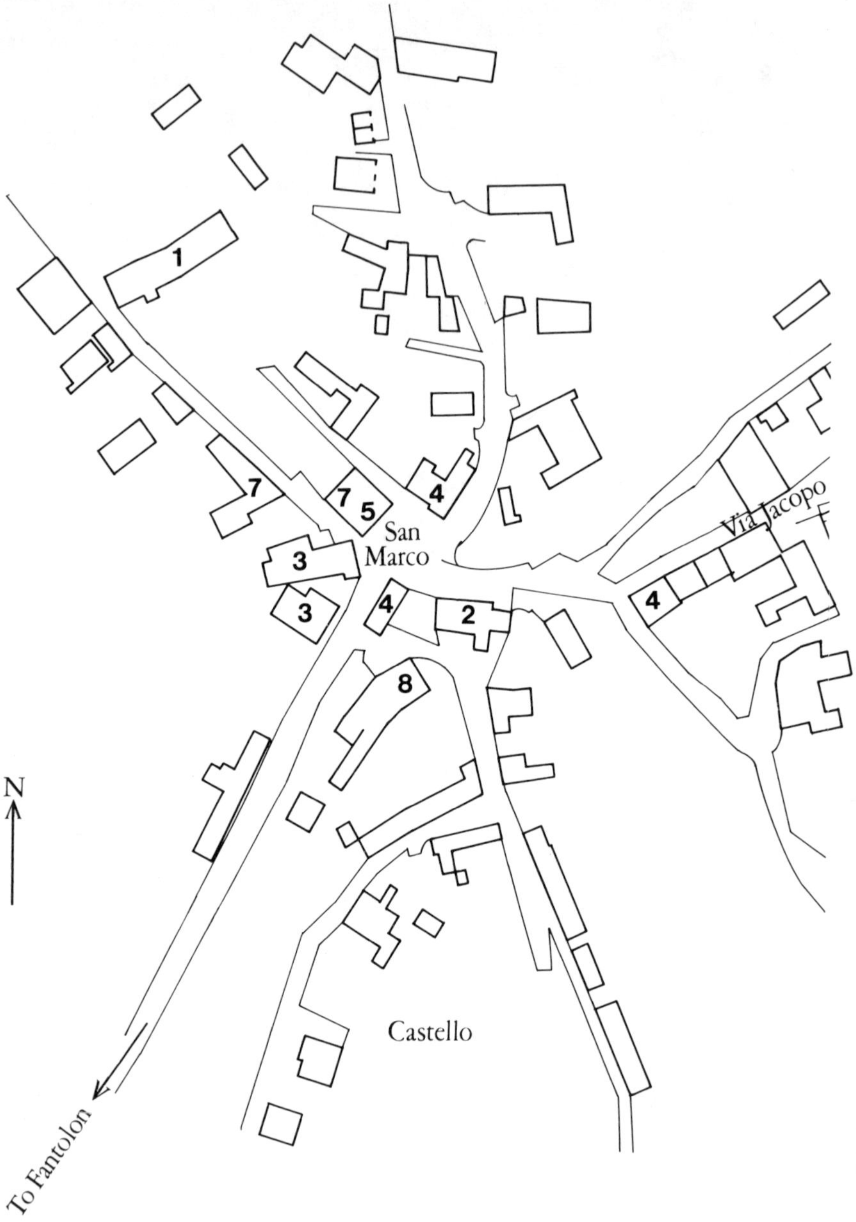

1
7
7
5
4
San
Marco
Via Jacopo
3
3
4
2
4
8
N
Castello
To Fantolon

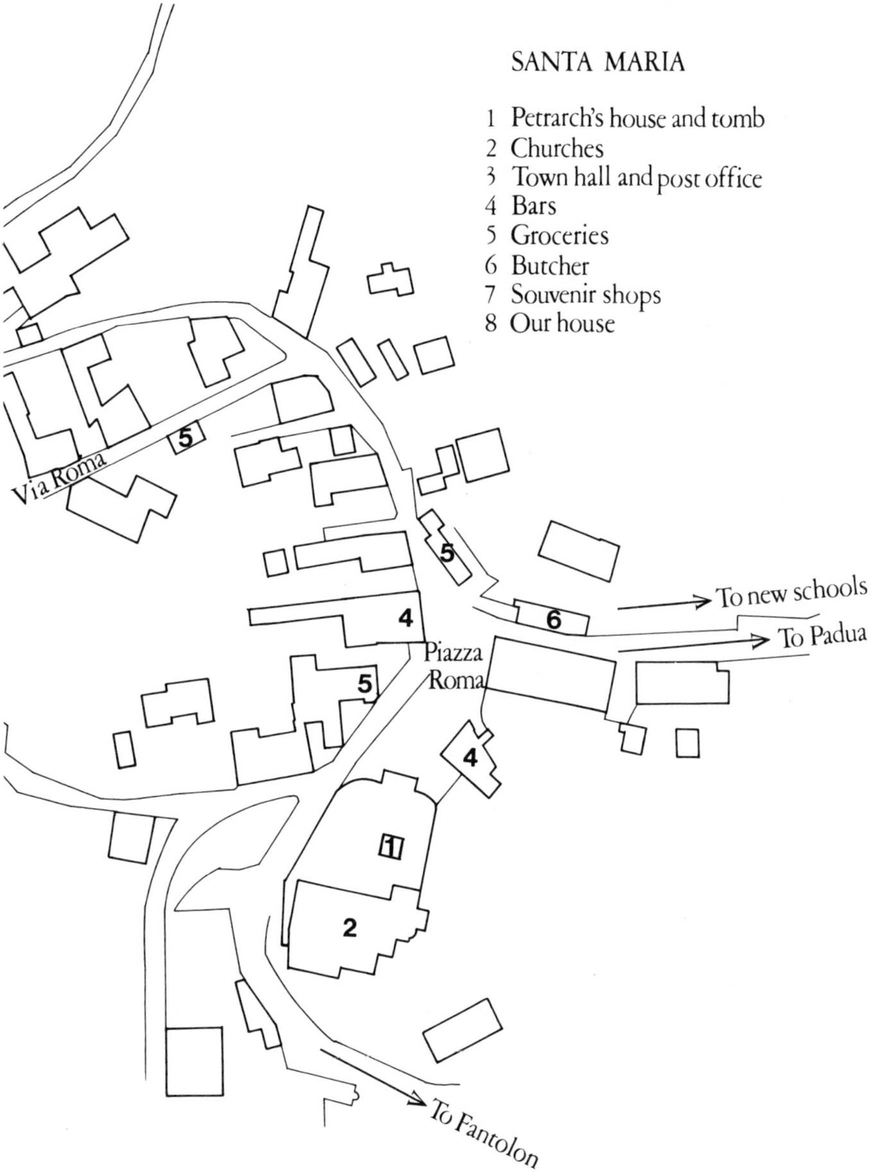
SANTA MARIA
1 Petrarch's house and tomb
2 Churches
3 Town hall and post office
4 Bars
5 Groceries
6 Butcher
7 Souvenir shops
8 Our house
Via Roma
5
5
4
Piazza Roma
5
6
4
To new schools
To Padua
1
2
To Fantolon

Via Jacopo di Santa Maria
(main street)

The parochial church

and flavor, while its generalized usage differentiates the Veneto from the more integrated regions of Central Italy. "It is a culturally and socially homogeneous zone . . . geographically, historically, . . . ethnically. . . . To cross the Po, in a certain sense, means to change worlds, not only geographically but also in what relates to culture, to the very attitudes toward existence considered in its entirety."[36]

Santa Maria, like other villages in fragmented Italy,[37] suffers acutely from campanilismo. The Mariani think of themselves as a very particular breed of Venetians and Italians—in that order. It is not only due to the pride they have developed as custodians of the mortal remains of the poet, but maybe to a subconscious remembrance of the medieval period of greatness when the Vicaria of Santa Maria controlled twenty surrounding villages and parishes. These are "good for nothing" and their inhabitants who come to the village "only create trouble, play with a knife and try to seduce women. Worse, they try to convince us to strike. They are all communists without God and without Law," exclaimed Adolfo Zancanaro, who works in Padua. He added, "We are better, more intelligent, Christians . . . and in any case make wine while they can only grow corn, God dammit!" Certainly to the observer, Santa Maria and its inhabitants do not have traits that would render them unique; in fact they are far from atypical. But in their own minds, the inhabitants remain persuaded of their distinctiveness, of their originality that makes them different from other Italians, a special kind of Venetian subject. These traits contribute to the mosaic that is Italy.

Today the village has entered into the major stream of communication in the Veneto: Padua is the largest pole of attraction to the northeast. Fantolon, four kilometers away from Santa Maria and on the main line of communication between Padua and Bologna, is served by excellent railroad and autostrada connections. Since the mid-fifties a well-paved road has connected these two centers and is linked with the village's lower and upper squares, while another state road joins Santa Maria directly with Padua, closely following the contour of the hills, the last mountains that jut out into the plain of the Adige, standing out like islands in the sea.

Very little of Santa Maria's earlier grandeur survives. Less than a century ago its inhabitants wore a typical costume; it has disappeared. The tradition of earrings being worn by men to indicate the owner's trade has almost totally disappeared. I was able to find only one instance of this habit, in Qualto, six kilometers away from Santa Maria. Only the local dialect remains, slightly different from "classical" Venetian, more Paduan, with even smoother intonations, a softer "s" and the open vowels typical of Chioggia and Burano on the coast,[38] allowing one to distinguish a Mariano from his neighbors a few kilometers away.

Santa Maria is in the midst of an area of ferment and tension. A careful analysis of the Veneto, taking into account religious behavior, agriculture, economic development, political orientation and levels of education, reveals the existence of three different homogeneous zones:[39] Santa Maria is caught between the northern and southern ones in a growing industrial band that extends from Venice to Verona and serves as a cultural and economic pole of attraction, conveying and living in a totally different system of values. The village straddles the northern zone, where the sociocultural fabric is solid, and the southern zone, characterized by a rejection of the traditional values and patterns of life of the extended family. Change, and rapid change, sweeping through the major Italian centers has extended to the countryside, engulfing the smaller communities which, emigration notwithstanding, constituted the backbone of social and political stability in the peninsula and the heart of tradition and conservatism. A careful analysis of the community may give some indication as to the future changes in the nation: the long period of isolation it has known necessarily creates a time-lag with the rest of the country, but this time-lag, created in great part by the physical environment, is becoming shorter and shorter.

Today Santa Maria occupies 1,252 hectares (about 3,120 acres) on the southern slope of the Euganean Hills,[40] the Blue Hills as they could be called for the particular color they take on during the warm summers. Sixty-one percent of the village's territory is in the hills proper and the other 39 percent is in the plain. The average size of a family's holding does not exceed 2.9 hectares or 7.5 acres, a condition at best suited to a subsistence type of economy.

The rich black soil of the plain, reclaimed at the end of the nineteenth century, contrasts sharply with the limestone and *scaglia* hills, constantly subject to erosion, where the topsoil is seldom more than one foot deep. To cultivate this terrain is a hard and ingrate task. The hills have to be terraced and if possible irrigated; in the plain a constant battle takes place with the seeping waters. Watering the hills and reclaiming the plains are two antithetic operations, seldom performed successfully. The problem is rendered more complex by the sub-mediterranean climate, where in summer rainfalls are essentially storms that lead to flash-flooding and considerable erosion, or even worse, to hail storms which in a few minutes destroy the year's crops: for the peasant *la tempesta* is the equivalent of the plague. Since 1657 when the prayer was first used on the feast of the Holy Trinity, the priest and his flock ask God to "curse Satan, all unclean demons and associates, so [they] may have no powers on the clouds in the skies and be unable to send hail, thunder, and lightning and all that is bad for the human race." Temperatures are moderate and olive trees grow extremely well.[41] In winter the fog that invades the plains seldom reaches Piazza San Marco, while in the summer a soft breeze descends in the evenings to moderate the heat of the day. Hence the major problem for agriculture is the nature of the soil and its distribution. However, more important for the general welfare of the village is its isolation.

For nearly five centuries Santa Maria has had to contend with the problem of communications with the outer world. The older illustrations[42]—and not only the romantic ones of the nineteenth century which delight in presenting tormented landscapes—provide us with pictures of mountain paths that linked the village to Fantolon over Monte Ricco to the south, while the only road prior to the 1870s (della Costa) is described by travellers as nearly impassable. With the draining of the plain a new link was established towards the east and Padua, as well as towards the west and Este, but until 1947 it could not be used year-around, since it was subject to constant flooding and sinking under the weight of trucks loaded with peat. As the notable Marastoni puts it, ". . . the roads need to be redone *ab imis*."[43] To the north very little communication was possible because of the higher mountains, but it had to suffice because

Santa Maria was virtually the same in 1950 as in 1880, when the prefectoral commissioner termed it ". . . a rural commune of no importance whatsoever."[44]

This situation had not always existed. Petrarch chose Santa Maria, among other reasons, for the facility of communication with Padua and Ferrara: the village was directly linked to Venice by waterway—still remembered by the site named "the harbor." Following the poet's death it became fashionable for the Venetian and Paduan nobility to live in his shadow. In 1493 the village was frequented in summer as "a great place for recreation"[45] and at the same time an academy to honor the poet was extremely active.[46] When the Venetians discovered the convenience and pleasures of villas on the Brenta at the end of the sixteenth century, Santa Maria returned to its lethargy.

Mariani and Change

The epithet coined for the Mariani by Pietro Chevalier in 1830—*rozzi montagnardi* (crude mountaineers)—stayed with them. There is an admonition still mentioned in the surrounding villages: always be cautious when dealing with a Mariano! A schoolteacher who lived in the village at the end of the 1940s declared that from a social and cultural point of view the people were no different from those she had known in the Apennines, residing over a thousand meters above sea level, a true mountain population.[47] But the epithet should come as no surprise if one remembers the peasants' miserable lot. Even Petrarch remarked on the Mariani's tendency to seek refuge in oblivion, calling them a "drunkard people for whom life is not in blood but in wine."[48] Chevalier's comments, when considered in this light, become more understandable. He says, "So rustic is the place, so crude the fiber nature has endowed those people with, and so hardened are they by their bad habits, that any well born soul can only dislike them."[49] In fact, the chronicle declares that so much medieval ferociousness remains, they maintain no relations with their neighbors, whom they greet "first with stones and then with knives."[50] Arguing with a Mariano was somewhat like challenging him to a duel and the old men still recall the village feasts ending in knifings, or the period when people would kill "for apples on the ground," or "for a handful of earth robbed from a field." More recently we can remember an incident concerning a Mariano who, riding the bus to Padua, had to get off because he felt uncomfortable going to the city without the pruning knife he always carried in his hip pocket and had forgotten when putting on his Sunday suit.

Gloria wrote a century ago about the "*fieri colligiani*"[51]—proud men of the hills—and we too found the Mariani "good, coarse and generous . . . , but proud, terrible in their anger, implacable in their hatred."[52] Isolated, the Mariani have in the past resisted change, and any initiatve in such a direction is viewed with suspicion. "The winds of progress have not changed their ignorance and eradicated their old habits; ignorant of discoveries and knowledge, they live a patriarchal life, faithful to their customs."[53] But today, the peasant society is no longer isolated nor able to resist the changes that have followed the Second World War. It is undergoing rapid transition, while attempting to hold on to a system of values and a way of life. Nowadays a true peasant is the exception, even in the surroundings of Santa Maria. Luigi Gaddoni, who has worked the family farm for over forty years, declared, "Of course in town there are movies, supermarkets and all the modern conveniences. But look, in town nobody knows each other. You are better off here. Sure, it would be nicer with central heating, running water and all that. Maybe my kids will be able to afford them. But I prefer Santa Maria where you are never alone."

Nevertheless, inbred traits die hard; and for the *fieri colligiani* the most important values center around honor and shame, the critical elements in both conflict and conciliation, and providers of a basis for the peasant's system of life and ideology.[54] Derived from natural qualities as well as from education, honor means a concern for one's reputation and a willingness to defend it: a distinction is made between *maschio* and *manso*, manliness and castration. Under these circumstances the willingness to use a knife and the frequency with which fights occurred in the past should not be surprising. Today such means are still ethically valued if a man's honor has been offended by an unfaithful wife: in 1965 the village almost unanimously excused a peasant who had knifed his wife twenty-one times after having surprised her committing adultery.

Pride is reflected in the strong desire to *fare bella figura,* to cut a fine figure, and the equally strong desire to impress people in the strenuous effort to be in debt to no one. The first trait we came to know well. More often than not the generous hospitality we received in the homes we visited was clearly above the means of the host. At the same time the first trait reinforces the second, that of putting someone under an obligation, but one that is not reciprocal. The Mariano always attempts to pay for a service, even if it is rendered gratuitously, to avoid incurring an obligation. After a few weeks I became the village "photographer" and would give out duplicate prints. This device, though it was not intended to do so, kept my wine cellar adequately supplied. It is as if the peasant were conditioned to try to be one step above his fellow man: to owe nothing but to have others obliged to him. Thus, an informal mechanism for gaining power and influence is present, although when exacerbated the sense of honor can lead to generational feuds that divide the community.

"I work, I work, night and day, and what do I get: more callouses!" said Livorno, thrusting out his earth-eaten hands. As could be anticipated, I found many illustrations of "the image of limited good," surprisingly enough not only among the peasants, but also among the "intellectuals" (including some of the schoolteachers) and "bourgeoisie." Many seemed to be of the opinion "that out of Santa Maria you could only get so much and no more." Any attempt to do more could only lead to ill feelings, jealousy and hatred which eventually would destroy your reputation. As Foster puts it, ". . . a peasant's cognitive view provides moral and other precepts that are guides to—in fact may be said to produce—behavior that may not be appropriate to the changing conditions of life he has not yet grasped."[55] These attitudes naturally lead the peasant to express his individualism, his conservatism, his refusal to change: in brief to reject the twentieth century. The peasant who refuses to commit himself—to leadership roles or to anticipating the size of his crops—cannot view the future with optimism and must be content to accept passively the established patterns of life and authority in the family, in the Church, and in local politics. But what was true because of the village's isolation no longer applies to the younger generations and to those who commute from Santa Maria to their jobs in the cities.

Since the unification of Italy many forces have worked to break this isolation, and what had been a natural condition for centuries has been transformed in less than fifty years. In the conflict between a subsistence economy and a market economy the former has not been able to resist the latter, and the history of the twentieth century records its defeat. The process began a few years after the unification when, for reasons not under consideration here, the State attempted to curb the power of the Church and confiscated the holdings of the monasteries and religious orders. In Santa Maria the parish and some forty monasteries held property, providing employment for the population. Because of papal obstinacy few Catholics bid for these lands and most were acquired by large landowners, at times Italians of Jewish descent, or speculators. Large domains were thus created and Santa Maria, which had been a village of medium land holdings given out to farmers, saw its economy dominated by large-scale enterprises. Capitalism had entered; and a problem that Venice had never seriously attempted to solve because of the distance and lack of funds became a major issue: reclaiming the plains from the waters. The early capitalistic developments as well as the founding of a silk industry created a false and short-lived feeling of security—work was available—accompanied by a rise in the birth rate and demographic expansion. Before the end of the century the population was growing poorer and poorer, and very soon the industrial and rural revolution led to the first waves of emigration from Santa Maria and to the strengthening of patronage. Landowners found it impossible not to give to charity—"for years the miserable peasants have appealed to the philanthropy of the Diani-Martello family"[56]—thus creating a considerable accumulation of hatred and resentment among the population.

At the end of the First World War these repressed feelings exploded. In less than two years over 50 percent of the large estates were redistributed to the peasants. However, what appeared to be a blessing soon proved an economic blunder, but a blunder which enabled the community to go through fascism and the depression enjoying a relative prosperity. This act contained the seeds of its own destruction: none of the holdings exceeded three acres. The end of the war coincided with a resumption of demographic expansion at a time when the older generation was passing away and properties were being further divided by inheritance. Confronted with the prospect of near starvation, the population first took to seasonal and then to massive and permanent emigration. It was only stayed by the Italian "miracle" and the creation of small industries in the province of Padua affording the farmer new sources of income: peasant no more,[57] yet living on the farm, he became a peculiar breed of rural commuter.

In less than a century the entire economic, social and political structure of the village had changed. It is this period we shall now focus on in more detail, exploring the changes in the attitudes of the population regarding political, administrative and religious authorities.

2. Political Development in Santa Maria, 1866–1951

SANTA MARIA BECAME PART OF THE ITALIAN KINGDOM in 1866. The Catholic Church reached the peak of its influence in the Italian republic in 1948. Between those years numerous political, economic and administrative changes occurred that provide clues to understanding the community's present political situation. The following summary of Santa Maria's political development considers not only the dramatic highpoints but also the less sensational events that characterized its political life. Both aspects are important to the creation of political attitudes. To understand Santa Maria today we must comprehend how its political norms and culture evolved.

During this period two critical cleavages emerged that dominated life in the community. Their resolution has had a definite bearing on its political development. One, the Church-State conflict, indicated the progressive assertion of a secular political culture. The other, the landowner-tenant dispute, altered the economic structure of the village. These issues also affected the perception of authority and the process of socialization. A study of the cleavages thus reveals the crystallization of new economic relationships, the secularization of political attitudes, and the alteration of views toward authority.

To analyze these trends we must divide the period into several segments. We begin by considering Santa Maria's heritage to provide the background for the era. Then, a review of the local administration touches upon the individuals and issues that have shaped Marian attitudes toward their political leaders. The next section deals with the economic transformation of Santa Maria, followed by a discussion of the community's political crystallization.[1] A brief review of the effects of the Second World War and its aftermath concludes the analysis of the development of Santa Maria's political attitudes.

The Heritage

Santa Maria joined Italy following three hundred years of Venetian rule and sixty-five of Austrian domination interspersed with a few of French military occupation. Integrating the community with its proud Venetian heritage into the nation proved a difficult task and a heavy burden for the newly formed State. It had to oppose regional autonomies, create a new centralizing administrative structure—one that compared unfavorably with the efficiency of its predecessors in the Veneto—and, above all, overcome the influence of the Church, a bastion of stability that had successfully weathered the rapid succession of regimes.

In 1789 Santa Maria had 977 inhabitants;[2] by 1873, during the first years of Italian administration, the population had jumped to 1311, an increase of more than one third in less than a century. This demographic expansion, due among other factors to the progressive disappearance of cholera epidemics (the last was in 1886), allows one to surmise that the condition of the inhabitants must have hardly improved since Venice ceased administering them. At that time the population divided into four classes:[3] the first class, or *benestanti* contained 16 people; the second class, or *mediocre*, 106; the third class, or *infime,* 700; the beggars, or *mendicanti*, 85. The average family size was 4.78 persons, though 8 percent had more than ten people. Of the 204 families accounted for, 24 were beggars, 18 tradesmen and 162 depended on agriculture for their livelihood. The professional divisions among the men reveal that 11 were tenants of large estates, 76 of small estates, 9 were animal drivers, 1 was a shepherd, 4 recruiters and 61 daily laborers. Ten percent lived on charity, a percentage no higher than in other Venetian centers of the period.

At the time of the French occupation of Santa Maria in 1803 the territory of the commune was divided between a multiplicity of small proprietors in the hills, mainly religious orders, and three large landowners: the heirs of the Venetian Lanzoni family, and Emilio Zagati and Giovanni Moscardi who had purchased the Franciosi and Andreoli properties during the eighteenth century. Tenant farming was the rule. A majority of the contracts provided for long-term tenancy and 41 percent of the population directly or indirectly controlled some land. When the State confiscated and sold the religious properties in the 1870s as a result of the Church-State controversy, not all the peasants were able to purchase the land they had tilled for generations.[4] Italy had formally rescinded the divisions of the population into classes but, simultaneously, it contributed to the pauperization of the poorer classes on the eve of the capitalist revolution by denying them security of employment. When Santa Maria became part of Italy the primary objective of the people, placed under a new landowning structure and confronted with demographic expansion, became one of physical survival. At the same time, the rapid succession of political regimes they had witnessed predisposed the population to cynicism toward the new State and its efforts to create a united national policy.

The Venetian inheritance left a definite mark on the political and social history of the village under the Italian monarchy. The community remained a marginal entity, suffering from geographic isolation and strenuous demographic, economic and political limitations; it was hindered in its political and social development by administrative laxity, not to say incompetence; its development was further held back by the particular type of religious faith and practice imbued with values of the eighteenth century. These three elements were constants of the system and changed only during the last half of the twentieth century.

Physical isolation, in spite of the attraction of Petrarch's burial place, reduced the stream of visitors during the nineteenth century to a trickle. Connections with the outside were invariably bad, and the state of the roads remained lamentable as late as 1940, when the regular bus link with Padua still required a five-hour journey to cover the short distance separating the two cities;[5] a good walker could cover the distance in the same amount of time and a horseback rider cut it by half. Not only were communications bad, the exact location of the village was unknown to many would-be visitors, even men of letters. On the occasion of the celebration of the fifth centennial of the poet's death, the official speaker, Giosué Carducci, coming from Bologna, stopped at Santa Maria Polesine, some thirty miles away in the plains of the Po, delaying the ceremonies by several hours. Still, some distinguished visitors came to Santa Maria, such as the Minister of Finance in August 1878 and the Emperor of Germany in September 1890.[6] For those taking the waters at Abano or Battaglia, Santa Maria located a few miles away made a pleasant excursion. All recognized the charm of the village idealized by Ugo Foscolo in the *Last Letters of Jacopo Ortis,*[7] but they agreed with Foscolo that it lay in an unfortunate state of decay. Many of the buildings were in ruins, as were the streets linking the poet's house to the main squares and the tomb,[8] and most remained in this state until 1966. The occasional tourist had no reason to stay beyond a few hours in this squalid environment where he was hard put to find a place to rest or eat as late as 1948 "without having to bear the songs of drunkards" and "their blasphemous language."[9] The municipality derived little actual benefit from the poet's house, beyond providing work for the Marian guardian, because the property had been bequeathed to the city of Padua in July 1875 by Cardinal Silvestri, its last private owner.

Notwithstanding the well-established reputation of Santa Maria's agricultural products, oil and wine in particular, only small quantities found their way to the market. Production was limited by the ownership system aimed at rendering the farms autonomous and devoting a good part of the soil to the uneconomical cultivation of wheat and corn. Furthermore, natural calamities—the severe winters of 1880 and 1931, phylloxera after 1901—nearly wiped out the production of wine and oil. For the farmers who devoted a large share of their meager income to rent payments, the one and only aim was to survive from one year to another; the reputation of the quality of their products certainly reached the city—and whatever could be sold was sold—but too little was available to derive much profit, and even less to reinvest.

Isolation and poverty made the village of little political importance or relevance. At no time prior to fascism was the electoral body larger than 510. Only after the introduction of near-universal suffrage in 1911 did more than one hundred electors vote. As the prefectoral commissioner remarked in 1887, "the village is of no importance whatsoever."[10] Furthermore, the community was judged throughout the entire period to be politically safe by the governments in power, and no efforts were made to transform it.

The documents of the period lead to the conclusion that, at least until the fascist period, Santa Maria was a good example of a closed and politically marginal society. The basic ethos was one of subsistence, and the pursuit of private economic interests with physical survival was the primary aim. In this context positions of political power were rarely sought by either locals or outsiders; and very little respect was accorded these occupations which were considered to be a foreign import. Political power was neither sought nor respected; at most it was suspect, while economic power was to be feared. Until the 1950s politics seemed to be a marginal, if not useless, activity, while the encompassing problems of economics hindered the development of a political conscience.

Local Administration

From 1866 to 1951 the local administration was characterized by incompetence, laxity, and disinterest in the village's future. Local administrators sought not to call attention to themselves to the point that their very inaction and attempts not to "rock the boat" made them conspicuous to the prefectoral authorities that oversaw their activities. They acted only when involved in controversies they had wished to avoid or when circumstances beyond their control, such as war, made it imperative.

The Mayors

Seventeen men administered Santa Maria between 1867 and 1944 though only three were locals. Prior to 1889 when a maximum of twenty votes were cast for the fifteen seats on the municipal council, the office could hardly be termed elective. This was all the more true since the final choice of the mayor remained with the prefecture and the ministry of the interior, as it was during the fascist period from 1925 to 1944. Only once, in 1913, did universal suffrage play its proper role in selecting a mayor. In general, one can doubt the weight of the office or the prestige inherent in it: positions of authority came with religious or economic power but not with politics.

The local citizens who became mayors are impressive because of their limitations. The first, Orfeo Bardini, occupied the office from 1867 to 1875. He was a small landowner, and also a tenant of the Manzato family (that had purchased the Lanzoni property in the early 1860s), the elder of which, Giovanni, was a member of the municipal council. Bardini took his instructions from Giovanni and appeared little more than a prête-nom. The choice of Bardini was simple—no other person could be impressed into the job. The man was "esteemed," but had "neither a deep knowledge of administration nor a strong intelligence."[11] When Manzato asked him to resign in 1873 he promptly and gladly did so, not wishing to face the responsibilities involved with the up-coming celebrations in honor of Petrarch. It was to no avail; the Prefect, on instructions from the Minister of the Interior, refused to accept the resignation: the only alternative to Bardini was Angelo Tosi, a small farmer, "a crude man because he belongs to the class of the peasants," and ineligible "having been condemned to several years of prison for knifing an opponent."[12]

The next Mariano to be appointed was Giovanni Bardini, a distant relative of the first. He occupied the office from 1882 to 1895, attempting to resign like his predecessor in 1885 and 1892, on the pretext of "the poor economic conditions of his family" and his desire to emigrate.[13] In 1885 he had been reconfirmed as "intelligent enough for Santa Maria"[14] and in 1887 the motivation was hardly different: the larger landowners did not want the job while Bardini was "well liked . . . [and] functioned discreetly though of very limited culture."[15] Bardini's administration was not particularly dynamic and his favorite technique was to report to the authorities that all was well, even when this was a crying discrepancy with reality; he went so far as to report that the state of the roads was excellent, the schooling system efficient, and the sanitary system satisfactory.[16] In 1895 he received only 17 votes out of 75 cast.

The third local mayor, Silvano Tiberto, nicknamed "Water-drinker," entered the council the same year with sixty votes, became mayor in 1898, and remained in power until 1914. An innkeeper and small landowner, he was considered by the commissioner to be "uneducated," deriving his influence "from his large network of relatives and because he is well regarded by the population."[17] Until 1908 he was a political moderate, enjoying the support of the Church. However, he was unwilling to accept the instructions of the new parish priest in 1909 and (coinciding with the proclamation of universal suffrage) he provided the Mariani in 1913 with a true occasion to exercise their political judgment.

The local mayors attempted to maintain good relations with everyone and to avoid controversy. Outside appointees sought above all not to be involved. The more eminent men simply refused to serve, either because they resided elsewhere—for example, Dr. Stabilin, who lived in Padua and married into the Moscardi family, turned down the office in 1873—or because they were more interested in running in the larger constituency of Fantolon. This was the case with the landowners Manzato and Ferrari (heir to the Zagati fortune), though the latter did accept one brief term from 1879 to 1881. Those who agreed to the appointment seldom served longer than two years; for instance Professor Avvocato, Cavaliere, Tommaso Ruffini, of the Royal University of Bologna, was mayor from 1895 to 1898 and was called "a most cultivated man who enjoys the highest degree of public esteem."[18]

The community derived little or no benefit from the appointment of outsiders. Moreover, in 1905 Ruffini ended the practice of retting flax which had existed in Santa Maria for centuries, informing the Prefect that it was contrary to regulations. The true reason for his gesture was the odor emanating from the ditches near his house where the flax was left to rot. To say the least, his sense of responsibility toward the community was minimal. The same is true for Angelo Diani, who was appointed in 1914 and resigned for personal reasons in 1915. When Rome refused to acknowledge the resignation, the village was left without a mayor throughout the critical war period.

One man constitutes an exception for the period. Carlo Marastoni was drafted to the mayoral chair in periods of crisis, at the end of wars, or when the community sorely felt the need for an efficient administrator. Born in Padua in 1882, he was independently wealthy and acquired considerable prestige in Santa Maria where he had sought refuge following a series of calumnies relating to his personal life in Padua and Este. He purchased a large fifteenth-century palace which had belonged to Guido di Santa Maria, doctor of the Hungarian court in 1435. A man of intelligence and some artistic talents, Marastoni devoted his stay in the village to painting and the study of ceramics and literature, without neglecting the archaeology, history and anthropology of the community. He was the curator for the archaeological museum in Este. He also published a guidebook and several articles on local customs as well as contributing an article on Santa Maria to the Italian Encyclopedia. His intellectual qualifications and his position were such that he had no equal in the village and was a natural choice for mayor. Appointed in November 1920, he resigned in February 1923 but was maintained until 1925, in spite of his protests and letters to the prefect declaring he no longer considered himself to be mayor.[19]

During his brief tenure he reorganized the entire local administration and the tax structure, proposed the development of the aqueduct and lighting systems, and obtained funds from the State and City of Padua to restore the poet's house. The municipal council recognized him as "having deserved well of the community," so great was his success. The village had become his passion and represented to him part of the Italian heritage that had to be maintained at all costs. Thus, he entered into a long (and losing) battle with the local urchins who derived great pleasure from shooting stones at the lion of Saint Mark or defacing the few existing frescoes, not to mention their parents who sought building materials in the ancient monuments. Marastoni also built up a large correspondence with the ministry of education and culture, and obtained recognition for a folkloristic group he patronized and for which he designed the costumes. By 1938 he had managed to have the entire territory of the village classified as a national monument; ten years later he succeeded in having a communal road classified as a state road, and hence paved, to facilitate the flow of tourists to the village. Although he served as a catalyst and enhanced the mayoral position, what Marastoni did was not through the virtue of his office (in fact he was more successful out of office), but because of his intelligence, his very independence from the village, and even more through the network of personal friends he maintained in various ministeries.

No Podestà under the fascist regime lasted more than fifteen months. Appointments were either temporary or took the form of prefectoral commissioners who exacted a salary from the meager municipal budgets. In point of fact, Santa Maria never offered a broad enough political base for the office of mayor to be attractive to those who viewed politics as a career. All those forced into the municipal chair simply delegated their powers to municipal secretaries. The villagers could hardly look to the mayors for political guidance, nor did they receive administrative or political training from their example.

Municipal Secretaries

The municipal secretary occupies a critical place in the local administration but has the unenviable position of being the servant of two masters, the government that chooses him and the local council that pays him.[20] His main function is to run the local bureaucracy and serve the mayor as legal counsel. In a small town such as Santa Maria, where the municipal council is ignorant of legal matters and where the mayors are more often than not unconcerned, this position contains a substantial potential for power and authority, although with endless possibilities of being overruled. Unfortunately, the municipal secretaries appeared very eager to shun their responsibilities.

The two secretaries who administered Santa Maria prior to the fascist period were, like the mayors, men of limited means, and like their masters more concerned with routine than with innovation. Inertia being their guiding principle, they did not engage in local politics. Bruno Bertazzo was secretary from 1867 to 1880 and, since the man was an absolute nullity, the length of his tenure indicates the importance that Santa Maria was given by the prefectoral authorities. Not one of the semestrial reports sent by the prefectoral commissioner throughout the entire period fails to make derogatory remarks about the man. In 1868 mention is made of "his indolence and negligence . . . and belatedness in answering superior orders." In 1874 he is noted as "an absolute nonentity and of unqualifiable inertia," in 1877 as being "indolent and negligent," in 1879 he is accused of "indolence, neglect and carelessness."[21]

The appointment of Mario Favalli in 1880 was a necessary and welcome change for the community: "an intelligent and zealous man was substituted for an ignorant one, for the greater good of the municipal office."[22] The two years that followed were characterized by a flurry of measures which though of indisputable bureaucratic value were of little utility in an agricultural community, in particular traffic regulations "to insure that animals are not scared" and public hygiene, prohibiting the keeping of "oxen, horses, donkeys, mules, goats, sheep, pigs, geese, ducks and other animals which create odors and fumes that are harmful to public health"[23] in rooms intended for human residence. The appointment was made permanent in 1888. Favalli was given lodgings, an increase in salary and he married into the village. After 1890 one is struck by the decline of initiative on his part: only current business was expedited. The villagers, and particularly his daughter, recount that his main problem was to make ends meet on a meager salary and that above all he attempted "to offend no one and satisfy everybody." For forty-three years a man in favor of the status quo ran the village, dying just prior to the fascist takeover in 1923.

Administration

If the men who ran the village were weak or unconcerned, few effective measures that could have some bearing on the development or the respect for authority could be expected. During the period under consideration little was accomplished that reflected positively on the local administrators either in the field of administration or in that of conflict resolution. The period of greatest administrative laxity coincided with Orfeo Bardini and Bruno Bertazzo's tenure as mayor and secretary, respectively. Santa Maria appeared to be the most neglected and poverty-stricken village of the entire province, even unable to afford letterhead paper before 1875. The secretary was invariably late in answering prefectoral communications—when he did not simply ignore them—and the same holds true for the mayor as late as 1894 during the tenure of the second Bardini.

The budget was never given to the prefecture on time for approval. The accounts of 1873 had still not been turned in by August 1874, and had to be further delayed so the secretary "could join in the festivities of Santa Maria to honor Petrarch."[24] The budgets from 1874 to 1876 were submitted in 1878.[25] Certainly good reasons could be invoked, the secretary having failed to prepare a nominative tax role and having overlooked the taxation headings on horse-driven carriages, domestic servants and commercial enterprises as late as 1875. Appropriately, the commissioner noted "these could be of some relief to the desperate economic circumstances of the village"[26] where, for practical purposes, the most prosperous inhabitants failed to pay taxes from the unification of Italy until 1882. The failure to obtain an appropriate tax schedule made other administrative shortcomings appear somewhat minor; from 1871 to 1875 the register of births and deaths was not kept up to date, with no entry made for the period. The small capital, 15,000 lire, that Santa Maria possessed from the rental of communal propert was maintained in the form of bearer bonds rather than nominal bonds, against explicit prefectoral instructions;[27] and the municipality failed to forward electoral lists for 1876.[28]

Favalli's record as an administrator was better. During his entire tenure of office only one serious error occurred. In 1904 on the occasion of the election of the auditors to the municipal accounts there were more ballots than electors. Moreover, Favalli accepted the outcome which happened to favor the clerical party with which he sympathized, but nevertheless reported the exact count of the election! He received a reprimand, though the election was never invalidated.[29] The major problems were inherent in the collection of municipal taxes; it is difficult to condemn outright the man who failed to collect them, since he had to live in the village. The commercial tax and the tax on carriages and domestics were overlooked and in 1882 "the proposal [to collect these] was paralyzed by the demonstration of those communists [i.e., the inhabitants of the *comune*] who had seen their crops destroyed twice in August by hail storms. . . ."[30] In 1893 a surtax imposed by the Giolitti government was not even considered in Santa Maria, the only village in the entire province not to acknowledge the prefectoral circular letter. One can only guess that Favalli must have been under considerable pressure, since the purpose of the tax was to pay municipal secretaries in 1894!

The overall situation was hardly different in 1939. Santa Maria was ". . . a miserable village without resources, overburdened by taxes insufficient to cover the most impelling necessities of public service, nearly all of which leave something to be desired; [a village] where doctors and midwives only stay long enough to find a better post. . . ; [where] the financial situation of the *comune* is far more deficient than presented in the 1940 budget." Under fascism at least the budgets were presented on time, but, as usual, "the internal functioning of the offices" was of very poor quality.[31]

Under such conditions even minor problems became insurmountable obstacles and one can only sympathize with those who refused to become mayors, with those mayors who could not act, and with the secretaries who attempted to keep the good will of the population. However, their very lack of effectiveness did not enhance the authority of their office. Throughout the period Santa Maria's local administrators were unable to find solutions to any of its problems. For example, the organization of the local Centennial ceremonies was entrusted to the Pro-Petrarca committee in Padua where all the major celebrations took place. Santa Maria, though its situation had been explained to the Roman authorities, received no help and its streets remained mountain paths. The little work that had been commissioned—by one of the members of the municipal council since the mayor was in the process of resigning at the time—had still not been paid for by 1878. Rather than allow the case to go to court the Prefect ordered the Paduan committee to pay the bill, 121 lire.[32] Santa Maria was not totally inactive in preparing for the ceremonies, but the major initiative came from the Church, which refused to collaborate with the municipality and ignored the local authorities. The priest had no trouble in convincing the locals to refurbish the churchyard that harbored Petrarch's tomb and to build the enclosing wall that bishops had requested for over two centuries. The local gazette reported that "Men, women, children . . . inspired by sublime thoughts, forget feast-days and rest, and . . . spontaneously, enthusiastically, indefatigably work on Sundays. And for the greater part, these are peasants who offer the spectacle of abnegation, contributing with their sweat that turns into gold to the preparation for the centennial celebrations."[33] In fact, all initiative had evaporated from the town hall.

More important for the community was its inability to keep a doctor in residence. At the turn of the century the salary, less than 2,000 lire, was too low. In 1907 an offer was made carrying a salary of 2,450 lire with the specification that two thirds of the population were entitled to free services;[34] a year later the post was not filled: "Nine months of infestation have not been sufficient to find a doctor to take care of the physical well-being of these people subject, like others, to bronchitis and influenza and more than others subject to harmful knife wounds in brawls."[35] The situation did not change until the end of World War II; and Santa Maria had to make do with just an occasional midwife. Unable to hire a doctor, the town hall could hardly do more than provide a little relief or hospitalization for the sick and the poor. In a community where pellagra was rampant 286 lire were spent to hospitalize the poor in 1891, while (as a means of comparison) the town hall spent 62 lire for paper during the same period.[36]

A last item, the problem of water, gives an indication of the village administrators' lack of possibilities. Since 1547 Santa Maria had been dependent for its water supply on a single fountain in the main square. What was sufficient for 700 inhabitants was clearly not so for a population double the size in 1870 and more than triple in 1930. Consideration had been given to the question since the turn of the century but no funds were available. In 1937 the fascist government finally contributed sufficient monies—presented as Mussolini's personal gift—to build a cistern and an aqueduct so that water would be available in the upper square.[37] Once again the initiative came from the outside rather than from local authorities.

The village was in a vicious circle: its economic limitations meant a lack of funds so that its administrative limitations became self-perpetuating. Its public figures, mayors or secretaries, envisaged their task as the maintenance of peace and the status quo rather than the promotion of change. The small number of inhabitants made the community politically insignificant, so that it had no influence to bring to bear on the prefectoral administration. Poverty had an overriding influence on local politics and the local power structure, allowing only a few positions of authority in the leadership structure and even fewer visible leaders. Essentially, the only visible leader was the parish priest. This lack of positions did little to enhance the legitimacy of the local political offices. The mayor's and municipal secretary's offices were limited by the inability of the people who held them, as well as by the lack of interest they expressed for their positions. The consequences would be felt until the late 1950s, when a local elite appeared on the scene. However, before considering the political changes of Santa Maria, its economic transformation is worthy of attention.

Economic Transformation

The pattern of landownership in Santa Maria underwent two major transformations in less than sixty years. Italian unification and the ensuing Church-State conflict heralded the emergence of a capitalistic structure in the community. The sale of Church property benefitted the large landowners and led to an increase in the number of daily laborers, some of whom had previously been tenant farmers, while the traditionally long leases granted by the religious orders to their tenants were changed to short-term leases. These were more favorable to the new owners than to the farmers, who found themselves in a position of greater insecurity. The second change occurred when fascism radically altered the situation, forcing the sale of the largest property in the village, replacing it with a cooperative of small owners. The members quickly went from a progressive socioeconomic orientation to a conservative one that proved unviable in the post Second World War market economy. Economic changes of such magnitude had considerable influence on the crystallization of attitudes in the population, leading the people towards a greater participatory role in the community's political life. To separate, as we will do, the economic change from the political transformation is artificial but is necessary for expository convenience and clarity.

Until the end of the First World War, the leading force in the economic development of Santa Maria was capitalism. Three families, successors of the property divisions of the Venetian Republic and major beneficiaries of the sale of Church property, controlled two-thirds of all available land, or approximately two thousand acres. Only they had sufficient funds to invest in the draining of the plains, an objective recommended as early as 1556 by the Venetian Senate, thereby increasing the value of their holdings several fold.[38] In 1873 the Ferrari, who were succeeded by the Diani, had property in Santa Maria valued at 160,000 lire; the Manzato family was worth 70,000 lire and the Stabilin worth 26,000 lire.[39] These families were able to rely on an informal alliance with and the cooperation of the archpriest of Santa Maria, Don Alfredo Lumini, a landowner who did not have to depend on the prebend for his income. Local reports note he was ". . . one of those hypocritical priests who are priests only in their dress, conspicuously rich and totally dedicated to his vast farms and to his famous wine."[40] In 1880 at the agricultural fair in Ferrara he received a gold medal for the quality of his wine, and in 1885 a bronze medal for his oil.[41] The figures for 1789 show that the remaining thousand acres not controlled by the major families were divided between at least seventy-six families;[42] based on the system of inheritance it is reasonable to suppose that the number of small landowners was probably nearer to one hundred by 1870. To this figure one should add some of the forty small tenants who had worked the properties of the religious orders and some of whom were able to purchase the land when sold by the State. In all cases the average size of the holdings must not have exceeded 9 acres, while their location in the hills made their yield relatively modest compared to the large properties in the plains.

The larger estates were farmed out to tenants on a short-term basis. This led to maximum exploitation with a minimum of care since tenants were never certain of seeing their leases renewed.[43] Even by the standards of the time the farming methods used in Santa Maria were "antiquated."[44] The heavy hand of the landowners extended not only to the daily laborers but also, indirectly, to the small peasant landowner. Possessing too little property to be truly self-sufficient, he had to sell his services in competition with the laborers. In 1885, Manzato, whose enterprising spirit had brought a silk factory to Santa Maria, attempted to introduce in cooperation with other landowners a McCormick harvester-binder. Although a symbol of progress, this move was disastrous for the people, especially the laborers who derived much of their income from cutting and binding the wheat by hand. Rather than face revolt, the landowners abandoned the experiment upon prefectoral orders "consequent to political conditions in which the district finds itself," or, more concisely, unemployment[45] and peasant strikes.

Short of emigration, the men of Santa Maria had only one means to support their families: the trachyte and limestone quarries around Santa Maria, particularly at Fantolon. All the older villagers reminisce about the times when they worked at the Cave delle More or the Palazzina which overlook the plain of Santa Maria. Work was dangerous, hanging from ropes and blasting the stone, accidents frequent, and the cases of silicosis numerous. The Mariano sought to avoid this type of activity. The archives hardly mention the quarries in the village because problems rarely arose, though they provided a livelihood to many unskilled laborers. As the commissioner put it in 1873, ". . . here in the quarries of Euganean stone there are a good number of workers and it does not even enter their heads either to strike or to request increases in their daily earnings."[46] The situation remained unchanged throughout the century in spite of anarchists' disruptive activities: agriculture did not offer enough jobs and laborers were forced to accept the conditions of those who would hire them.

The peasants, 78 percent of the population as late as 1936, lived in dire poverty. They were forced to submit to the large landowners' conditions for employment and for food, to the few merchants ready to extend credit at usurious rates. The archives are replete with mentions of rural disturbances, and the living conditions of the period make the revolts understandable. According to the commissioner, contracted workers, such as oxen drivers, "live a life subject to great sufferings, and their daily salary which is 35 centimes in winter and 50 in summer should be increased." As for the daily laborers, this same official wrote, "their condition is disastrous."[47] In 1882 the Municipal Council declared that "the inhabitants of the *comune* will have to undergo many sacrifices to live through next winter."[48] On another occasion a subsidy was requested by the *giunta* "for the necessities of the laborers who clamor for work to break their hunger."[49] But the public works "to give some bread to the miserable class of workers" were too few and only lasted during the winter,[50] leading to revolts in the province, though not in Santa Maria. A few people lived in the plains below Santa Maria in houses "built of mud and bamboo canes, with roofs of straw and beaten earth floors, receiving light through the door which must be constantly kept open."[51] The commissioner noted in 1890, "Unfortunately charity . . . cannot hide the increasing specter of misery. . . . The wave of stealing of objects of prime necessity in the countryside and elsewhere is proof of the existence of impelling needs."[52] Little could be done to alleviate those conditions and the following year the commissioner concluded his report, "We must resign ourselves to the times in which we are living, observe and consider the stifled movements and agitations, the nervous tiredness of the poverty-stricken, their envy of those who are rich, and their rage at not being able to attain that state themselves."[53]

The laborers worked less than half of the year and their diet was hardly sufficient to assure physical survival: the man who could eat polenta (a type of corn mush) every day was considered "un signore." In 1905 when the old Moscardi who had managed, through hard work to buy a few fields, died, his last words according to his grandson were "Dammit! I'm dying now that polenta is plentiful." In 1898 Santa Maria had no baker; and when the mayor received a ministerial circular asking what had been done to reduce the price of bread he could answer that this was no problem since only the lucky ones were able to afford polenta regularly.[54] The older people still recall that gathering wild salad and vegetables was not a secondary pastime but a task that ensured survival, that women would fight over the possession of a patch of wild asparagus, "that eggs were split into four and even six," and that, on occasion of the most important religious feasts, women went to the market and asked for a piece of meat "as good as the one you gave me last year."

Under these conditions one is surprised that the general health situation was no worse than it was. Few families lived in the plains and the cases of malaria were rare even before the draining took place.[55] The isolation of the village prevented it from being contaminated by the cholera epidemics of 1849, 1855 and 1873, though the virulent epidemic of 1886 did touch Santa Maria.[56] Pellagra—an endemic disease often ending in insanity and death in which the skin reddens, dries and cracks and the epidermis peels off—was the major problem, to the point it became a natural and accepted illness. The disease was provoked by the regular ingestion of insufficiently dried corn, so the relatively dry climate of the hills meant that Santa Maria, despite its poverty, had one of the lowest rates in the province of Padua. Yet in 1913 more than 10 percent of the population still suffered from it.[57]

The economic welfare of the exclusively agricultural village was entirely dependent upon the weather conditions. The climate controlled the size of the crops, allowed farmers to pay rent or to pay off debts, and provided work for the laborers. One poor harvest meant considerable hardship for the entire population until the next one. Only if a good year followed could the peasants accept adversity as a natural lot. This was the case in 1885, 1892 and 1905 when hail storms struck the harvests.[58] But a series of crop failures offered no escape from famine or forced emigration, since it takes several years for a vineyard to return to full productivity after severe hail storms and wine was a critical product for the local economy.

In less than ninety years three catastrophic periods struck the village. The winters of 1879 and 1880 were extremely cold and destroyed the olive groves. In 1882 hail struck twice in July and August, wiping out all the fruit and grape crops.[59] Very similar conditions were repeated from 1895 to 1898, particularly in 1897 when a hail storm on June 11 destroyed the vineyards in the hills.[60] Between 1928 and 1932 hail in the summer was followed by very cold winters leading again to the destruction of the olive groves and the grape harvest, while phylloxera was also taking its toll of the vineyards.

The economic problems were compounded by a rapid population increase, more than doubling between 1873 (1,311) and 1943 (2,641). The peak years of demographic expansion coincided with the most serious agricultural crisis: The average annual increases for the periods 1881–1887 and 1931–1936 were 21 and 16.6 per thousand, respectively, while the average increase for other periods seldom exceeded 11 per thousand.[61] The conditions became more critical when emigration was limited or compensated by the immigration of unemployed laborers. In 1887, 78 people left the village, but the same number immigrated.[62] The situation was alleviated by emigration during the second major crisis (1895–1898) to the point that during the following six years, for the first time, the village population decreased by 32 units, or 3 per thousand per year. In 1898 the net loss due to emigration was 31; in 1904, 44.[63] New roads had opened up: in 1894 a few Mariani left for Central Europe and Austria-Hungary to build railroads,[64] while emigration to the Americas increased 40 percent between 1894 and 1895.[65] The third major crisis (1928–1932) occurred when fascism was seeking to limit emigration, thus aggravating the hardship in the village. In December 1935, despite the very harsh prerequisites, 14 men left Santa Maria for Italian East Africa, to be followed by 15 more the following year,[66] though few actually settled in Eritrea.

At the outbreak of World War I, as we will consider later, a political spirit was prevalent in the village coinciding with economic demands: misery made socialism attractive. Since 1898 no major economic calamity had struck, but the rise in prosperity was offset by the increase in population and the division of small properties through inheritance while the larger estates remained untouched. War artificially limited demands and brought a measure of prosperity to the village: the older men and women worked the farms, while the younger men in the armies were fed by the State. Though outside the combat zone, Santa Maria was nevertheless in intimate contact with the war; the king maintained his headquarters a few miles away, the plain of Santa Maria served as an airport, and several small hospitals were set up in the village. Its adolescents were brought into contact with a new mentality; and Marian soldiers, 25 of whom did not return, fought and believed they would be rewarded for their heroic sacrifices with more than medals. The rapid demobilization and return to civilian life of 290 men overloaded the economic and political systems in Santa Maria. Those who had fought wished to be paid for their suffering in land, but this land belonged to others. Since the traditional outlet of seasonal emigration to Austria and Germany was no longer available, considerable dissatisfaction developed; and for the first time a local organizer was present who could capitalize upon the discontent: Gino Baratella.

Born in 1885 in Beolco, a few kilometers from Santa Maria where his mother had relatives, Baratella pursued a career common to those of restricted means but endowed with a keen though not brilliant intelligence. He became an elementary school teacher.[67] He reached Santa Maria in 1910, having gone through training school in Padua and frequenting the University, taking courses in pedagogy and philosophy though he never earned a formal university degree. During his formative years he worked in the ranks of the socialist party, because he was convinced that the peasants' situation was basically unjust.

In 1911, the young man, being greatly infatuated with the niece of the priest of a neighboring village, attempted to break into her apartment and convince her of his love and ardor. Caught by the uncle (who had repeatedly discouraged the suitor, whom he considered an unworthy socialist-atheist), Baratella was accused of attempted homicide of the priest as well as robbery. During the legal proceedings both accusations were proved unfounded. In the first instance there was no substance to the *corpus delicti* in spite of the blows exchanged—the judge turned out to hold very anticlerical feelings—while in the second case again the facts did not support the allegation. At a time when the parish priest's popularity was waning, Baratella's popularity grew stronger: his violence and impulsiveness were attributed to his youth, although he was twenty-six. Thus, a new personage appeared on the local scene, enjoying an image of virility and machismo that served him well during his early career under fascism. In 1913, he was elected to the municipal council and kept his seat until 1922, when he was appointed justice of the peace in which capacity he served, ironically as we shall see, until 1926. Drafted in November 1917 into the infantry (81st regiment) and being "a noble and generous soul full of combative ardor,"[68] he rose through the ranks. He was admitted to the officers' school in July 1918 and commissioned second lieutenant in August. While serving with the fourth regiment of Alpine troops he returned to armed duty in the operational zone until the armistice. He was discharged in April 1919 and immediately returned to Santa Maria.

The thirty-four-year-old lieutenant, several times decorated, was soon able to exploit his status and prestige among the younger men, many of whom had been his elementary school pupils, to form a local association of veterans to promote the interests of those who had fought for the fatherland. In less than two years it became a cooperative, the aim of which, appropriately to his early socialist inclinations then shared by many of the returning soldiers, was to take over the large estates which had been neglected during the war. The Veterans' Association launched his political career. Baratella was a socialist for whom the word *Patria* held the romantic undertones advanced by D'Annunzio, and in 1920 he joined the Fascist party and the action squads of Padua. By 1921, helped by his oratorical talents and his activities in Santa Maria, he had gained enough prestige to be appointed secretary of the Fascist federation of Padua. In October 1922 he led the action groups of Paduans and Mariani in the March on Rome and by 1924 became the undisputed leader of the Fascist federation of Padua, also occupying the position of Provincial political secretary and Commander of the Second Cohort of the 54th Legion of the MVSN with the rank of consul. This was the man who would transform Santa Maria, leaving an everlasting image of kindness and generosity among the older generations in spite of all the excesses that would be committed during the period of his tenure.

Rapid demobilization and innumerable requests that could not be satisfied had opened Pandora's box. Political and economic turmoil reached its height in Italy during the period 1919–1921 when the maximalist-inspired socialist workers revindicated and seized the means of production.[69] In Santa Maria the years 1919–1920 witnessed little improvement in the cultivation of the Diani property, Bignago, because the owner had abandoned his wife and she left the care of her farms to administrators. Baratella had few problems in convincing his socialist partisans they were entitled to till the unproductive soil and in June 1920 the villagers rose en masse and invaded the Diani villa acting as "revolutionaries, bolsheviks, and a red horde singing proletarian and republican hymns, cloistering the owner and her children, attempting to brutalize them, acting as if they already owned the property."[70] The distressed Mrs. Diani conceded 240 campi (approximately 200 acres) to the Veterans' Association headed by Baratella in spite of the intervention of the carabinieri, or maybe because of their tardy arrival.

Quickly abandoning their revolutionary role, the men returned to their peasant status and sought to exploit the small plots given them, only to see their efforts thwarted and their revolutionary spirit rekindled by a major blunder of the Diani. The land that had been granted the association was entirely reclaimed but until 1880 had been under water. Hence it was essential that drainage be maintained at all times, particularly during the winter. In November 1920 the son of the owner nightly opened the sluice-gates that contained the waters and flooded the land, destroying all efforts so far expended and preventing the peasants from preparing the ground for the following season. Baratella, and it must be credited to his efforts, maintained his control over the men: rather than seeking blood they sued the Diani for damages.

Baratella had risen in the ranks of the Fascist party and was appointed Secretary of the Padua federation in 1921. The *Popolo d'Italia* was editorializing in favor of the working class, calling for "the diffusion of small properties in those zones and for those crops which allow it to be productive." The peasants and fascists of the Lazio swore that "the Italian fighting Fasci proclaim the right and the will of the peasants to conquer true, complete and definitive ownership of the earth, by means of adequate technical and economic preparation and a transitory form of co-participation."[71] This was exactly the situation in Santa Maria. In February 1921 the Veterans gave up their damage suit and agreed with the owner on the rent they would pay to use the property, indexing it to the average price of wheat during the preceding three years and agreeing to pay all expenses involved in draining the property. In early April they founded a cooperative headed by Baratella to distribute the fields to the various families. The cooperative did not, however, extend to the type of cultivation or to the selling of the products: the peasant remained an individualist. Simultaneously, Mrs. Diani agreed that she would not sell her land without conceding a first right of purchase to the cooperative.

The word "sale" had been mentioned, and the unoccupied part of Bignago was large enough to prove attractive to speculators if they felt they could get rid of the cooperative. Baratella perceived this clearly. The message from Rome was equally clear: he could count upon the support of the Fascist party; and further action could bolster his own position in the hierarchy. In June 1921 the peasants once again occupied the Diani villa. Obviously out of touch with reality, the owners considered Baratella a "red," a socialist, and called upon the Paduan fascists to defend them, but to no avail. By the time they realized their mistake and called the carabinieri, 200 more campi had been wrested from their control. The carabinieri were under instructions to prevent violence and were content to separate the antagonists, deserving, in the words of the municipal council (from which landowners and *popolari* were absent), "a word of applause for their intelligent and attentive intervention."[72]

The years 1922 and 1923 were difficult ones for Baratella who, through the Padua federation, was seeking to launch a national career which left him little time to devote to Santa Maria. In January 1922 the cooperative was invited to purchase the entire property, but it had no funds and sought financial aid from the Provincial Office of Assistance. Since time was essential, one of Baratella's tactics to delay any sale was to make the property as unattractive as possible to other prospective buyers. Throughout the entire period, contrary to the agreements reached in February 1921, he refused to agree to any increase in the rent. Lacking any will of their own, the peasants followed him blindly.[73] In February 1923 an offer was made on Bignago by a well-known speculator and preliminary agreements were drawn up. The property was escaping the cooperative. Baratella through the party brought pressure to bear on the buyer, who "agreed" to withdraw if the cooperative could purchase the land. In May part of the funds were raised, the Cassa di Risparmio (Savings Bank) in Padua offering 700,000 lire or 50 percent of the purchase price. The balance was to come from mortgages on the peasants' properties; but the latter proved reluctant to lose control of what was theirs and believed blindly that their leader could raise the full amount without their help. Baratella continued to negotiate with the owners. However, on the two occasions when final agreements were ready to be drawn up he was unable to provide the required deposit of 200,000 lire; and on May 7 the Diani lawyers informed the cooperative of its eviction. The entire property was to be free November 11, and all houses and stables to be unoccupied by June 13. The last interview between Baratella and the owners took place on May 17, 1923. On May 28 the Diani sold the property to a speculator from Lucca, officially for 1,775,000 lire or 350,000 more than the cooperative had offered.

Two means were left to the cooperative; and Baratella, with his previous organizing experience, used them well. On June 23 he wrote to the minister of Justice, Finzi,

> . . . requesting aid from your Excellency in this most saddening episode which once again reveals the base speculations which through swindles have become legal, but which must be absolutely condemned and prevented by the Government of Justice you so adequately represent.[74]

In September, to support the political pressure that was being put on the Prefect in Padua, violence erupted: the representative of the new owner was bodily ejected, beaten up, and prevented from returning to the farm by the peasants. Pressure was applied from all parts; and letters from the speculator to Rome and Padua remained unanswered, while the response from the prefectoral commissioner in Este was hardly better. The law no longer offered equal protection; and on November 3 an agreement was reached between the new owner and Baratella. The earth belonged to the peasants, at least to those who had sided with Baratella and followed him in his evolution from socialism to fascism.[75]

Two years later a similar assault was waged upon the other major landowner, the Manzato family. Baratella, since 1924 bolstered by the role he had played in the takeover of the Diani property, acted as a "ras," dictating and giving orders to all. The Manzato sought to evict thirty tenants in November 1925 but the representatives of the law were met by a hostile assembly of two hundred villagers: men, women and children convened by the volleys of the village church bells, which rang in spite of the strict orders given by the priest but not obeyed by his sexton. Baratella insisted that the eviction be delayed, and a new date was set for April 27, 1926. All requests from the prefect that Baratella mediate the conflict—after all he was justice of the peace in the village—were turned down. He wrote: "I cannot hide my preoccupation that the harvest is very advanced. No doubt if the peasants see the fruit of their labor wrested from them, they will not remain quiet."[76] The carabinieri, writing to the prefect, also sought to avoid responsibilities, requesting "at least fifty men on horseback and fifty to seventy carabinieri"—an exaggerated number to deal with a village as small as Santa Maria—while asserting that

> . . . the threatened peril to public order is at most relative and nothing would occur if the erroneous conviction among the expellees that they are supported by the political authority were removed; but they believe and say that Cavaliere Baratella dominates your Excellency and that consequently they will not be expelled.[77]

And the carabinieri were right: pressure was put on the Manzato family who finally agreed to renew the contracts, realizing that to oppose fascism and Baratella would eventually lead to the total loss of their property in Santa Maria.

In five years, with a minimum of violence, the regime of ownership that had existed for centuries had been swept away. For all practical purposes the two larger estates had been divided among about three hundred families, providing each one with approximately two acres of rich farmland in the plains. Santa Maria had become a village of small owners, tenant farmers and a cooperative. However, the cooperative spirit never entered the village: those who belonged to Baratella's group—and only a few *popolari* among the more prosperous of the small owners refused to join —envisioned the cooperative as nothing more than a purchasing association to acquire new land. Baratella, more concerned with a political career that depended on the good graces of fascism, abandoned his socialist ideas in 1926 and never sought to instill a spirit of cooperation among the peasants, who would have easily yielded to his influence. His aim was to

> grant the earth to the poor laborers in the name of the Flag of the Fatherland without offending the rights of private owner-

> ship; provide the veterans with the means for a vigorous and hardworking life; increase the yield of the earth through intensive culture; eliminate unemployment, increase patriotic feelings and create a privileged situation in Santa Maria that could serve as an example to other villages in the hands of the subversive parties that lead them to economic and moral ruin.[78]

In this he succeeded and could declare, "Now in Santa Maria there are no men out of work, and no other party lives that is not in agreement with a sentiment of absolute veneration of the Flag."[79] The peasants were ready to follow the Duce and his lieutenant, Baratella, because he had given them the means to survive. And survival it was: what appeared to be prosperity was nothing but an illusion that would carry Santa Maria through the years of fascism, preventing its evolution towards modernity. Every family was certain now that it could produce enough cereals and corn to survive; and the news led one family to leave the coal fields of Pennsylvania, taking their son out of high school to return and till a small plot of ground "at home."

The illusion of prosperity lasted briefly. The winters of 1930 and 1931 were the most severe in memory, destroying the olive groves that had provided a marketable product, essential for the peasant to pay off his debts. Furthermore, Santa Maria's tax assessment, while inadequate to provide for the village needs, was higher than that of any of the surrounding communities and proved an additional burden on the people's limited resources. By 1935 many were seeking to emigrate.

A total divorce between the elite and the polity had taken place. The two major families that had been a font of charity were alienated from the population, entertaining sentiments of hatred which are not extinct today. When Baratella's influence waned they were not ready to provide alternative leadership, so sour was their state of soul. Carlo Marastoni, tied by friendship to the Diani, retired from municipal politics and devoted his attention to the preservation of monuments. Two other landowners adhered to the ideals of fascism, as they still do, depriving the community of potential leadership. Even the local Church, the best equipped to resist Baratella, was forced to bow to his authority, since its clientele preferred to own a field rather than receive spiritual rewards in another world: the *popolari* soon dwindled to a handful of faithful. With few exceptions the socialist leanings of the population had been coopted by fascism.

In brief, the social split was total; but it also created total economic unity, since nearly all the families had benefitted from Baratella's actions. Nevertheless, a new dimension was introduced among the farmers: motivated by the ownership of fertile lands in the plains they gave them top priority, neglecting the hills which until then, at considerable cost and effort, had provided them with a limited means of survival. In doing so they wrote their own long-term defeat: the hills had provided poor cereal crops but were essential for wine and olive oil, the two commodities that generated a cash income. The plains allowed them to live. However, divorcing the mountain from the plains and, after the winters of 1930 and 1931, neglecting the former in favor of the latter, soon pushed the peasant back to his original state of poverty. Many were obliged to leave the village after years of toil spent repaying their debt.

The future of the community was linked to its leader's, and if the man was suited to be king at home, he was too limited to become a leader in the new fascist regime: his downfall signified the continued isolation of Santa Maria. A domineering personality, Baratella never encouraged the creation of an elite within the cooperative, refusing to challenge the individualistic peasant with a true spirit of cooperation that could have helped him weather his economic woes while learning the virtues of organization. In the name of obedience nothing was done to develop a true political conscience or elite. The capitalistic system that had dominated Santa Maria since unification and forced the local Church to seek its alliance was defeated by the association between the peasantry and the fascist movement. After the downfall of fascism all that remained was an old elite alienated from the village and a loose association of owners who had little sense of cooperation. Following a brief and unsuccessful attempt by the left to organize the community—after all, Mariani who had seen fascism give them the earth had never envisaged the movement as one of the right—the village proved easy grounds for conquest by the right-wing Christian Democrats acting with the blessing and support of the local

Church (which had been thwarted by capitalists and fascists alike).

Political Crystallization

The years of Austrian administration in the Veneto were characterized by a different response to the Church's status in the community than the first years of Italy's control (1866–1895). Under Austria the local clerics supported and endorsed the most Catholic Francis Joseph. And he was ready to support the Church as long as it was content with its spiritual role and its privileged position, without attempting to intervene directly in the region's politics.

Under Italian rule, the Roman question poisoned the relationship between the Church and State and led to the *non expedit* which forbade Italian Catholics to participate in politics and the confiscation of ecclesiastical properties. Don Alfredo Lumini, the archpriest of Santa Maria and a landowner in his own right, therefore refused to collaborate with the new State. His income was sufficient to make him independent of his yearly stipend (39 lire in 1884) or of the collection fund (184 lire the same year).

His flock came to church regularly (it was the only weekly occasion for a social gathering of the entire community), and the church bells regulated everyone's life. Don Alfredo could call upon the collaboration of all and could refuse to extend his cooperation to the local administrators whenever he desired. Between 1874 and 1885 efforts by the prefect to survey the prebend budget were opposed by Lumini, who advised the prebend responsible to ignore all prefectoral requests. For the priest it was a question of principle; for the responsible it was a question of necessity since it appears he had diverted a good share of the funds (300 lire) for his own purposes, leading the prefect to suspect "grave incidents of embezzlement" and to send an inquiry committee to Santa Maria.[80] To this group Lumini suggested that nothing should be done and threatened the committee, leading the inquirer to write the prefect: ". . . the matter is odious: consequently I would be exposed to the hatred and vendetta of the people of Santa Maria, who are of a rather proud character."[81] No further mention is made of the matter: Lumini controlled the population well enough to resist the political authorities.

The effect of papal pronouncements and the archpriest's control is more evident in the local elections. In the eight elections held between 1871 and 1884, political participation was reserved to a minority, by choice and by necessity. The population exceeded thirteen hundred of which four hundred were adult males, but only one out of four was entitled to vote and only one out of twenty chose to exercise his rights. The occupants of the fifteen seats on the municipal council were usually picked by twenty electors. Abstention was the dominant trait and the few Mariani who voted (17 in 1873) were men of sufficient substance not to need the priest's patronage and thus able to resist his dictum. Despite their political independence, which addressed itself only and exclusively to local administration, their political ideas did not differ considerably from his. They were all landowners. The members of the municipal council remained clerical conservatives throughout the period. At least this is true for the locals who constituted three-quarters of the council's membership. The other quarter was composed of outsiders who were considered conservative liberals. In Santa Maria any competition that took place had "no political color but was exclusively personal, characterized by private interests and rancor."[82] Local political activity was essentially apolitical and even the outsiders had few reasons to oppose Lumini, though they could have easily manipulated the village representatives, some of whom were their tenants, men with little formal training or education and comparatively limited economic means.

What little opposition existed was "extra legal," oriented as much against the government as it was against the Church, finding its expression in the local anarchist-socialist movements. Their membership and their influence, however, was limited, but the seeds they sowed would flourish after the war. The group in Fantolon was led between 1877 and 1885 by the future parliamentarian Angelo Galeno and a young student of independent means, Carlo Monticelli, who resided on the eastern edges of the *comune* of Santa Maria. In 1873 the commissioner could find little trace of the movement, known only through the newspapers. The group had 27 adherents when in 1877 Andrea Costa came to Fantolon to write up the statutes of the local Socialist Society. In 1878 the party had grown to 68 members, at least two of whom were from Santa Maria, Silvano Stefani, a forty-year-old tailor and Giuseppe Tognin, a nineteen-year-old medical student.[83] In 1884 it claimed a membership of four hundred, though its efforts to move the peasantry were futile and the strikes called for in 1885 failed, leading to the arrest or voluntary emigration of its leaders. Only intermittently were they able to publish a one-sheet newspaper, *Il Pioniere,* having the motto "Proletarians of the World Unite" and containing articles by Monticelli.[84] Their ideas were more strongly felt in the area immediately surrounding Monticelli's and Galeno's habitations, particularly in the sector known today as Mandonego or Corte Beghin, where the inhabitants are surnamed Galeni and have expressed socialist-anarchist opinions since the late 1870s.[85]

In 1885 a majority of the Marian population was politically nonsecularized and nonparticipatory. Between 1895 and 1926 Santa Maria entered its critical period of political development. During this thirty-year span the war brought the crisis of development to maturity. Obviously this crisis cannot be separated from the rapid population increase (from 1,650 to 2,200 inhabitants), the agricultural crisis, and the attainment of temporary economic satisfaction that have been dealt with elsewhere.

Two major factors were the transformation of the electoral laws expanding the electoral body, and the informal raising of the *non expedit* in 1895. The electoral law of 1882 increased the electoral body from 98 to 360. The enfranchised population increased nearly fourfold while in twenty-five years the voting population progressed from 20 in 1884 to 309 in 1913, increasing fifteenfold. The new qualifications to become an elector radically modified the composition of the municipal council. In 1895, 50 percent of the electors took part in the vote, rather than the average 20 percent as in the past. The returns expressed a vote of no confidence for the previous administration, since only four members of that council were returned to office, and the incumbent mayor obtained only 17 votes out of a possible 75. The commissioner, who had forecast no changes, was obliged to revise his opinion and recognize that the council now had only three clericals, but twelve moderates.[86] The swing of the village mood, reflected also in the hostility many felt for the new parish priest, was evident in the returns of the political elections: in 1903, 26 votes went to the liberal candidate and 39 to the conservative; in 1909, 43 went to the liberal and 32 to the clerical; in 1913, 159 to the liberal, 7 to the socialist and 135 to the clerical. The 1914 provincial election confirmed the trend with 211 votes cast in favor of the radical candidate while his clerical opponent only garnered 125.

This transformation and the appearance of an opposition can best be explained in terms of a single personality, Don Francesco Lanzoni, and the active role he played in politics. In the summer of 1908, following Lumini's death, he took possession of the rectory and made it clear he intended to dominate the village and to dictate its political choices. He attempted to become friends with Silvano Tiberto, the mayor, "to keep him under his influence and consequently to be consulted and kept informed of the decisions to be taken in the municipal council."[87] The mayor, a man of character, had been elected to the council in 1895 and had been mayor since 1898. He was a supporter of the moderate liberals and later of the socialists and refused to bow to the priest's pressure. Lanzoni interpreted this refusal as outright hostility and made it clear that accepting his orders "would have been better for [the mayor] and his supporters." While Tiberto, the owner of an inn, was popular, Don Francesco was not: in 1909 another conflict broke out that led to an inquiry by the carabinieri. The priest had attempted to remove the choir master, which was well within his prerogatives. However, the move was opposed by the choir singers and the municipal band, which the Church helped support. In their effort to oppose the change the singers and players gathered at the mayor's establishment, no doubt with his blessings. Sensing possible defeat, Don Francesco addressed the singers in Church the following Sunday "blessing good Catholics and cursing their enemies, threatening them with the evil eye."[88] The feud was open and the village started taking sides, supporting the rectory or the town hall. Although there was no final confrontation then, a third episode came to the fore in 1911 which proved decisive. In May, the mayor approved the building of a public weighing station to be located in the main square. One can argue that the location was reasonable and convenient since the village's principal roads converged on it, but it was an ill-advised choice. Locating the weighing station so close to the church gave the impression that the mayor was taunting the priest; and if it were built in front of his own inn, there were few doubts the mayor would benefit. Above all, putting the station in a direct line with the poet's tomb, one could easily argue, endangered the aesthetics of the square. A crime of lèse majesté had been committed. The rectory rapidly counterattacked, referring to the "retarded intelligence" of the mayor, pointing out that the weighing station "was being built to favor the mayor's private interests" and that it would destroy "the aesthetics of the monument to the poet."[89] Here was an occasion to force Tiberto's resignation. On May 27 the campaign went from whispers into print, with the appearance of an anonymous manifesto on the village walls. Without having to consider the printer's mark, that of the Apostolic press in Este, its origins were clear. The message itself left no doubts.[90]

> Hosannah! Hosannah!
>
> The municipal *giunta* has done homage to the poet's tomb! Today on the Unique Square in front of Petrarch's tomb a new monument is being built:
>
> The Public Weighing Station
>
> Tomorrow the Poet will not only receive the homage of visitors from all over the world, but also those of bovines that will drop their fecal memorial.
>
> The Citizens

The prefect inquired immediately. In his reply the mayor pointed out that the station was in a lower part of the square, somewhat separated from where the poet's tomb stood, but that all work had stopped and would not be resumed.

The rectory anticipated resignation and spread the rumor "that the mayor, rather than digging the pit for the weighing station, was digging the tomb of his own administration."[91] With the priest's encouragement ten municipal councillors resigned: a quorum no longer being present, the appointment of a prefectoral commissioner appeared normal. However, such speculation ignored Tiberto's fighting temperament. Elections were at hand. The crucial dimension was no longer the weighing station but the choice between the list inspired by the rectory (led by Avvocato Lumini, who had penned the manifesto) and the Tiberto faction from the town hall proclaiming the need for civilian-inspired, independent government.

> During the electoral period Don Lanzoni was most active; he did not hesitate to enter the family dwellings to propagandize in favor of the list developed in the rectory where the mayor's opponents gathered every evening, the list that was rejected by the electorate.
>
> The man is anxious to acquire popular ascendency over the population of Santa Maria he wishes to dominate, and cannot suffer to be considered as a negligible entity in this village outside of his church.[92]

His hostility to Tiberto, the town hall, and indirectly the state, knew no limits. In 1916, when Italy was at war, he went as far as "exalting the Austro-Hungarian monarchy and its army."[93] However, the village had made its choice and had broken away from the domination of the Church. Don Francesco later mellowed with age, but he was never able to enjoy the total loyalty of his parishioners.

The conflict revolved around personalities much more than political ideas. However, the population for the first time had been able to make a clear choice, putting the principles of the autonomy of civilian administration above personalities and choosing autonomy over control. This analysis is the consensus of those with whom we talked in the village. The Church and the right had been contained, and the outcome of the confrontation indicated the progressive secularization of the people. This situation, and the split in the village it provoked, continued after the war when Church-oriented *popolari* and socialist supporters of the town hall opposed each other.

From 1920 to 1926 was a period of voluntary economic unity and forced political unification. Baratella's redistribution of the estates among the peasants made the village a single economic entity based on the ownership of small plots of land from which only the most obstinate excluded themselves. Because of Baratella's influence and the intellectual qualities of Carlo Marastoni, Tiberto's effective successor, Lanzoni's hold on the citizens was totally undermined. Yet, though all the odds were against him, he did not give up without a fight.

In 1924 the local doctor, Michele Bertazzo, only held a temporary appointment. He was a supporter of the *popolari* and had Lanzoni's backing, while the fascists believed it was imperative he be forced to leave. In a move prearranged by Baratella a certain Doctor Gastone Stocco won the competition for the official appointment.[94] Lanzoni lost neither time nor occasion to embarrass the fascists and immediately cast doubts on the legality of the proclaimed winner. The village divided itself along political beliefs, and in one case two brothers went as far as dividing the house they owned in common, as well as the garden. The *popolari* sided with Bertazzo and four councillors resigned; for the socialists turned fascists intimidation was a natural recourse to force his departure. On September 14, 1925, the doctor's residence was attacked by a band of local fascists, and on the fifteenth he sent in a telegram of resignation: "This night pistol shots inside residence. This morning decline all responsibilities of service."[95] The municipal council was short of a quorum and could no longer operate. The government appointed a temporary administrator. By 1926 the office of mayor was no longer elective; and during the twenty years to follow Santa Maria would be administered by ten different appointees, outsiders who had little sympathies for Lanzoni and the Church.

The fascists' domination was as complete as the parish priest's defeat. Only a handful of socialists had clear enough ideas and strong enough convictions to resist Baratella's espousal of fascism and go on proclaiming their opinions. Remo Davi was the exception who unfalteringly taunted the local fascists, often forced to escape through the windows of the local bars after heated political discussions, and usually successful because he was an excellent runner. When two castor oil treatments did not silence the man, Baratella ordered he be roughed up more "efficiently." The orders were too literally interpreted and he was beaten to death in 1926. Baratella's power insured that no inquiry was ever ordered.

Santa Maria had become thoroughly fascist. In 1924, 448 of 457 votes went to the national list and 3 to the *popolari*. Honorary citizenship was offered to Mussolini.[96] In 1929, of 315 electors, all

296 who voted endorsed the regime. The nascent democratic spirit had been eliminated. The commissioner, writing to the prefect in 1929, noted:

> The reverend archpriest has devoted his energies for the success of the electoral plebiscite. He was helped by the chaplain. They have maintained a praiseworthy attitude, have propagandized individually among the electors and held no public speeches.[97]

The Concordat had been signed and spelled Lanzoni's defeat in the greater interests of the Church. Yet, while forced to accept fascism, he refused its methods and retained some dignity, propagandizing individually but refusing to march the faithful to the voting booths, as many of his colleagues did in the surrounding parishes.

More than the regime, Baratella destroyed all democratic tenets in Santa Maria, turning the village back fifty years in terms of political development. Between 1926 and 1943 the village was an unwavering stronghold, though it had a peculiar brand of fascism based on socialist ideas of land distribution, which, once accomplished, easily evolved into the conservatism of small ownership. Fascism was not Mussolini, fascism was Baratella, and he could accept no opposition. Viewed and acting as the supreme being, the ideal fascist man, a "ras" in his own right with his feudal domain and vassals, he based all his decisions on the tenets of his fascist ideals. Thus whatever apoliticism might have existed in municipal politics—as it did in other Italian villages—was unacceptable in Santa Maria. The show could be run only by Baratella and the village had provided him with unlimited power, so that its future depended upon his future.

Relying upon such a person appeared to be a reasonable course. He was a member of parliament after 1923 and the political secretary of the federation in Padua. He should have been able to provide Santa Maria with enough manna to make the village prosperous. Many envisioned the spoils of the regime flowing to the hills, especially since Baratella had expanded his power base by becoming Podestà of the adjoining Qualto in 1926. But his very acceptability to the countryside made him suspect in the city; and within a few years he fell into disgrace.

In 1926 the prefect wrote Mussolini's secretary:[98] "[Baratella was an] elementary schoolteacher in Santa Maria. . . . It is correctly known that [he] has retained that mentality and has neither the necessary qualities nor the preparation to direct fascism in a highly intellectual province such as Padua." Political secretary Baratella believed he could deal with the town and the University in the same high-handed way that he had dealt with the peasants. Seeking respectability, fascism had to be purged of the violent and arbitrary image that Baratella incarnated so well. He was therefore accused of political factionalism and eliminated from the federation in Padua. The prefect wrote Mussolini:[99]

> The elimination of false fascists has been neither easy nor always peaceful. . . . This should be no occasion of surprise if one thinks that the government of Padua since the early days of fascism was in the hands of a band of suspicious characters made up of old radicals, some moderate clericals and a few deluded young men. Naturally during this period, though the leaders cannot be called dishonest, many not-too-honest things took place, and many mischief makers and demagogues satisfied their ambitions for power and honors. It should be considered, however, that especially if the Hon. Baratella, who was the representative element of the clique, is kept at a distance from Padua, things should promptly return to order.

In 1929 he was appointed to the rather insignificant post of general secretary of the provincial union of fascist agricultural syndicates as well as commissioner and later Podestà of Santa Maria. Fascism no longer needed thugs; instead, it sought men of culture. Santa Maria had bet on the first, lost, and soon fell back into its prior isolation, though many villagers still retained their illusions that Baratella was a powerful man with great pull.

Though still a member of parliament, in 1931 he was exiled to Bari in the south. The previous year had been marked by great festivities, a wine exposition, a grape festival and a bicycle race,[100] and the local choir had been invited to sing at the crown prince's wedding.[101] These events became memories of a past that would not be repeated. With Baratella's exile the local party faltered. His wife resigned her position as head of the feminine organization. For the feast of the Befana—coinciding with the Epiphany when a mythical old and ugly woman brings gifts to good children—and which the regime had appropriated and called *Befana fascista,* Santa Maria was one of the thirteen villages that did not contribute money to the provincial fund.[102] The Balilla group, the association of fascist boys under 12, had only thirty members in a village where the children of that age were at least four times that number.[103] The frigid winter doomed the summer harvests and put Santa Maria in "desperate financial conditions."[104] By March 1932, 103 men were out of work.[105] In 1934 the Fascist party no longer endorsed Baratella, who thus lost his parliamentary seat, and the prefect declared:[106]

> He is a respectable person, but as a man of limited culture he does not possess those general characteristics required to properly perform the delicate functions of parliamentarian. If one also considers that by disposition of the Party the Hon. Baratella must take no part in the political activities of the Province, it is illogical that he should be one of its political representatives.

The village adhered to the rites of fascism and 100 percent of the population voted for the list that no longer contained their hero's name.[107] The inhabitants of Santa Maria could only be disillusioned with fascism as a form of politics. Their dislike was compounded by the economic crisis.

The depression struck with great severity. During 1935 and 1936 29 men left for Italian East Africa.[108] In 1939 four families sold all their belongings and went to Libya,[109] while 18 men and 6 women sought temporary employment in Germany. In 1940 the Party reported that 362 men and 135 women were unemployed,[110] an exaggerated figure that probably represented the total working force, but expressed the state of mind that existed in the village. The little relief came from administrators, certainly not from Baratella. In 1938 Marastoni had the town classified a historical monument; in 1937 and 1940 Podestà Bertoni obtained monies for the aqueduct,[111] but in 1940 the village was snubbed by Mussolini, who visited Fantolon, Este and Beolco but neither received Baratella nor came to Santa Maria.[112]

The prefect received anonymous letters criticizing the local administration and the central government signed "The People of Santa Maria. We will win," the fascist war cry that could be interpreted "win the war" or "overthrow the government."[113] Respect for existing authorities declined and new alignments began to emerge.

The War and Its Aftermath

Alfredo Valeri, an administrator of properties born in 1906 in Villafranca near Padua, was the last Podestà of Santa Maria, governing between June 1943 and April 1945.[114] He attempted to play the role of a conciliator. This was no easy task in a village occupied by the Germans, the Republican Fascist Black Shirts, and a population influenced by the ideas of the Resistance and willing to help escaping American and British prisoners. He had no municipal building, since the town hall and the tax records had been destroyed in February 1943 by arson. He also had to face an influx of refugees from Padua; there were 130 present in June 1944.

The Germans stayed on the outskirts of the village in the villa Diani: their task was to insure the defense of Padua. In this period of scarcity they extracted food from the peasants though the locals boasted an equally successful record of accumulating durable goods: one young man appropriated twenty tires, which provided him in 1945 with sufficient capital to get married. The eight Marian Black Shirts were in charge of keeping order and recruiting men to work for the Germans. The bombastic attitudes they passed for patriotism, the threats they made to use their weapons, the frequency with which they spent their evenings drinking did little to endear them to the citizenry. However, some people still remember that they distributed the little food and tobacco available. At the end of the war two were jailed while a third escaped to Milan.

The Resistance in Santa Maria was never extensive; however, its influence was felt. Two partisan detachments existed in nearby Qualto and Torreglia,[115] and in October 1944 a few isolated snipers shot and injured three Black Shirts on Piazza Roma. The "rebels" seized cattle on the Manzato farm in November. Two young men who sought to organize their friends were caught and died in Matthausen; and the village chaplain was jailed briefly. Following this incident Santa Maria turned to passive resistance and the Black Shirt recruiters usually came away emptyhanded. In April 1945, with the Germans in retreat, the partisans occupied the military installations in the Euganean Hills. But Santa Maria remained calm, because Valeri discouraged armed activity and the Liberation Committee (CLN) acted rapidly. The war, nevertheless, took a heavy toll: 22 soldiers were killed, 29 were taken prisoners, 7 of whom never returned from the Soviet Union, 2 civilians died in concentration camps, a deaf old man of 73 who failed to heed an order to stop was shot by the Germans in June 1944; and a 24-year-old woman was killed in April 1945 by the retreating troops.

For the next 18 months the left dominated Santa Maria, at least in appearance. Four communists and 11 socialists controlled 16 of the 22 positions on the CLN, "Camera del Lavoro," and municipal council. Only 3 of the men were not Mariani (2 communists and 1 socialist); and only one, a communist, had been a political prisoner. Strikingly, half of the representatives of the left in the CLN and the Camera del Lavoro (there were 10 leftists and 2 democrats) lived in the eastern part of the *comune*, at Mandonego, which in the nineteenth century had been under the influence of the anarchists and early socialists Monticelli and Galeno. The area turned prosocialist in the twentieth century and constituted the strongest nucleus of resistance to fascism after September 1943. Their organization and early resistance could not, however, counter the fact that local Mariani considered these men outsiders. Known as "the dishonest Galeni," they were Mariani for administrative purposes but not true members of the community. This fact and their lack of education allowed the chaplain and Carlo Marastoni, who had been called back in May to administer the village temporaily, to manipulate the CLN. This body chose four socialists (one was elected mayor) and two democrats from Catholic Action to sit on the municipal council. Only one socialist came from Mandonego. He emigrated in early 1946 with the two non-Marian communists who had constituted the driving forces of the CLN and the Camera del Lavoro.

The problems the new administration had to face were serious. The people lacked food and work. Angelo Bardini, the socialist mayor, resigned in December 1945, declaring the people wanted more than he could give. The socialists were also suffering from the fact that in Santa Maria more of them had compromised with fascism and accepted Baratella's leadership than had the *popolari*. The Veneto by early 1946 became a Christian Democratic stronghold. The Christian Democrats in Santa Maria found a leader in Don Arturo Ferlini who officially succeeded Francesco Lanzoni as archpriest in August of 1946. His credentials were impeccable. Born in 1913 in the province of Treviso, he had been chaplain of Santa Maria since 1937, and was untouched by the hatreds and resentment of the twenties. A Venetian who knew his people well and who was endowed with a jovial character, he could joust and bout with the men, play cards and not hesitate to stand up to the most formidable drinkers. There had been tensions between him and Lanzoni, whom he defines as a man "not always easy to deal with." His devotion to the people was endless; he served not only as pastor, but also on occasion as doctor or even midwife. The left found his record in the resistance flawless.[116] He had been arrested by the Germans for a brief period in Santa Maria while attempting to calm a crowd demanding more tobacco. He had been jailed for a longer period following the arrest of a young man of Catholic Action accused of being a member of the Resistance and had been freed by his bishop who, accompanied by two other priests, visited him in jail, gave him a cassock and walked out with Ferlini in his entourage. Don Arturo had also let it be known he saw no reason to fight for Mussolini's puppet regime in Salò. However, the right realized he had never encouraged the Resistance, and it soon was known he had granted asylum to the last federal secretary of Padua, Primo Cattani.

At the end of 1945 the only moral leadership that stood either redeemed or uncompromised in the eyes of the people was the Church. Its leaders had no particular inclination towards democracy, yet, after fascism, it could hardly be ignored. The people of Santa Maria now saw that the fascist regime had brought them war and misery. But most of the men in the municipal council were born after 1908, had lived their adult life under fascism, and were short of political experience. Furthermore, they had not been directly exposed to the Church-State conflict which had reached its height from 1909 to 1913. The Republic witnessed the progressive domination of the Church over the village's politics and the very slow development of a true sense of participation and opposition which are the basic elements of genuine democratic institutions and life.

This domination can be traced by examining the role played by the clergy in the elections. Angelo Bardini, the socialist mayor appointed by the CLN, resigned in December 1945 and Paolo Cattin served as acting mayor. In March 1946 elections were called to select new administrators: for the first time since 1924 the people exercised their political will, and for the first time women were allowed to vote. As in so many other small centers the personnel at hand was limited in numbers and in quality. Those who had been compromised by fascism, such as Baratella (who had returned to the village), were excluded from the competition. The socialists and the left in general who administered the community were evidently available and anxious, though their energy was exhausted by the innumerable problems that faced the village in the aftermath of the war: hunger, refugees, returning soldiers, the prisoners, unemployment, the rebuilding of roads, etc. Above all, they were no longer acceptable to the Church, which instead endorsed the Christian Democrats. Paolo Cattin, deprecatingly nicknamed *polentina* (little mush), was forty-two and had led the Catholic Action groups during the last years of fascism. He had acquired some experience in the town hall as a temporary administrator. He appeared to be the best suited and most reliable candidate: he was a man of exemplary piety and devotion and a member of Catholic Action. This appraisal, however, overlooked part of his character: his ambition and authoritarianism.

Only "democrats" were suitable candidates, and Don Arturo endorsed their list in full, pushing Cattin, who was in his same age group, into the limelight. The socialist-communist list was played down, and the third list, led by liberals of extreme rightist inclinations, had few chances to succeed. On March 24, 1946, 86 percent

2.1 PARTICIPATION IN LOCAL ELECTIONS MARCH 24, 1946

	M	*F*	*T*
Entitled to vote	684	688	1,372
Voted	580	603	1,183
Did not vote	47	85 }	189
Military	57		

2.2 RETURNS OF LOCAL ELECTIONS MARCH 24, 1946

	Votes	*Seats*
Christian Democrats	752	12
Social-Communists	129	3
Liberals	66	—
Others	149	—
Nonvalid votes	87	—

of the people of Santa Maria went to the polls and following Don Arturo's advice produced a triumph for the Christian Democrat list led by Cattin. Many electors split their votes between the lists and the outcome was even more conclusive: the highest number of votes for a Christian Democrat councillor was 831, the lowest 788, while the socialist-communists could muster no more than 171.

Don Arturo and the local tacticians, however, had committed two errors. First, Paolo Cattin proved to be unsuited for the position. Secondly, they had not understood that the system allowed them to choose their own opposition. With three lists running and the winner taking four-fifths of the seats, judicious vote-splitting can favor either the second or the third list, since every elector can distribute his vote over twelve candidates from any of the three lists. Don Arturo had not encouraged vote-splitting and it soon became clear in the council that the socialist-communists were far more embarrassing an opposition than the liberals would have ever been. This error would not be repeated.

The incapacity of the favorite, Cattin, was more disquieting. He soon came to see himself as a new Baratella and sought to threaten the state authorities and his fellow councilmen. Where joint efforts could have been productive, Cattin antagonized the protagonists. In 1944 parts of the poet's tomb (the bust on the arch) and other art treasures had been entrusted to the custody of the Fine Arts. A speedy return could possibly entice more tourists to visit the village. Like other state administrations the Fine Arts were characterized neither by speed, nor haste; but Cattin never ceased sending them insulting letters accusing them of pettiness.[117] Similarly, a local entrepreneur wished to build a hotel near the village and the required building permit depended upon the Fine Arts' approval. Cattin wrote the superintendent and the prefect: "Serious events will occur [if the permit is not granted] for which I decline all responsibility."[118] In December he wrote Manzato, a large landowner: "If you do not employ more war veterans acts of vandalism could well take place on your properties."[119] Such tactics were no more acceptable to the authorities than they were to the majority in the council, who forced his resignation. A bitter man, he slid from the republican group to the socialist and then communist parties, with a single objective in mind, to obstruct any initiative from the town hall. In spite of all this he has not left the Church and acts as a devout Catholic.

Facing Don Arturo during the same period was a more important and sinister problem which put the village into the regional limelight. When Primo Cattani, the last federal representative of fascism in Padua, sensed the end of Mussolini's Republic of Salò, he sought to hide. Don Arturo, as a neighbor (Cattani was also mayor of Qualto) and out of charity, provided him with a refuge in May 1945. Without informing Lanzoni, he first hid him in the nursery school and then in the rectory itself: only the priest's immediate entourage knew where he was. Cattani died of a heart attack in the spring of 1946, a few weeks before he was to be tried *in absentia*. The situation was delicate and the only solution appeared to be to hide the corpse. In great secret one night Don Arturo and six other men carted the body through the village and buried it in a garden near the upper square. What appeared to be the end of the story was only a beginning: the man's children raised the issue of his trial, pointing out that he was dead and there was no longer any reason to proceed; furthermore, because he was dead they were entitled to their inheritance. Yet the death had to be proved. The magistrate issued an accusation of concealment of a corpse. The issue became serious and the conspirators decided to exhume the body. Again, during a summer night, the decomposing cadaver was carried through the village and was abandoned near the cemetery, to be "discovered" the next day. The issue was no longer Cattani's trial but an accusation of concealing a corpse, violating a tomb, and removing a corpse. The gruesome affair was judged October 10, 1947. Nobody in the village could be found to testify and the tribunal included only Christian Democrats. Don Arturo acted as his own lawyer and pleaded not guilty because as a priest he was held to the secrecy of confession and could not reveal what he might know as a man. The *Unità's* headlines read: "Cattani's corpse travels while the priest remains silent." The verdict for him, the family, and six other codefendants was not guilty due to the lack of evidence. Don Arturo had created a bond with the village and returned triumphant.

He had become the most important personage in the village—he had formally succeeded Lanzoni as archpriest on August 15, 1946. His patronage became essential for those who desired employment; and well known in the province and Padua, by now entirely dominated by the Christian Democrats, he did his faithful justice. Between 1946 and 1949 he was relentless in his search for positions, procuring through his good offices work for over 300 people, and writing innumerable letters of recommendation for the emigrants.

In a short time Don Arturo created a patron-client relationship that reinforced the spiritual links existing between the priest and his parishioners. In most cases the patron-client relationship extended to the entire family of the individual; with the six men who had participated in the Cattani incident (four of whom were connected with the municipal council or the town hall) a bond of complicity existed. As in all similar relations thanks are not expected and seldom offered, the client believing either that the debt can be extinguished or that his patron has good reason to continue backing him. But one indirect way of acquitting oneself, at least in the Santa Maria of the late forties and fifties, was to heed the priest's instructions at election time.

In June 1946 the Italian people had to choose the form of political regime they desired, monarchy or republic. The Church clearly favored monarchy and the Christian Democrats inclined to be of the same opinion. Santa Maria had always believed in strong government and perceived the king as a necessary father figure. The outcome of the vote was never in doubt in either of the two electoral sections that divide the village. (See Table 2.3.)

2.3 RETURNS OF REFERENDUM, JUNE 1946

	Section I	*Section II*	*Total*
Electors	709	584	1,293
Void or cancelled	99	60	159
Republic	114	149	263
Monarchy	496	375	871

Section II represented the countryside, and in particular the eastern zone of the *comune* outside the parish limits. It appeared far more inclined to the left, if republicanism can be called left. It also followed this trend in voting for its representatives at the constituent assembly (Table 2.4).

In Santa Maria 66 percent supported the Christian Democrats (DC) while the left garnered slightly less than 20 percent. In the village proper (Section I) the DC led the left 74 to 13 percent,

2.4 RETURNS OF ELECTIONS TO THE CONSTITUENT ASSEMBLY, JUNE 1946

	Section I	*Section II*	*Total*
Voted	668	584	1,252
Void or cancelled	37	41	78
Christian Democrats	493	340	833
Communist Party	15	28	43
Socialist Party	66	121	187
Four other parties	57	54	111

while in the countryside the DC mustered 58.2 and the left 25.5 percent. The relative independence of the countryside, which is in more direct contact with other centers and above all is not entirely part of the parish, is a constant trait in Santa Maria's politics: the further from the center the more difficult the population is to control.

The election of 1948 was presented in very simple terms: for or against Christ; saving Italy from the Marxist hordes; freedom versus enslavement. The dichotomy was total and the DC campaigned virtually unopposed. But to say the DC is not exactly correct since in the village the party had no formal organization. Cattin had left the municipal council and could not be expected to play his role as head of the Catholic Action groups. The provincial committee of the DC, in a letter dated September 9, 1947, and addressed to the mayor, Catholic Action and the parish priest, lamented the nonexistence of a formal organization in Santa Maria ". . . when preparations are being made for an electoral campaign during which Italy's future as a democratic and Christian nation will be at stake." In April 1948 the Italian organizations of the United States sent a letter exhorting their brothers to be faithful to democracy and defeat atheistic communism. The major propaganda center became once again the rectory and the altar. The instructions were clear; the only vote to be cast was DC and no votes should be lost. The women in particular were instructed on this last item; less then one percent of votes was wasted while in 1946 the proportion had been over six percent. The returns for the House and the Senate are presented in Table 2.5.

The DC scored a resounding victory. At the national level it carried 48 percent of the electorate; in Santa Maria, 85 percent. The attempts to polarize the situation had worked. Santa Maria's rural section, in spite of the very strong DC showing, still manifested its relative independence and sympathies for the left. The socialists lost across the board, conceding votes to DC and PCI, the latter gaining 45 votes or 4 percent of the total, thus doubling its 1946 standing. The returns for the Senate, where the qualifying age is twenty-five, indicated the left had done far better with the older generations, particularly in the rural section, with the PCI tripling its 1946 returns. Finally, in Santa Maria practically the whole

2.5 RETURNS OF 1948 ELECTIONS

	Section I		*Section II*			
	votes	*%*	*votes*	*%*	*Total votes*	*%*
			LOWER HOUSE			
DC	625	92	498	79	1,123	85
PSI	19	6	36	15	55	11
PCI	21		57		88	
7 others	15	2	34	5	49	3
			SENATE			
DC	543	91	412	77	955	85
PSDI	6		19		25	
PSI	28	9	40	22	68	15
PCI	20		60		80	

female population voted DC. It has been estimated that in Italy 70 percent of the DC vote is female.[120] Considering that in Santa Maria 49 percent of the population is female, if only 70 percent had given their vote to the DC, the DC would have received more male votes than there are male electors. Consequently, it would appear under the most favorable circumstances of 1948 that if 90 percent of the females voted DC, no more than 60 percent of the male population gave their vote to the Christian Democratic party. The men inclined towards the left and were less susceptible to the Church's orders, at least on issues concerning national politics.

In local politics the situation was different. In 1951 apoliticism governed. Don Arturo had carefully chosen the list of councillors, convincing Angelo Bardini, who had run as a socialist, to join the DC list. A second militant from the socialist party, professor Mario Fortuna, also joined the DC forces. He was a "favorite son." A soft-spoken and well educated man, he had, against many obstacles, completed his university studies to become a professor of letters specializing in the study of Petrarch. Fortuna was well known and liked by all. He had an extended family clan that could be relied upon for support. His relatives had always been present in the municipal council; and one of the most influential members in the village, the broker, was his uncle and ready to back him. Don Arturo had no doubts that he would be elected.

Once again the DC won easily, and again, the rural section indicated its opposition proclivities. The victory was even more astounding considering the preferential votes. Mario Fortuna received 859, making the mandate clear. He was, therefore, elected mayor by the Council. For the first time Santa Maria had a political leader who was not only qualified, but who also desired to help his fellow citizens. When the Italian miracle erupted he was still in power, and well prepared to exploit the political and economic possibilities. This will be dealt with later, in chapters 5 and 6.

Santa Maria's political development was strongly influenced by the economic transformation at the end of the nineteenth century, essentially the introduction of capitalist structures in the community, and the revolution of the landholding system brought about by fascism. These radical changes made a frustrated population that was inclined toward socialism turn to the conservatism that goes with landownership. The first decade of the twentieth century and the introduction of universal suffrage witnessed the progressive secularization of the people when forced to choose between the Church and the State. The village's experience with local administration from unification until 1951 was essentially negative and explains the people's passive acceptance of authority and their reticence to accept local political roles.

The most important element that influenced the political development of Santa Maria was the Catholic Church. Following Italian unification the papal *non expedit* led to a policy of Church nonintervention in politics until 1895 when the socialist party appeared on the electoral scene. It was opposed because the Church believed it atheistic. Without decreasing its charitable and social activities, the Church engaged more actively in politics, rescinding

2.6 RETURNS OF MUNICIPAL ELECTIONS, 1951

	Section I	*Section II*	*Total*
DC	390	353	743
Opposition	45	99	144

the *non expedit*, and supporting, in turn, first *popolari* and then Christian Democrats. Progressively, the legitimacy of the Church was transferred to the party it supported and to which it lent its local organizational network. An essential element in the transfer was the parish priest, which led at the local level to confusion between Christian Democratic party and Church. They were often viewed as a single entity and even today the older Mariani repeat that "the DC is the parish house."

In Santa Maria, the confusion was possibly greater than elsewhere. Until the end of the Second World War the village was physically isolated. The only figure of authority its inhabitants knew was the parish priest. During the period of nonintervention, Don Alfredo Lumini, though he took little interest in his parish, remained the major personality and encountered few challenges from the municipal leaders who were either no more interested in the community than he was, or simple peasants who shied away from responsibilities.

Had Don Alfredo been more involved, Santa Maria undoubtedly would have felt the influence of the Catholic Congress movement which was particularly vigorous in Este, a few kilometers away. Instead, the village allowed itself to be swayed by the socialists from Fantolon. Francesco Lanzoni, Lumini's successor, lost the battle against the socialists and the fascists. Don Arturo Ferlini, first chaplain and later archpriest, was the only legitimate guide the population could follow in 1945. His legitimacy was transferred to the Christian Democratic party that he came to represent. His position was such in this village of small landowners that he could use, for example in 1948, arguments that hardly belonged to the realm of politics: he convinced men that their souls would be saved if they supported the Christian Democrats. His strong personality, his paternalism, and his prestige slowed the secularization process and hindered genuine participation in Santa Maria. This very slowness may, however, augur well for the democratic future of the community.

3. The Population and the Economy

A COMMUNITY WHOSE LIVELIHOOD IS ENTIRELY DEPENDENT upon agriculture can only support a determinate number of inhabitants. People are forced to leave when they can no longer find adequate means of support for their families.[1] Population movements are closely linked to the village's situation. Knowing the demographic trends that affect emigration and the variations of the working population is essential to the understanding of the changes that have occurred in the local economy.

Population Movements

Over Time

On January 1, 1969, the official population of Santa Maria was 2,040: 1,042 males (51.08%) and 998 females (49.92%).[2] Ninety people who lived elsewhere maintained their official residences in Santa Maria, reducing the total number of actual residents to 1,950. One-third lived in the village proper, 38 percent in the hills, 20 percent in the plains, and 10 percent in the relatively small but distinct groupings known as *corte* or nuclei.[3]

The population is extremely homogeneous, sharing similar traditions, language, and cultural and physical traits. Three-quarters of the residents were born in Santa Maria and one-fifth moved to the village from other centers in the province of Padua. Only 5 percent came from other Italian regions and 1 percent from abroad. Eighty-two percent of the males and 65 percent of the females living in Santa Maria were born there. Thus, the ethnic unity is not simply Paduan or

Venetian, but above all Marian. The community is a living reality based upon a shared past and an intimate knowledge of the events that have influenced, favored or hindered the development of every single family of the community. Significantly, ten family names comprise over 60 percent of the total population, revealing a clan structure which reinforces the unity of the community.

Until 1904 economic uncertainties and emigration limited the growth of the population. (See Table 3.1 and Graph 3.1 for population variations.) Continuous expansion marked the first half of the twentieth century. The large estates required manpower; the outcome of World War I and fascism temporarily closed the traditional destinations of emigration; the peasants' land seizures, Mussolini's family legislation, and the influx of war refugees all led to a population increase the economy could hardly support. In 1948 Santa Maria had 2,694 inhabitants, 1,052 or 64 percent more than in 1888. Several poor harvests in the early 1950s led people to abandon the village en masse. Only ten years later, when work became available in the province of Padua, did the population size begin to stabilize.[4] Santa Maria, an agricultural society, could not support more than 2,000 inhabitants.

3.1 POPULATION VARIATIONS

Year	*Population*	*Absolute Increase*	*Average Yearly Increase*	*Average Yearly Increase Percentage*
1888	1,642			
1904	1,729	87	5.56	3.2
1911	1,876	147	21.0	11.6
1921	2,090	214	21.4	10.7
1931	2,292	202	20.2	9.2
1936	2,487	195	39.0	16.6
1943	2,641	154	12.8	5.0
1948	2,694	53	10.6	3.9
1951	2,544	–150	–50	–19
1956	2,376	–168	–33.6	–13.7
1961	2,125	–251	–50.2	–22.2
1969	2,040	–85	–12.1	–6.0

GRAPH 3.1 ABSOLUTE VARIATIONS OF POPULATION

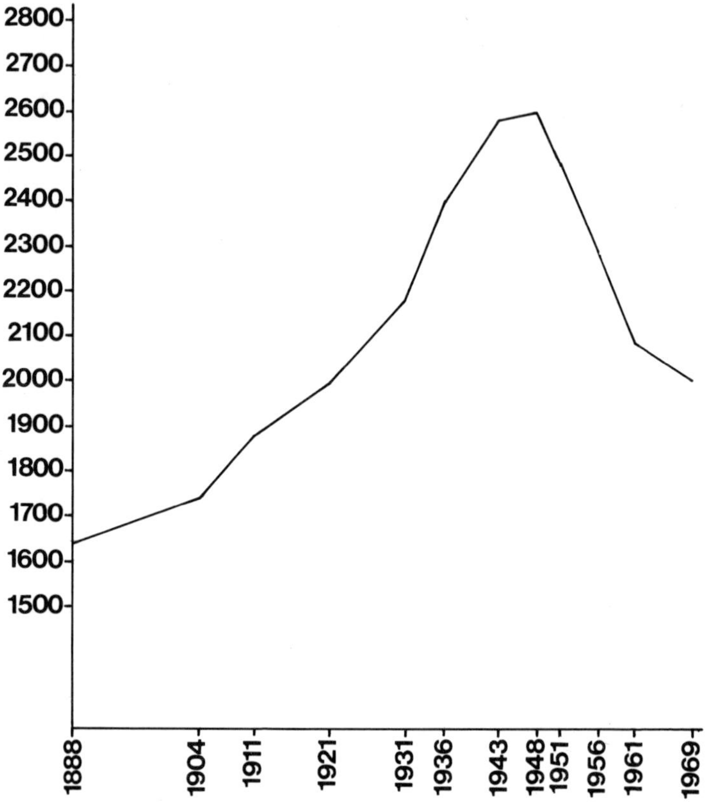

In Space

The changes over time have been accompanied by changes in space. The 1948 population density of 215 people per square kilometer declined to 162 in 1969, coinciding with a trend to move into the village from the countryside.[5] This change appears to be connected with the decline in agricultural activities and a search for greater physical convenience (water, light, etc.). The trend was gradual until

3.2 POPULATION DISTRIBUTION IN PERCENT

Year	*Village*	*Countryside*
1939	27.5	72.5
1954	32.9	67.1
1961	33.3	66.7
1969	41.2	58.8

the end of the fifties but pronounced in the sixties, leading to a physical expansion of the village along the two major access roads. Prosperity at home coincided with the return of the emigrants who often invested their savings in a new home. The village thus acquired a higher percentage of older people than any other part of the *comune*. (See Table 3.3.) The nuclei, while they contained proportionately the highest percentage of young people, also had the lowest percentage of workers, reflecting the strong pressure to emigrate from the *corte*.

The distribution by sex presents some points that are at variance with the overall Marian norm: in the village there is a higher concentration of widows and young girls, and women are more numerous than men (50.55%, while the average is 48.92%); but in the nuclei men represent 66 percent of the population, a considerable variation indeed. This is due to the extremely harsh life of the women in the *corte*, leading to shorter life spans and inducing the younger girls to leave as soon as possible. An analysis of marriage trends reveals that girls in the *corte* marry at a younger age than village girls and emigrate more often.

Graph 3.2 presents the age pyramid of Santa Maria as of January 1, 1969, and reflects the population variations of the last fifty years; it is

3.3 POPULATION DISTRIBUTION BY ZONES AND AGE IN 1969

	Percentage	*0–20*	*20–65*	*Over 65*
Village	32	32	55	13
Nuclei	10	47	47	6
Hills	38	35	57	8
Plains	20	40	53	7

GRAPH 3.2 AGE PYRAMID, 1969

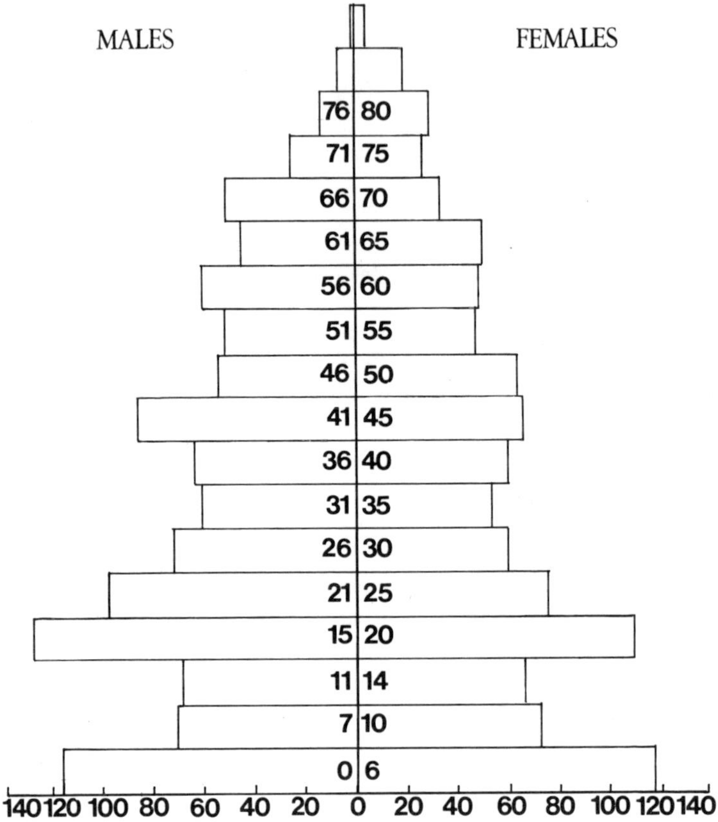

an irregular pyramid much in contrast to that of 1953 before the impact of massive emigration.[6] The age group born between 1893 and 1903 that benefitted directly from the redistribution of the earth in the mid-twenties, was subject to the fascist laws on emigration, and was too old to leave in the 1950s is still very much present. The size of the age group born between 1918 and 1923 is noticeable, a consequence of the end of the war and of the soldiers' return, though this group bore the brunt of the military effort in the Second World War. In contrast, the classes born between 1923 and 1933 constituted (with their children) the mass of the emigrants leaving the village after 1950. The weight of the older generations created an imbalance with economic consequences we shall discuss later.[7] A decade of emigration between 1948 and 1958 has made a clear impact on the younger age groups. Between 1975 and 1985 trends of low natality and high mortality will lead to a further decline in the population, which, if the younger people are forced to emigrate, would have long-lasting consequences.

Emigration

Emigration is the main demographic and social problem in Santa Maria; one is tempted to say it is eternal, a state of mind. Faced with poverty, the Mariani have traditionally sought employment in northern Italy and abroad, in Germany, Austria-Hungary, France, and after 1879 in America, particularly in South America. "Those tormented by misery leave for foreign lands, offering the strength of their arms and the sweat of their brow, to seek the food they cannot or do not know how to find at home."[8]

The explanation given in 1902 was similar to the ones we gathered in the summer of 1969 when we talked to emigrants who returned for their vacation. Gianni Sivieri said, "I left in 1953 and went to Vercelli before moving to Alessandria where my mother's cousin found me a job in a canning factory. I started sweeping floors but now I'm a foreman. I left because I was hungry. There was no choice. My brother helped my parents on the farm and you can only prune a vineyard once a year. Sure, I could eat at home if you call a salted sardine and polenta a meal, but it was humiliating to look for work, find none and always depend on the others. Even the girls who went bare-foot knew you couldn't make a living. There was no work for me and the priest wouldn't help because I didn't go to church. So I left."

Until 1950, when it became apparent that the land available was too limited, if not too poor, to insure anything more than a family's physical survival, leaving the village was considered a temporary move. The emigrant returned when he had accumulated a small capital, often attempting to provide his family with a better life by purchasing one or two fields. But when the disastrous harvests of 1951 coincided with industry's claims for manpower, the emigrants were no longer fathers or bachelors but entire families, often headed by the youngest sons, who owned no farm land. During the early 1950s the average age of the emigrant dropped to 5.8, resulting in the depopulation of the younger age groups.

In the span of twenty-five years between 1943 and 1968, Santa Maria lost 2,281 inhabitants to emigration. Material gathered from the provincial archives indicates that Santa Maria lost 4.2 percent of its population yearly between 1887 and 1905. Since World War II the percentage of emigrants has seldom been less than 4 percent, reaching peaks of 6.6 and 9.1 percent in 1957 and 1961. Abandoning Santa Maria were 1,040 (45.6%) males and 1,241 (54.33%) females. Excluding 321 women who left after marrying outsiders, 53.1 of the emigrants were men and 46.9 percent women. Considering only those over age 18, 654 males and possibly 182 females (taking one-third of the female emigrants to be members of the work force), or 836 people, left the village, relieving it of a laboring class larger than the present gainfully employed population. Ninety percent of the males declared themselves to be farmers or peasants; 5.34 and 4.66 percent belonged to the secondary and tertiary sectors, respectively.

3.4 EMIGRATION, 1945–1968

	Under 18	*Non-married*	*Married or Widowers*
Male	387	211	443
Female	373	140	406
Total	760	351	849

Only 62.77 percent of the emigrants were born in Santa Maria (compared with 74 percent of today's resident population). In other words, 37.32 percent of the emigrants, it can be presumed, did not have strong roots in the village and could leave with relative ease, representing "flow-throughs,"[9] a fluctuating population of agricultural laborers or tenant farmers who were the most prone to suffer from the adverse agricultural conditions.

Unfortunately we have not been able to ascertain the jobs obtained by the emigrants. Those to whom we talked when they returned to the village definitely shunned agriculture, finding employment in factories, commerce and trades in the larger cities of Piedmont and Lombard and in the city of Padua itself, particularly after 1960.

A case in point is Adolfo Zancanaro who left in 1954 and went to work as a common laborer for Olivetti in Biella. Going to night school he became a lathe operator. In 1960 his father died leaving him six acres in Santa Maria to which he returned. By 1961 he had a job in a factory in Padua. As he put it: "I don't mind working the fields but you can't keep a family happy with them. Every third week I take a night shift and that gives me enough free time to keep up with the farm. We make our own wine and grow our vegetables. That's about it."

The emigrants sought to remain as near as possible to their own province, and the percentage who went abroad was insignificant. Prior to 1963 a large share (42.68%) went to the more industrialized parts of northern Italy and the industrial triangle (32%), establishing "colonies" in the cities of Milan, Alessandria and Vercelli. Trying to locate a place to live in Santa Maria, on the advice of the parish priest we visited in June 1968 an usher, a florist, a mechanic and a butcher in Milan, all Mariani of the Pittoni family! Reflecting the changed economic conditions of the province, three-quarters of the emigrants of the second wave stayed in the Veneto, 75 percent of these in the province of Padua. (Contrast Tables 3.5 and 3.6.) Thirty-six percent reside in Fantolon and 12 percent in the town of Padua. Thus, about 48 percent of all recent emigrants live within a twenty-five kilometer radius of Santa Maria. The proximity to Santa Maria allows the emigrant to feel that he has not left his village and circle of friends. In many cases a choice has been made between commuting and residing as near as possible to one's work.

Today emigration appears to have reached reasonable limits: 3.16

3.5 EMIGRATION AND DESTINATION, 1945–1968

Destination	*Numbers*	*Percentage*
Padua (province)	1,144	50.13
North	1,058	46.36
South and central	53	2.32
Abroad	9	0.39
Unknown	20	0.87

3.6 EMIGRATION AND DESTINATION, 1964–1968

Destination	*Numbers*	*Percentage*
Padua (province)	277	74.46
North	87	23.39
South and central	8	2.15

percent per year between 1964 and 1968 and only 2.1 percent in 1968. However, it is far from certain the younger generations will accept holding two jobs with the ease that their fathers did. Consequently, it is imperative that either some industrial development take place in the village or that employment be secured in the immediate vicinity. However, this latter possibility is beyond village control.

The Economically Active Population

The changes that have taken place in the gainfully employed population are summarized in Tables 3.7, 3.8 and Graph 3.3. First of all one must note that the proportion of economically active to resident population declined between 1951 and 1961 as a result of emigration. In spite of the higher concentration of older age groups after 1965,[10] more young people have been able to find work in or around Santa Maria and are no longer forced to emigrate. This is particularly true for those employed in secondary activities.

3.7 ACTIVE AND RESIDENT POPULATION, 1951–1969

	1951	*1961*	*1969*
Resident population (PR)	2,544	2,125	2,040
Active population (PA)	996	657	707
Primary active population (PA1)	675	290	117
Secondary active population (PA2)	234	277	452
Tertiary active population (PA3)	87	90	138

GRAPH 3.3 ACTIVE AND RESIDENT POPULATION

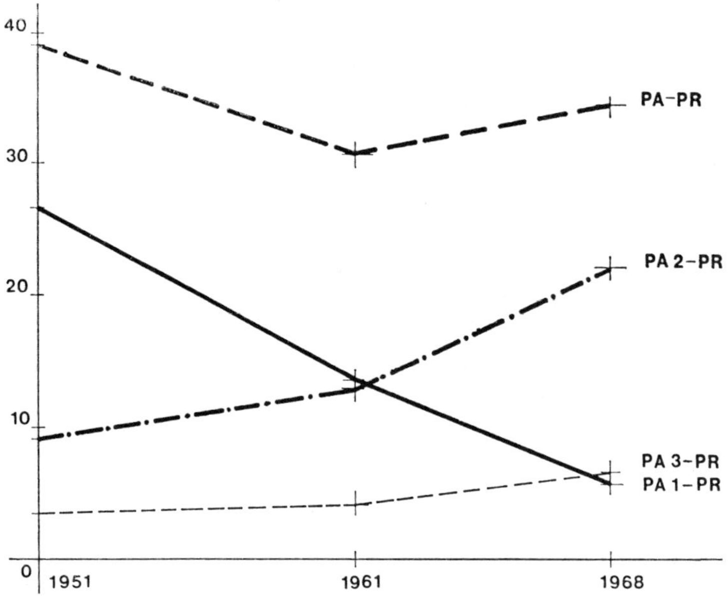

In agriculture the transformation was brutal. The ratio of farmers to total resident population reached a low point of 5.73 percent in 1969. This figure is open to various interpretations, since it is directly derived from our system of classification. We defined the primary sector as those whose major source of income came from the farm. This system

3.8 ACTIVE POPULATION/RESIDENT POPULATION, IN PERCENTAGE

	1951	*1961*	*DI 51–61*	*1969*	*DI 61–69*
PA/PR	39.15	30.92	−8.23	34.65	+3.73
PA1/PR	26.53	13.65	−12.88	5.73	−7.92
PA2/PR	9.20	13.04	+3.84	22.15	+9.11
PA3/PR	3.42	4.23	+0.81	6.76	+2.33

excluded many factory workers who are also part-time farmers. Generally, in particular among the younger generations, a clear choice has been made in favor of the factory over the farm. But a dual allegiance still survives, and the decline in agriculture has not led to a radical transformation of the value system of the peasant culture even though it is going through a slow process of change. In fact many aspects will remain because the smaller farms that are run by retired men over sixty-five also employ their middle-aged sons on a sporadic basis, and their young grandsons more regularly, maintaining a respect for farming.

The limited change in tertiary activities (+3.4 percent, 1951–1968) is due to an increase in the number of state employees, schoolteachers in particular, which has compensated for the decline in commercial activities.

The economically active population, excluding all people over the age of sixty-five who benefit from a pension scheme, is distributed as in Table 3.9.

Between 1961 and 1969 the working population increased 3.76 percent to become 35 percent of the total population while the latter declined. Seventy percent of those employed are concentrated in secondary activities, an increase of 27 percent. This is a good indication of the changes and newly acquired prosperity in the community. The economic situation is further improved by the pensioners (294 or 14.75 percent of the total population), many of whom continue to work on the farms as long as they have the ability and strength, though one-third received a yearly income of 480,000 lire, or above $770.

3.9 DISTRIBUTION OF ACTIVE POPULATION, BY PERCENTAGE

	1936	*1951*	*1961*	*1969*
Primary	78	68	43	16.5
Secondary	14	13	43	70
Tertiary	8	19	14	13.5
PA/PR	37	39	31	35

The Economy

The question one must ask when dealing with a rural community such as Santa Maria is: under what conditions can agriculture survive today? Can a village remain basically oriented towards the production of agricultural goods in the twentieth century, when the towns no longer put an exclusive reliance upon the countryside, but envision themselves a part of the national and at times international economic system?

Santa Maria, located in the southern part of the Veneto that has no major industrial centers, is caught between several poles of attraction including Padua, Rovigo, Verona and Ferrara. Yet to all appearances a peasant culture survives there. The image traced by Foster remains true in many respects.

> Broad areas of peasant behavior are patterned in such fashion as to suggest that peasants view their social, economic, and natural universe—their total environment—as one in which all the desired things in life such as land, wealth, health, friendship and love, manliness and honor, respect and status, power and influence, security and safety, *exist in finite quantity and are always in short supply,* as far as the peasant is concerned. Not only do these and all other "good things" exist in finite and limited quantities, but in addition *there is no way directly within peasant power to increase the available quantities.*[11]

This attitude is hardly conducive to change. The peasant is an individualist, a conservative, and a defender of the status quo. He remains attached to beliefs antedating the nineteenth century and opposed to the values of a modern market economy. Obviously, this abstract characterization refers to a generic and closed peasant civilization. But we have had many occasions to witness this pattern of behavior in Santa Maria.[12] Peasant mentality there has decisively negative effects on the economy. The problem has deep roots that are more human and psychological than economic, explaining the need for a transformation of the local culture and an alteration of the economic system.

The Agricultural Tradition

The 1961 census classified 43 percent of the population as agricultural, and based on first impressions one might feel that this is still true. However, the situation has changed, even if it is not always reflected in outward appearances. Until the downfall of fascism the entire economy revolved around agriculture. But the economic structure changed rapidly under the Republic and by 1961 the primary and secondary sectors were on a par. In 1969 the agricultural sector employed less than 20 percent of the full-time working population.

The work of part-time farmers allows Santa Maria to maintain the image of an agricultural center. Approximately 450 people own a piece of land in the community, deriving some benefits from their ownership and devoting part of their free time to its cultivation. But in the Veneto[13] three-fifths of all income is from industry, and the rapid development of motorized transportation has radically transformed the Marian way of life. The peasant has become a peasant-worker and a commuter. His village tends to become his dormitory. This phenomenon has taken on massive proportions in Santa Maria. Sixty-two and a half percent of the laborers work outside the physical boundaries of the *comune*. Under these conditions it is difficult to ignore the change of mentality that ensues, the tensions that result, and the new status of agriculture. Today the local society is in a period of rapid and acute transition without having assimilated all the values of the new industrial society; it is bewildered but still attached to the earth, its symbol of security.

The Latin epigrammist Martial lauded the quality of the products of the Euganean Hills and there are many remarks in the documents of the courts of Este and Carrara that mention the exquisite wines of Santa Maria. The noble Paduan and Venetian families made it a practice to hold property there and a sixteenth-century list notes that 1,200 campi (464 hectares) were held by Paduans alone. But today

3.10 PERCENTAGE EMPLOYED IN AGRICULTURE

1789	*1936*	*1951*	*1961*	*1969*
80.1	78	68	43	16.5

there is no longer general agreement as to the "supreme" quality of the wines; they do not keep well and do not always please the refined connoisseur. Although this is true, it detracts little from the genuine naturalness of the products. In an Italy that has redefined "sophistication" as the art of making wines without grapes, this attribute becomes an asset.

Until the twentieth century all agricultural activity was concentrated in the hills on the arc from Sasso to Monte Ricco (Stone to Rich Mountain). The arc was intensively cultivated and terraced, planted with vineyards, olive groves, and orchards.[14] The older members of the community remember the efforts needed to carry water up the side of the hills. Each handful of earth was precious and susceptible to theft, which led to fights and knifings. Under these conditions there was work for all and in spite of low yields few understood the meaning of the expression to give up: the peasant was morbidly attached to the earth. When fascism in its onslaught on local capitalism gave the earth to the peasantry, there were definite psychological effects on the population. For the first time all were landowners, the village was one, tempered in the same fight for survival. For the first time the peasant had obtained property where he could cultivate cereals rationally.

A dialogue between the mountain and the plain was thus established with the village serving as a link. Increased communication was beneficial to the community, as was the creation of new loyalties with regard to the village, but in perspective this development also had the negative result of creating an artificial and false sense of security among the people "who [as one mentioned] thought of themselves as signori who no longer relied solely on polenta and who even purchased meat once a month." Since the plains were easier to work, when the harsh winter of 1930 and the phylloxera nearly destroyed all the vineyards and olive groves on the hills, a majority concentrated their efforts on the plains. Only the most obstinate and intelligent perceived that the production of wine and oil was in fact more advantageous and started replanting on the hills. When a true market economy became a reality, the plains no longer insured survival. The late fifties, which saw the peasant extinguish the financial debt incurred under fascism, also marked the end of a peasant culture in Santa Maria.

Today one can no longer talk of a mountain-plain dialogue. The interaction now exists between village and city. When one sees men moving through the village toward the fields, it might seem that agriculture still thrives. But the appearance is false. Only 16.5 percent of the working force is concentrated in agriculture, and these are mostly old men who continue the agricultural tradition because they know no other trade. However, among a handful of young men a new mentality appears in the making. Stimulated by a few of their elders who possess some capital, with the sense of newly discovered initiative, they are returning to the hills and bringing them back to life. During the last five years many new vineyards have been planted. Olive groves have also been started though these will take twenty years to reach their production peak. New cultures such as lavender and basil have been tried. The farmer has realized that the cereal-producing plain is no longer his best source of income, and that wine and oil might insure his prosperity.[15] Patience and courage have appeared anew in the village.

Distribution of Crops and Productivity

In Santa Maria today the distribution of crops is rational and is a function of the terrain, while in the past it corresponded to abstract ideals of pure autarky, family or state dictated. The hills are dedicated to the cultivation of grapes, olives and a few early crops such as spring peas (for which the village is famous). The plains are given to the intensive cultivation of herbaceous plants on short rotation, such as corn and wheat, often interspersed with a few rows of grapevines in promiscuous cultivation. The last few years have witnessed successful experiments that devote part of the plains to vegetable production, in particular Treviso chicory.

A variety of crops are produced (see Table 3.11) and the surface planted in vineyards has more than tripled since 1940, while the promiscuous plantation of grapes has nearly doubled. Even the olive groves are attaining levels reminiscent of the 1930s. The peasant-worker has reinvested part of his added income from the factory into those crops which, through intensive labor, provide greater financial benefits. Above all the village is orienting its agricultural production toward only two products: wine and olive oil.

3.11 CROPS IN HECTARES[16]

Crops	*1929*	*1939*	*1949*	*1963*	*1970*
Wheat	172	170	190	255	210
Spring corn	136	120	175	160	205
Rotation pasture	79	160	140	75	118
Permanent pasture	192	170	173	172	166
Vineyards	133	100	60	135	346
Vineyards, promiscuous	333	485	372	205	579
Olive groves	45	25	20	20	16
Olives, promiscuous	—	—	—	25	55
Sugar beet	17	4	5	7	16
Orchards	22	40	8	6	12

The habit of promiscuous cultivation has not disappeared. Grapes, fruit trees and vegetables such as beans are grown simultaneously with corn. This type of plantation affords a more intensive exploitation of the soil, but will not survive. This method, calling for numerous trips to the fields for very short periods of work, is not economical. With greater specialization more efforts will be put on larger plots of land that facilitate mechanized operation.

Other crops have disappeared from Santa Maria due to the increased competition from better equipped zones or to technological progress. Flax, linen and the silkworm industry are memories of the past. Today the orchards seem to be moving in the same direction and represent a very limited source of income. The cultivation of peaches and apricots is practically extinct. The no more than one hundred cherry trees are far from producing the thirty tons the statistics noted in 1963, a figure that was half of the 1929 harvest. A more interesting future appears reserved to the jujubes, of which approximately one ton is harvested annually, as they are rare and very much in request on the local markets. The tree itself requires very little attention, though harvesting the crop is costly. The same applies to the peas, which are so well known they command prices on the Paduan market twice as high as southern peas. Ten years ago everyone planted them, but today it is becoming more difficult to find the manpower to harvest them before dawn, while the middlemen can extract the prices they want from the unorganized producers. The local market does not provide more than 20 to 30 tons. Since irrigation and mechanization are difficult in view of the incline of the slopes, this commodity will soon disappear or be limited to family consumption.

Considerable problems were encountered in gathering precise figures regarding oil and wine. The peasant is reticent to talk about his sources of income. Presently the production of olive oil falls short of its 1930 level. However the only olive press active locally cannot satisfy the demand and many (for the sake of secrecy, or because they are in conflict with the owner of the press) have their harvest refined elsewhere. The production reaches from 10 to 12 tons per year, most of which is sold at $2,000 per ton, four times the commercial price of vegetable oil.

The yield of wine is low, since at best a production figure of 18,000 hectoliters can be estimated. Wine sells for three to five hundred lire a liter (a high price) and production is insufficient to satisfy demand. The most renowned grapes are the red and white muscats which are blended with garganega and pinella grapes. They possess delicate colors, splendid bouquets and reasonable body, and contrary to most muscats are dry wines that accompany red and white meats most adequately. Barbera, Pinot and Cabernet are also of fine quality, while the Corvello and Marzemino have become rarities. These are mountain wines that often retain the flavor of the stones on which they have grown, and, because of the late harvest, have a high alcoholic content (12-15%), reaching 19 percent in exceptional years or when particular care is taken in choosing the grapes for the press. Unfortunately, quality is often locally judged on the alcoholic content and not enough importance is given to aspect, bouquet and especially acidity. Much remains to be done with regard to the vinification and preservation. The problem is not new: in 1890 the Royal School of Agriculture declared that the wines from Santa Maria, often among the best, fell short of their reputation because of their poor preservation.[17]

The promiscuous type of plantation in the plains is not economical, while the plantation system adopted in the vineyards corresponds neither to the peasant's interest nor to EEC criteria. The rows are extremely narrow which hinders the use of tractors, calls for an

Shredding wheat under Petrarch's balcony

Hoeing in the valley

Grape harvesting

Making salami

intensive use of fertilizers, and makes harvesting more cumbersome. A habit derived from promiscuous plantation, placing a few rows of each quality in the same field, calls for staggered harvesting. This system requires patience and increases costs. Such an approach is still possible because of the many elderly folk who can devote their time to this occupation and who are not paid for the work. With larger farms, when speed becomes a factor, this solution is no longer available if the grapes are to be picked at their optimum.

But the negative aspects are not predicated on economic factors alone. They are the product of psychological orientations. The peasant often refuses to learn and does not want to renounce the past and the methods of his forefathers. Above all he rejects all forms of cooperation which could decrease his costs, and he even more strenuously objects to all forms of control. In 1969 the entire territory was included in a zone of VDQS-OC—limited production wines of superior quality and controlled origin[18]—similar to those of Piedmont and Tuscany. The meetings organized by the ministry of agriculture were well attended and at least 45 producers were on hand. The ministerial representatives insisted that enrolling on the list of recognized producers was an opportunity that would not be repeated. Yet at the end of 1970 only eight people in the village had met the deadline, although they gain considerable advantage from the promotional value of the label and also command a higher price for their products. The farmer who accepts the VDQS-OC quality label agrees to use fixed percentages of specified grapes in blending and determined methods of pressing that are only slightly different from those called for by tradition. If he does not respect these standards in certain years the only penalty is that he cannot use the label VDQS. People simply refuse to change, even while acknowledging in private that their wines would be far better if produced under the new conditions.

In the same vein little has been done to exploit common market subsidies for the plantation of new vineyards in harmony with standards that would allow for mechanization, in spite of examples in surrounding villages—one in particular on the property of a Mariano, which has proved very successful. Again, the peasant has not yet tried to plant vineyards in the plain, also a VDQS zone, respecting the tradition that this part of the land is reserved for wheat and corn, even though in many cases it is well suited to wine production. The uneconomical principles of family autarky continue to prevail in the agricultural sector.

Size and Location of Farms

The multiple problems inherent in Santa Maria's agricultural situation cannot only be attributed to a peculiar form of mentality, heritage from a distant past, but should also be connected with the particular type of landowning pattern which resulted from the fragmentation of the large domains during the fascist period.

Tables 3.12 to 3.15 provide a summary of the situation.[19] Since 1930 the number of productive units has decreased 10 percent overall, but by 33 percent since 1949 when fractionalization reached a peak, while the total amount of productive acreage has declined 25.7 per-

3.12 FARMS, SURFACES AND AVERAGE HOLDINGS

Year	*Number*	*Productive Surface/Ha.*	*Average Ha.*
1930	347	1,200	3.4
1949	459	1,207	2.6
1961	364	1,033	2.8
1970	310	892	2.9

3.13 FARMS IN 1961

	Farms		*Surface*		
Type	*No.*	*% Total*	*Ha.*	*% Total*	*Average Size/Ha.*
Direct farming	347	95.3	714.69	69.7	2.06
Salaried personnel	6	1.7	206.71	20.1	34.45
Tenant farming	9	2.5	111.23	10.8	12.36
Other	2	0.5	0.97	0.1	0.48

3.14 FARMS IN 1970

	Farms		*Surface*		
Type	*No.*	*% Total*	*Ha.*	*% Total*	*Average Size/Ha.*
Direct farming	299	96.4	652.39	73.1	2.18
Salaried personnel	7	2.2	175.72	19.7	25.10
Tenant farming	4	1.3	64.61	7.2	16.15

3.15 NUMBER AND SIZE OF FARMS IN 1929 IN HECTARES

n = 347

Hectares:	up to 0.5	0.5–1	1–3	3–5	5–10	10–20	20–50	over 50
Farms:	53	39	141	72	27	12	1	2

cent, due to the abandonment of less productive areas in the hills that have turned into woods. Today 73 percent of the productive soil is controlled by 96 percent of the producers (4 percent control 27 percent), who personally exploit the very limited holdings that are divided between hills and plain. Excluding the larger properties which average 25 hectares (62 acres), the average holding is only slightly over five acres. In 1930, 40 percent of the farmers owned over 8 acres, while in 1970 only 27 percent did; no more than 20 percent of the farms can be considered a profitable size.

In Santa Maria every family is a landowner: the official statistics note 310 farms, but a survey conducted in 1969 where the criterion was whether a person had a piece of land revealed that 450 people considered themselves owners. The average surface would be less than 6.3 acres if one included the entire community territory, but only 3.3 acres considering the arable land and excluding the eleven larger farms. Fractionalism has divided and subdivided the plain of Bignago and the hills into mere strips of earth. The boundaries are not marked by irrigation ditches but more simply by a stone or a stake, making it impossible to distinguish the strips from another when they are planted in the same crops. The physical divisions brought by fascism were exacerbated by the equal inheritance system. Recently, however, few sons express the desire to become full-time farmers. Not only are these farms hardly suitable to produce adequate returns, their very inefficiency forces the peasant to seek out alternate sources of income. In the past it was emigration. Today one becomes a peasant worker. Although at first the income appears supplementary, it soon becomes dominant.

The typical Marian farm is a handkerchief of earth tended after the worker's return from the factory or the building site. In some cases it lies idle; in others, in particular those belonging to the local shopkeepers, it is farmed out so the owner can still have "his own" wine and polenta flour, a source of pride rather than of income. The larger properties are entrusted to tenant farmers or run by the owner using salaried workers. The adequately sized farm, seldom exceeding twenty-five acres, is usually a combination of land that is owned and of land that is rented, dispersed over the entire territory. For this reason, and not because of a lack of means, tractors are scarce in the village. More often than not the twenty pieces of machinery that can be seen in the fields are status symbols, purchased by a father to keep a son on the farm. The drover of the past has been replaced by the tractor driver hired on an hourly basis; the oxen have given way to the mechanized hand-driven plow.

Agricultural Balance Sheet and Relative Incomes

A long-time observer of the Euganean Hills notes

> . . . that when one factor of production is scarce in relation to other resources, in this case the soil, the productive structure that results is typically rigid, the general economic situation precarious and difficult, and the producer can only increase his income by intensifying the productivity of each acre. In fact the possibilities of his toils yielding greater returns, which are great enough with a larger farm or a radical transformation of productive crops, are, in this case, limited and modest.[20]

In Santa Maria productivity is low and is hindered by the system of ownership. The farms as they are cannot compete in the present market structures and have survived only because they have never been faced with establishing a salary structure. In 1963 a study of the farms in the region of the Euganean Hills indicated that the gross yield per hectare averaged 318,000 lire ($513; at the 1970 rate of 620 lire per dollar), with a minimum of 260,000 lire ($419) in Santa Maria and a maximum of 546,000 lire ($881) at Vo, a nearby village that produces mostly wine. The average return per man is 516,000 lire ($832). But in Vo with an average surface of 11 hectares per farm the average return per man is 1,034,000 lire ($1,668), while in Santa Maria on farms of 4.7 hectares the average drops to 339,000 lire ($547). The larger the property and the more specialized the production, the greater the income available. In 1967 the average yearly income for people in agriculture in the Hills was 325,000 lire ($525). The data we gathered in Santa Maria indicated for 1969 an overall average of 619,000 lire ($990) in contrast with the Italian average of 685,000 lire ($1,150) and the Venetian average of 671,000 lire ($1,082) for 1968.[21] The overall figure is broken down as follows: agriculture, 519,000 lire ($836); secondary employment, 694,000 lire ($1,120); tertiary employment, 902,000 lire ($1,454); and retired, 378,000 lire ($609). The relationship of income to property ownership is illustrated in Table 3.16. In these figures no consideration is given to the advantage the peasant derives from living on the farm, for himself and for his family: a good share of his food and in many cases his dwelling. These, however, are balanced by the production expenses incurred and the time and energy consumed which could be more profitably rewarded in other trades.

The contrast between the peasant's and the factory worker's incomes is evident. Eighty-three percent of the farmers have a yearly income less than 837,000 lire ($1,350 per year), and 39 percent less than 480,000 lire ($774), while only 60 and 23 percent of the secondary group fall into these categories. Under these conditions it is easy to understand why many are ready to abandon their farms.

It is essential to distinguish between abandoning the farms and leaving the community. Prior to the 1950s when life in the village was truly miserable, while people left farms and village they did so with the firm intention of returning to their natal environment as soon as

3.16 INCOME AND PROPERTY[22]

Yearly Income in Lire	Less than 4 ha. (396)		4–10 ha. (44)		More than 10 ha. (10)	
	%	No.	%	No.	%	No.
+1,800,000	3	12	5	2	40	4
+ 840,000	35	140	29	13	30	3
+ 480,000	30	119	41	18	30	3
− 480,000	32	125	25	11	0	0

3.17 INCOME AND ACTIVITY IN PERCENTAGES

Yearly Income in Lire	Primary	Secondary	Tertiary	Retired
+1,800,000	1	1	14	4
+ 840,000	16	39	52	11
+ 480,000	44	37	16	29
− 480,000	39	23	18	56

possible. One left, accumulated a little capital, and returned, purchasing a little more land in the hope of a more secure if not necessarily more comfortable life. Today such an alternative seems to be unavailable to the emigrant of the 1950s: the social pressures of his new life in the city, the greater comforts available to him, the considerable differences between city and village life, make returning a far less attractive alternative than in the past when the immigrant was an outcast in the city. At the end of the sixties it became clear that while the young peasant abandoned farm life with relative ease, he found it far more difficult to desert the community in which he lived, understanding its virtues over those of the city, and motorized transportation afforded him the best of two worlds. "It is a link . . . with values and with a community that are in the place where the peasant lives, and not a necessary link with life in the fields." that prevents him from leaving. The peasant believes "he is not as well off" as the city worker; the young are convinced that the possibilities of improvement in agriculture are limited (in the province of Padua only 16 percent think they can improve); 87 percent believe they earn less than if they were employed in industry and 91 percent of the young girls would prefer not to marry a peasant. But in contrast to this negative data 86 percent would be content to stay in agriculture if economic conditions were equal and 90 percent do not want to leave the community. These figures reflect adequately the situation that exists in Santa Maria.[23]

Commuting has considerably modified the emigration phenomenon. The younger generations constitute the largest share of the new commuters; 68 percent are under the age of thirty and 90 percent under forty-five. Men predominate over women by a two to one ratio except in the 15 to 20 age group, when the girls find employment as domestic servants with relative ease. In the critical age group of 20 to 30 the young women, married or not, and representing nearly 5 percent of the total labor force, continue to work outside the community, while the decline is considerable in the older age groups. (See Table 3.18.)

3.18 OUTSIDE EMPLOYMENT OF MARIANI IN 1969

Age Group	*Males*	*Females*	*% Total*
15–20	47	55	32
21–30	89	33	36
31–45	70	4	22
46–55	31	2	10

The generations born after World War II, whose parents were sufficiently prosperous not to have to emigrate in the 1950s, have known the hardships and privations of the past only indirectly. Familiar with the virtues of hard work through the example of their parents, the image of limited good was never a reality with which they had to contend, no more than they encountered amoral familism, if it ever existed, in a society where the class structure was still a reality. Children of the post-fascist era who did not live through the fight for the earth or the trauma of the liberation, the new generations grew into adolescence when consumerism swept Italy and filtered down to the Veneto countryside. In 1969 the young believed blindly they could find employment and their peers provided them with a living example.

Many now go to school beyond the age of 14 and acquire technical skills; more than half of the males under 30 and one-third of the females have found work outside Santa Maria. Many under 18 officially do not work as their parents can receive social benefits. Increased educational opportunities and increased contact with the outside have led to new ideas, above all that the individual is as much responsible to himself as to his family, religion and community. The individualism and anonymity of the townsman are becoming part of the young Mariano's intellectual baggage. In school he has been taught to defend his ideas while at work he has learned independence and self-reliance. The greater availability of money has changed many of the traditional relationships in the community. It is the amount of money available for spending that gives the youth his status among his peers. Salaries are no longer turned over in their entirety to parents. The first paycheck often serves as a down payment for the status symbol of youth: a motorcycle, the first step towards a car. Optimism, individualism and faith in the future characterize the youth of today. As Paolo Ficcanaso, who is only twenty-one and commutes daily to Padua, puts it, "I've got a job and few can do as good work as I can. My company needs me. And if worst comes to worst I'll get in the car and drive to Milan where they just can't find a guy with my talent."

This attitude has affected those born during the last years of the fascist regime. Though many were forced to accept seasonal emigration in the 1950s, they realized and were eager to exploit the opportunities of the 1960s. In 1956 for the first time the young indicated their belief in the possibility of change by organizing politically as a group and challenging, though unsuccessfully, the local establishment. Collective action can no longer be discounted. In the summer of 1969 some of the more enterprising young farmers were airing the idea of creating a common machine pool, a first step in cooperation, which became reality in 1974. Similarly, they believed in the necessity of establishing a sales cooperative for spring peas to bring up the prices set by the middlemen. New interpersonal relations have evolved and the jealousy that characterized Santa Maria in the past, and still marks the older generations, has given way to sharing and more simple monetary relations. Today, Frasson, the earth-moving contractor, no longer considers with whom his parents are not on speaking terms before taking a job, but rather if, and how much, he will get paid.

Antonio Tiberto works Adolfo Zancanaro's fields with his tractor in exchange for labor whenever needed, an agreement not all to his advantage as Adolfo is a full-time factory worker. In brief, relations are based on cooperation or on a financial basis, a far cry from the descriptions of the local society twenty-five years ago.

The community has a clearly positive value for its youth. Santa Maria is an object of pride for the young. Thus, in 1969 they created a youth center not only for their convenience but also because it reflected well on their village. In an unprecedented effort the group went as far as cleaning up the village, removing the old and forgotten garbage in what proved to be a major beautification project. The situation was highly unusual and the older people in the bars could only think this was being done intentionally to offend the municipal street sweeper. Maurizio Terron got into the clean-up against his father's advice that "one shouldn't do anything for nothing." His son responded that the village was theirs and a clean-up could make it more attractive to live in. If he had his way, he concluded he "would damn well oblige every Christian to grow flowers in boxes on their windows, just like in Holland!" With the help of the town hall the young people improved the soccer field, freely contributing time and labor. Finally, they challenged the political establishment by asking for a greater share in decision-making. The young are no longer passive or resigned; and they have few reasons to reject their community. They wish to see it change for the better and are willing to make the necessary sacrifices.

The consequences of these new patterns of thought can be considerable, leading to a better equilibrium between the agricultural resources available and primary sector work force. However, for the overall well-being of the community it is essential that those who turn to new occupations remain in the village. Commuting has created the singular problem of the worker peasant, of part-time farms, and mixed income families where the older generation is helped by the very young to keep the farms going, a transitory phenomenon which maintains the image of the community and keeps its agricultural traditions alive, but must, of necessity, have strongly negative effects in other sectors. If the younger age groups still have the desire to work in the fields, as many do, but cannot find a farm that will provide them with a suitable income to raise their families, then they, too, will abandon the earth. In time this would lead to a rapid depopulation of the village.

A restructuring of the farms is desirable but difficult. Certain pieces of land are claimed by as many as thirty-two owners! Among the older generations the attachment to the earth is still strong. But changes in the mentality of the young, the new necessities that factory life engenders—and it is no coincidence that the rate of absenteeism is higher among the peasant workers—the progressive decline of the older generations, all these factors make more likely the eventual concession and renting of the abandoned or poorly worked fields to those who will be ready to devote all their energies to this task. Today many plots of earth are left uncultivated, particularly on the hills and at the periphery of the village; others are farmed by men and women as old as eighty who will soon be replaced by their grandsons, who will be less likely to spend their evening hours in the fields when they return from the factory, and more inclined to rent if not to sell the family holdings. Antonio Tiberto, the municipal councillor, owns 15 acres of vineyards and sells the product in his wine store. He also rents 12 acres from three different owners. In spite of the considerable investment required he has agreed to plant these in vineyards. "It will have to pay off!" he says. "My wine is the best in the village and I can sell more than I can produce. Even if I have to hire a man I can come out on top. I already buy extra grapes and producing my own is bound to be cheaper."

The possibility of specialized production, wine, oil and vegetables that are profitable, the proximity of the larger centers for which Santa Maria can be a garden, prospective irrigation of the hills, all are assets the young are ready to exploit. They are rejecting the uncontrolled individualism of the older generations in favor of a new community spirit no longer totally alien to cooperation. In Santa Maria the traditional values of peasant civilization appear to be on the way out.

Secondary Activities

The variations among the active resident population in Santa Maria have been considerable during the last twenty years, as is noted in Table 3.9.

The development of secondary activities is a direct function of emigration and the decline in agriculture. Between 1951 and 1969 the ratio of primary to secondary workers was totally reversed. Primary and secondary sectors were in equilibrium in 1961, which was also the year with the lowest percentage of working population, a direct consequence of the waves of emigration of the previous decade. Available jobs in the province led to an increase in active population with 70 percent of Mariani employed in secondary activities in 1969.

The types of employment are limited, an indication of the recent evolution from agriculture to other forms of occupation. In brief, one third of the 452 secondary employees are connected with the building trade (bricklayers, carpenters, painters), which requires very little or no training. The rapid expansion of the building industry in the neighboring cities of Padua, Abano and Fantolon, not to mention Santa Maria itself, has allowed a speedy and rapid transition from agriculture. Furthermore, the trade is subject to seasonal variations and allows the peasant a certain portion of time to devote to farming. Approximately 5 percent work in the more traditional jobs in the quarries and cement factories, a low figure but easily understandable if one notes the long-known reluctance of the Mariani to work in the quarries. Many of the younger men have found employment in automobile repair and body shops, which require some initiative but call for limited technical skills and on-the-job training. About 20 percent of the labor force is made up of specialized workers who find employment in the Paduan factories, especially young men who have received training in the technical institutes, or older men who after a stint in the industrial triangle have returned to the village with experience and a trade. These are the privileged who set an example for the younger generations. The salary is good, they all have cars, and they have taken on some of the city mannerisms that can appear attractive. Many have ceased working in the fields.

The women who traditionally found employment as domestic servants now shun this work despite some obvious economic advantages. Having discovered a new dignity, they prefer to work for lower salaries in the plastic factories of Fantolon or at home making doll dresses for the factories, though these activities, particularly the latter, are poorly remunerated, since the workers are paid by the piece and not on an hourly basis. Fantolon, "doll capital of the world," provides employment for over half of the female labor force in Santa Maria.

3.19 SECONDARY EMPLOYMENT BY SEX AND AGE

	Male		Female	
Age Group	*No.*	*%*	*No.*	*%*
15–20	57	18	57	53
21–25	67	21	32	30
26–30	38	12	6	5
31–40	76	24	10	9
41–50	50	16	3	3
50–65	30	9	—	—

Table 3.19 reflects the general distribution of male/female workers in Italy and illustrates the prevalence of the younger generations in secondary activities in Santa Maria. This prevalence would be even more evident if one considered only the more specialized trades requiring some training and excluded the men employed in the building trades and the women working as domestic servants.

Tertiary Activities

Tertiary activities are of necessity limited in Santa Maria and depend on small trade and tourism which has not reached its full potential. There can be only a few jobs in the local administration. The town hall and the post office can hardly hope to provide work for more than ten people; the school employs a dozen teachers, all but two of whom are outsiders.

Emigration and the population decline is one explanation for the scarcity and decrease of commercial activity in the community. Similarly, the limited income of the farming population, its attempts at economic autarky, and the absence of any industrial activity are not factors to encourage the development of small business in the village. Possibly even more important is the rapid development of transportation and Santa Maria's proximity to larger centers that allow the villagers to shop in them with greater frequency and convenience.

Santa Maria and the Euganean Hills have never had a solid and lasting artisan tradition.[24] In 1962 nine enterprises were classified as artisan. Today it is hard to locate six (2 building construction, 1 tailor, 1 oil mill, 1 floorlayer, 1 bulldozer operator). The more traditional activities of carpenter, blacksmith, barber and mechanic have disappeared. The building contractors provide work for a dozen men with seasonal variations. The oil mill employs three men including the owner for three months a year; the tailor works with his wife; and the floorlayer works with his son. The earth-moving company employs one villager and the owner, who also runs the gas station and since 1972 the newspaper stand.

The small commercial enterprises that depend exclusively on the village trade find survival difficult. The butcher, the baker, four grocery stores (two of which are also tobacconists), the cobbler-bazaar, the fertilizer store, and the pharmacy, *the* stores in Santa Maria, have to compete with motorization, tradition and population decline or find new activities. Thus, the butcher breeds hogs, the baker owns a bar and a restaurant; the pharmacist runs another pharmacy in a nearby village. With the exception of bread (and even then one baker delivers from Fantolon), one purchases in Santa Maria only perishable goods or what was forgotten on the weekly market trip. Santa Maria lost its own market in the sixteenth century and today only a stall selling clothes and underwear is set up on the square Saturday afternoon. A travelling salesman loads his bicycle with sewing needs and cloths; on Fridays fish is sold from the back of a three-wheeled Vespa; twice a week an enterprising gardener sells fruits and vegetables from his truck; twice a month butter, cheeses and oil are peddled door to door. All these tradesmen come from the outside. Tradition has it that on Mondays one goes to market. By bus, by car, by bicycle, and even on foot the village covers the five kilometers to Fantolon. It is a social occasion and many would rather work on Sundays than miss the market the following day—an occasion for fun, leisure and business, where one meets relatives from the neighboring villages, friends, middlemen, fiancés, and lovers. The younger people promenade and eye the opposite sex; wives shop and search out the bargains since prices are lower, goods fresher, and the choice greater than at home; the men sell the harvest or simply talk, eat, and drink in the cafés and *osterie*. Fantolon is so near that with a car it is often convenient to shop there more than once a week, particularly if one lives in the plains. Some of the more enterprising now prefer to visit the supermarkets in Padua where prices are even lower. In practice this trend is the death knell for the local shops which can hardly hope to survive for long. When the owners die their shops will close never to open again.

More fortunate are the few store owners who have faced the issue squarely and chosen to orient their activities towards the tourist trade, such as an antique store, or more accurately a junk store, and a souvenir shop that opened in 1969, selling mementos of Petrarch, the owner's bottled wines, decorative objects, and small furniture of rather good taste.

Tourism

The village has rapidly adapted to tourism and the expansion of inns, taverns, bars, trattorie, restaurants, and hotels, not to mention the *frasche*—wine cellars that sell their own products—appears to be the catalyzing agent for a new village mentality. Long past are the days of 1938 when Marastoni lamented in one of his letters "there was no place to stop . . . not even a toilet," or 1948, when "nowhere could one have lunch or dinner without having to submit to the songs of the local drunkards." Today's tourist has a large choice; in recent years eight new restaurants and two modern hotels have opened their doors, four between 1969 and 1972. It was sufficient that a young man, an outsider, with reckless energy and courage as well as moral support from the town hall, start building a new establishment for others to follow in his footsteps. The typical *osteria*—only one remains active—has been replaced by the modern bar restaurant, unfortunately not always in the best of taste.

It is difficult to estimate the economic contribution of this industry to the village since most of the enterprises are family run, and only three restaurants use about fifteen outside employees. However, if we consider the total number of people who work, at least fifty find employment in the trade, generating an overall salary equivalent of 60 million lire or $100,000 per year. Also the trade is a large contributor to the town hall budget, in terms of family tax and food tax. The municipality has encouraged and supported activities that cater to mass tourism with the final aim of transforming the community. The poet's house and tomb, the monuments and medieval buildings, the climate and the limpid air, the quietness and tranquility of village life attract people, while the proximity of Padua, easy communications, and the tradition of consuming the Sunday meal in the Hills, as well as the existence of the nearby thermal spa, Abano, insures a constant flow of Italian and foreign visitors. In 1969 the number of visitors to Petrarch's house averaged nearly one hundred a day with peaks of three hundred on Sundays. To this one should add some 70,000 meals consumed in restaurants. By now at least 100,000 people come through the village every year. Certainly one can note that "the tourist influx is that of tourists in transit which can only be exploited with some difficulty"[25] but until recently no attempt had been made to exploit it intelligently. Encouraged by the town hall, animated by a new spirit, the Mariano is seizing on new opportunities. Souvenir stores are opening, bars have become more attractive, and the village shops attempt to display goods that will attract the visitor. The municipality has drawn up a town plan that would close the central part of the village to automobile traffic so the visitors can enjoy the calm and rustic streets and gardens, admire the beauty of the village and be tempted to buy what it has to offer. At long last the tourist will be able to sit in the village squares and cafés without having to submit to the noise and stench of motors.

Some, already attracted by the tranquility of the Hills, have started to settle in the community; and "weekendismo" is becoming a factor in the local economy, with consequences in the political system, social organization and value system.[26] Between 1969 and 1972 ten new houses were built and four older ones restored by families from Padua, Venice and Ferrara. The town plan, in an attempt to limit land speculation and above all disorganized expansion which has destroyed the harmony of other Euganean communities, has created zones of expansion for this particular type of building, attempting to encourage more people to come and enjoy the village's atmosphere.

The town has oriented its future development toward tourism. Santa Maria, "Pearl of the Euganean Hills," well preserved and maintained, aspires to become the "capital" of a future national park that would encompass all the Euganean Hills. It feels attracted to such a role not only because of its beauty but also by its past that has been recently resurrected with the foundation of a national Center for the Study of Petrarch. It proved its organizational talents during an

3.20 QUARRIES IN SANTA MARIA[27]

	Dimensions in Meters			*Production in Tons*		*Workers*	
	width	*depth*	*height*	*1961*	*1965*	*1961*	*1965*
Active							
Bignago	100	80	35	10,000	8,300	12	2
Costa	450	100	50	280,000	553,000	4	6
Inactive							
Lovo	40	10	5				
Laghetto	20	8	5				
Le Motte	400	150	25				
Castello	70	40	30				

international congress of Petrarch scholars in November 1970 and the sixth centenary celebration of Petrarch's death in July 1974, and is ready to serve as a pole of attraction for the hurried tourist as well as for the one who has more time.

Industry

No industry exists in Santa Maria, unless one so designates the small building companies or the local lime factory which employs less than ten people throughout the entire production cycle. The marginality of industry is in fact surprising in view of Santa Maria's subsoil, 450 acres of which belong to the cement factories of Fantolon. But only one quarry is truly operational, the Costa, from which 831,000 tons were extracted in 1969. While the figure is noteworthy, mechanization and automation have greatly reduced the manpower needs. Considering supplemental activities such as transportation—three or four trucks are operated by Mariani—it is clear that quarrying brings limited benefits to the village.

In fact, industry's contribution so far has been essentially negative and its development should be considered in relation to tourism, which requires that the hills not be indiscriminately mined, which creates, as in the case of nearby Fantolon, "a lunar landscape."[28] What mistakes have been made—the eastern slope of the village gazes into the immense white wall of the Cava della More—must now be controlled and a vigorous program of reforestation has been undertaken. That no new quarries should be opened in Santa Maria is a wish that appears to have come true. In 1969, Italcementi, the largest Italian cement company, proposed to open a quarry on the hill facing Petrarch's balcony: the considerable opposition this generated led to the passing of a law in November 1971 preventing the opening of new quarries and forcing the closing of all those that mine "vile materials," while permitting those that continue their activity to do so only on the basis of five year permits and constant reforestation.[29]

Local industry is nevertheless necessary to compensate for the decrease in agricultural employment among the younger Mariani who, between the ages of 15 and 25, constitute 20 percent of the population in the community. Because of the expansion of the Italian economy few are unemployed, but the temptation to leave remains great and will increase with the slowing down of the national economy.[30] A study of the Euganean Hills notes, "It is difficult to believe that the industrial sector can naturally play a larger role in absorbing the excess manpower that presently exists, or its increase, due to the progressive exodus from agriculture."[31] Hence, the industrial future of Santa Maria must be considered in a larger context: in the future the industrial zone of Este-Fantolon plans to make several thousand jobs available. Unfortunately this plan is the object of political conflict between the two towns and its realization has been seriously hindered to the point one is entitled to doubt if it will ever become a reality.

If Santa Maria wishes to offer its younger classes an alternative to emigration it seems essential that it generate some activity in its own territory, however limited or symbolic, in an attempt to attract other small industries. During the 1950s rumors of the establishment of a Zoppas (appliance) factory circulated, though they appear to have had very little foundation. More recently, possibly for electoral purposes, a football factory was supposedly considering settling in Santa Maria. The local administration has promised large financial and tax incentives and the town plan has set aside a zone for a possible industrial park. In Santa Maria capital is scarce but one must hope outside industry will consider investing there, so the village can stay alive and not become only a museum.

Transformation

The transformation of the Marian economy may be attributed to several factors, notably the demographic changes in the village, new perspectives of the younger age groups, the end of an emigrant complex, and the gradual disappearance of the peasantry as a social class. After a strong wave of emigration the population appears to have stabilized, containing its losses through natural replacement. While the population is stable, the younger age groups are becoming proportionately more numerous and more educated, indicating potential for future development. Furthermore, among those who live in the village one notes an extremely strong attachment to the community, to its way of life and overall value system without a systematic rejection of new values. Given a choice the Mariano prefers remaining in his immediate environment rather than seeking work far from home. When this option is not available to him a psychological crisis of serious proportions is created.

Since the middle and late sixties for the first time Santa Maria has adequate prospects of economic development. A specialized agriculture can provide means of livelihood for possibly as much as 10 percent of the total labor force, while tourism, which should undergo considerable development in the years to come, can support at least 15 percent. The nonexistence of local industry is certainly a negative factor that should be remedied, but the possibility of working in the immediate environment has rid the Mariano of his emigrant complex. Today one leaves Santa Maria by choice and no longer out of dire necessity. The reasons to depart are personal; noteworthy among others is the attraction of the city, where pay is higher and commuting unnecessary. The city is most tempting for the better educated youth who can find opportunities for employment in the city and more conveniences at the same time.

Under these conditions one can wonder about the future of the peasantry and the agricultural economy that has been the basis of the village during the past. Can the peasantry survive as a social class? The elders do not change and appear to be the prophets of defeat, believing that little good can come from Santa Maria's soil if not sweat and fatigue. Refusing to consider the possibilities offered by specialization and mechanization, they are the defenders of the image of limited good that the younger generations have explicitly rejected. The prospect is for a transformed society espousing a new economic value system that refuses limitations and will lead to a more dynamic and social community. Nevertheless, such a transformation is predicated on two conditions that can be realized only very gradually and which make the changes that have already taken place less apparent. It is necessary that the peasant-worker give up his dual allegiance and make a definite choice between the fields and the factory. This in no way forces him to renounce his community or his home. He must simply turn his fields over to others, either by selling or renting them. In this way a new agricultural class can be brought into existence where the farmer will control sufficiently large farms to make an adequate living. Seen against the backdrop of the present family structures and overall community patterns this appears to be wishful thinking. Nevertheless, the process is in an active phase of evolution.

4. Socialization in Santa Maria

THE FAMILY, THE CLAN, THE SCHOOL, AND THE COMMUNITY itself, probably the most effective agents of socialization, are dealt with in this chapter.[1] Socialization, an on-going process, calls for the study of the individual's entire life cycle; however, the most deeply rooted values are acquired during childhood years and consequently we will emphasize this period. The family is particularly important in dealing with the social (rather than the psychological) aspects of socialization and some attention will be devoted to objective factors that determine its social standing in the community, such as housing conditions or income.

Our final objective is to provide an overview of the Mariani's system of values, the system's acquisitive mechanisms, and its effects on political learning: the maintenance or transformation of shared or divisive values among the citizenry will have a definite impact on the traditions and the future of the community.

The Family

The family, the primary frame of reference in village society, affects the outlook of its members by placing them in a network of social, economic, and at times political relationships. The family leads to involvement in the community and influences the overall community identity. Thus, before dealing with the family and its role in creating values, particularly political ones, it is important to consider the objective conditions of Marian families.

Objective Conditions

In a 1969 survey, 262 houses in the community, or some 75 percent of all dwellings, were studied.[2] From this date it was possible to derive a picture of the objective conditions of the 347 families that constitute the population of Santa Maria. The distribution of the sample is given in Table 4.1.

The typical Marian dwelling is a two-floor house (98 percent); 81 percent of the dwellings had 3 or 4 rooms on the first floor, 68 percent, 3 or 4 rooms on the second floor. In a majority of cases two rooms served as a cellar or granary, leaving four to six rooms as habitable space: three or four bedrooms, a large kitchen, or a kitchen and a living room. The theoretical density was 0.98 persons per room. Of the houses 25 percent were in good structural condition, 54 percent in mediocre shape, and 21 percent in a very poor state; only 43 percent contained indoor hygienic facilities (39 percent with a bathtub or shower), 49 percent had an outdoor privy, and 8 percent no facilities at all.[3] While one-quarter of the families lived in housing meeting modern living standards, two-thirds of the heads of the household declared they were satisfied with their living conditions, in contrast with the fact that 64 percent wanted a complete bathroom in their house.

Housing conditions in the village were clearly better than in the *comune*, reflecting a division in society between those who lived "in town" and in the countryside, a result of the past development of Santa Maria and the recent efforts of returned emigrés who settled in the village. Thus, 33 and 17 percent of the houses were, respectively, in

4.1 POPULATION AND HOUSING

	Dwellings	*%*	*% Resident Population*
n=262			
Village	92	35.11	32.19
Nuclei	21	8.01	9.57
Hills	100	38.16	38.89
Plains	49	18.70	19.35

good or bad condition in the town versus 25 and 21 percent in the country. There is a further division in the village where 14.5 percent of the houses around the upper square were in poor condition while 54 percent of those around the lower square were in this state. The distinction made by the locals between those who "live at the top" and their counterparts "at the bottom" applied not only to geographical location but also to greater prosperity, if one can judge by their residences. If the distribution of property of the 1920s had some leveling effect (as we believe it had) some of it had been overcome by the 1960s. It was possible to see in housing conditions new patterns of social stratification and of a class structure that went beyond the simple division of peasants and landowners, or rich and poor. These social divisions were compounded by the effects of the Italian economic miracle and education. New groups substituted themselves for the old elite that withdrew from the local society either in the twenties or following fascism's fall and for the peasants of the past: the peasant-worker of the 1960s has had to live with a new elite based either on money, education, or both.

Typical of the new elite that disposed of well over $3,000 per capita income per year (3.5 percent of the population) were those who went into the restaurant trade. The most representative family is that of Bruno Beghin. He was born in the *corte* of Mandonego where his father was a sharecropper; he is now the most prosperous man in the village. His story is worth telling. During the war Bruno headed crews of local workers for the Germans, avoiding military service and work in Germany. Immediately after the war with practically no capital he rented a small restaurant on the outskirts of the *comune*; in the mid-fifties he started a new *trattoria*, La Fontanella, which specialized in large wedding parties and advanced bookings, low prices and good food. The motto "the client must be satisfied" made him successful. Borrowing heavily Bruno purchased a large farm in the plains in 1959. Within a year he sold one half to pay off most of his debts. He hired his brother-in-law to run the farm that produced vegetables, wine, and hogs used in the restaurant. A faithful member of the Church, he was supported by the parish priest and was elected to the municipal council in 1964. A dynamic assessor for public works, he brought water and electricity to the remotest parts of the *comune*. He also brought the Christian Democrats a sizeable portion of the traditionally leftist vote of Mandonego when he joined the party. His success and the quality of his food made his establishment a preferred meeting place for the politicians of the region, notably Mssrs. Gui, Bisaglia and Rumor. In 1969 a new, larger Fontanella came into being, accommodating up to three hundred patrons. With varying degrees of success the restaurant trade was followed by five other villagers and two outsiders, who with their families are among the most prominent members of the community. A few young men born after the war have reached a degree of eminence in the local society by following a different route. Education has put them above the common villager. One, an accountant, is a dispatching clerk for a company in Padua, another is a land surveyor (*geometra*) who also designs houses for local residents, two others are schoolteachers who live in Santa Maria and teach in a neighboring town. They have been at the root of the movement that challenged the established political system of the village.

Social divisions among the Marian families have become a reality which supersedes the earlier geographical lines of demarcation that characterized the community. From a society of equals, essentially peasants, Santa Maria has evolved into a stratified community which has a clear effect on the socialization process and the political life. The greater diversity has led to tensions and jealousies between the groups and individuals, with the rich being the combined object of admiration and resentment. The increase in prosperity and the visible presence of prosperous citizens has led to greater demands on the political system. Beyond the more common status symbols (refrigerators used in summer, washing machines displayed but seldom used, and automobiles), the locals now want bathrooms. These are difficult to accommodate in medieval buildings without adding to them, pitting the population against the municipal administration whose responsibility it is to prevent any change in the exterior aspects of the buildings. (This issue is discussed further in chapter 6.) But if new problems have arisen the expanding local elite provides for a greater capacity for their solution. Outcomes are discussed rather than accepted in resignation as in the past, making municipal administration and politics an element of greater importance than ever before in family life, and opening up the possibility of a political system based on bargaining and consensus.

Toward the Unicellular Family

The overall changes in objective conditions that we have mentioned above and discussed in some detail in the previous chapter have had an impact on the family structure. The size of the family and the evolving structures it embodies are dependent upon the type of economy in the community. Thus the impact of industrialization, though it has not led to a visible decline in agricultural production, has brought about a shrinking of the peasant class and of the size of Marian families. These have declined from 5.5 persons in 1951, to 4.9 in 1961 and 4.8 in 1969, well below the provincial average of hill farming families that stood at 5.7 in 1967.[4] The average family has 2.8 children. The extended patriarchal family is now a small minority, with only 2.7 percent having nine or more members.

The patriarchal family of the early 1900s is a memory of the past and has succumbed to the impact of emigration, industrialization, and the creation of the worker-peasant. The absolute authority of the father or the elder brother has followed its demise. This has clear repercussions on the socialization process. We noted that when a son takes over a farm the father's authority ceases to exist. Thus Piero Buzzachi, whose family had been a tenant of the same farm for over two hundred years, was only sixty-three, a vigorous and hard-working man, when he said, "It's clear. My son must take over because it is the rule of nature that the old must submit to the young. I can still work but will have to learn to obey. It is God's will." A faithful Christian Democrat, he added ruefully, "If only our politicians could figure that out. . . ." Similarly when children take in their parents to live with them, as one-quarter do, they seldom solicit advice, and when counsel is sought, the elder women carry more weight than do the men.

4.2 FAMILY UNITS IN SANTA MARIA, 1969

People per Family	1	2	3	4	5	6	7	8	9
No. of Families	23	44	51	89	67	68	39	15	11
Percentage of Families	5.7	10.8	12.5	21.9	16.5	16.7	9.6	3.7	2.7

Within the families a new pattern of male-female relationships is evolving. By all appearances life in the village is male oriented and male dominated. In all social acts the male has precedence over the female: men sit in the front of the Church, women in the back; men address women first in public, and the contrary is frowned upon; men frequent bars which women must avoid; drunkenness is no shame for the man but means opprobrium for the woman; at home she serves the man and seldom sits at the same table. Villagers consider the male superior to the female, believe that "inequality is a necessity of marriage," that the woman "must be less intelligent than the man." She is known as *la* donna, *the* woman. As the village priest exclaimed in a homily, "Wives who do not accept their husbands' observations lack humility."

Yet the woman is as important as the man because of her role in the family. It is her task to maintain domestic tranquility and religious faith, to define the accepted and acceptable values for the adolescent, to provide the cultural and religious upbringing of the children, often through the example she sets by her own behavior. Until recently in Santa Maria the female dominated the family, content to leave the male his apparent role of superiority, free to devote some of his attention to politics, a topic in which she seldom allowed herself to get involved. The woman's effective position is well reflected in two expressions commonly used in Santa Maria. A woman is judged by her ability to govern: *governare*. Primarily it applies to running the household, keeping the house clean and orderly, but it also means running family life and making decisions, often administering the farm, from which in the past men were frequently absent. To govern means to hold the purse strings. This is made explicit in the expression "Qui, comanda la Francia," France (feminine) commands here. The origin of the expression is uncertain, its reality is not. Some mention the belief, brought to the village by the Napoleonic soldiers, that in France women reigned supreme. It is more probable that when temporary emigration became common in Santa Maria—we also heard the expression "Qui, comanda la Svizzera"(Switzerland) —the men left the administration of the family wealth to women. In brief, emigration undermined male supremacy just as it weakened patriarchial authority.

If aspects of matriarchy predominate among the older generation where the man's and the woman's worlds are separate,[5] the situation is somewhat different among the younger couples who have benefitted from greater employment opportunities, more education, and increased mobility. In 1969 parents were more often together and no longer subject to the influence of their own parents. They had other choices besides working on the family farm. It appeared to us that decisions were reached after careful discussion and that decisions by fiat, paternal or maternal, were avoided. The younger husbands and wives not only lived together as their forefathers did, but went out together. Symbolic of this change, two young women were included in the opposition list for the 1975 municipal elections, and more importantly, were elected. The trend to discuss rather than assert, to bargain rather than dictate, to live as a single unit rather than as individuals under a common roof, though a long tradition weighs against it, will have pronounced effects on the socialization process. While patterns of the past are hard to overcome, it is in this unicellular family that children are born today.

Life Cycles

We have considered the objective conditions that have some bearing upon socialization, notably the more visible factors such as income or size of the family. Socialization is nevertheless an essentially psychological process by which belief systems are acquired, developed and transformed through imitation and osmosis. The major factor in this process is the family, and the critical period that of childhood and adolescence.

Childhood and Adolescence

In the Catholic society of the Veneto children are a gift from God, perpctuators of the race and a source of manpower. Describing the situation in Santa Maria in the early fifties a study concluded[6] ". . . children are everywhere; 'it is the only resource of the village' they say jokingly while all know these children constitute its greatest problems." The economic transformation of the society, the de-emphasis on the procreative function of marriage by the people first and the Church later, greater opportunities for education, and the preeminence of the nuclear family have given children a privileged place in contemporary Marian society.

The child (born at the nearby hospital in Fantalon) enters not only the family but also the community. He is part of an extensive series of links and kinship ties, and even his name is dictated by society. Because surnames are so few, parents debate among themselves and with the town clerk to insure there will be only one Stefano, Carlotta or Lidia Sbandellon in the records! A second series of links is established by baptism which, through the choice of godparents, associates the child with other members of the civilian community. Following the ceremony of purification of the mother, which still survives in Santa Maria, the infant is baptized. Until recently this was a private, individually oriented ceremony. Now, to mark the entrance into the religious community, the Church strives to celebrate several baptisms simultaneously, though it appeared to us this ceremony did not please parents, since it de-emphasized the individuality of the child and, unconsciously, introduced status and competition among the families.

The central figure at the ceremony is the godfather. The godmother is relegated to a secondary position by the norms of the society though not of the Church. Emphasizing the importance of the community in the ceremony may diminish in part the importance of the godfather and is thus another reason the parents do not like the new orientation. Traditionally, the godfather is an instrument that reinforces clan, family, or friendship ties and often he has served as first witness at the wedding ceremony. He is then known as *compare d'anello* (ring godfather) and the proverb states "*Compare d'anello, padre del puteo,*" "The ring godfather is 'father' of the child."

> The relationship between parents and god-parents, who are most often cousins, is much like that which might exist between brothers and sisters. Fruition of ritual alliances is sought in the reiteration of preexisting bonds between "compari," while joint dedication to the welfare of the child serves essentially as the instrument by which the identification of kinship ties is accomplished.[7]

In the past, seeking a high-placed protector was frowned upon in Santa Maria. It was viewed as an unethical means of advancement or an indiscreet use of patronage. This is no longer the case. Friendship appears the most important element while patronage per se is de-emphasized, though the search for means to advance the long-term future of the child is not forgotten. The mayor, a prosperous outsider, flatly stated that he did not wish to be called upon as godfather or wedding witness and that he would refuse any and all such offers. In brief, the choice of a godfather today is reflective of the changes that have taken place in Marian society since World War II. Parents, while conscious of their objective social and economic situation, seek out a godfather for their child not only in terms of family ties or prestige but also on the basis of true friendship, an indication of their search for a more open society, the gradual lowering of rigid clan barriers and the weakening of kinship ties.

The major role in the education of children is, naturally, entrusted to the mother who, until the child has reached the age of six or seven (the so-called age of reason for the Church), appears to have the exclusive responsibility for the child. She delegates her powers quite frequently to her older daughters and less frequently to grandparents, who seem to be used essentially as pacifiers for the younger children. Only in exceptional cases is the authority of the father called upon to impart corporal punishment, "to show," as one proud father declared, "who really commands in this house." The husband exercises final authority over his offspring, but the aspects of matriarchy we indicated earlier certainly diminish his importance in the eyes of the adolescent children. At least they are put in the situation of perceiving that the formal and the effective source of authority are at time different.

From the earliest moment a child is trained to behave according to the norms that regulate the conduct of his sex: sexual dichotomy regulates family and social life in Santa Maria, and the separation of the sexes throughout childhood and adolescence reinforces and complements the natural divisions and affinities of the family. The separation applies from the earliest ages (3 or 4), and children of opposite sexes are never encouraged to play together, "cosi non vanno a fare porcherie" (so they won't mess around). It is something that is not done in reputable households, and while protecting the female's integrity it reinforces the male's sense of superiority, since boys are taught not to play with girls, who are not worthy of them. This is well documented in the very games the children play. Among those of ancient origins we may note *a gamba sopra,* played by girls, and *salta caselotto* and *pin decca* for boys.[8] Certain ritual pastimes are the exclusive preserve of boys, such as the singing of the *Ciarastela* during Epiphany. The boys chant in dialect the simple story of the trek of the three kings to witness the Savior's birth, and the boys are rewarded with wine and money.[9] However, these activities hardly survive and more modern games are favorites. Little girls imitate their mothers and play with the plastic dolls manufactured in nearby Fantolon. By age ten they are expected to take care of their younger brothers and sisters, and to help in the house. Boys are soldiers or cowboys, but soon turn their attention to card games or soccer. Complicated and costly mechanical or electric toys had hardly appeared in the village in 1969 and very few families purchased coloring books or reading materials for their children. Children are expected to play with their peers and with what is around them. Toys are viewed, it seemed to us, more as an assertion of the family's status in society than as a distraction for the child, whose natural tendency to discover "what is inside" is seldom rewarded, if not with a spanking.

In the process of bringing up their children, parents attempt to inculcate values that have been the guiding spirit of their own lives. Throughout the process of education, for boys and girls alike, authority, deportment, honor and pride are emphasized.

Acceptance of authority and obedience are expected from the child as soon as he becomes mobile. These attributes are reinforced by verbal and corporal punishment. A rather negative approach, where reason seldom enters, permeates the period of early child-rearing. It is not that the child *should* not wet, run in the streets alone, open a dresser, etc.; he *must* not do so. At first efforts will be made to shame him if he contravenes orders, but if he continues to disobey he will be paddled, slapped across the face, and even belted rather than derided. Discipline and corporal punishment teach respect and parents feel entitled, if not duty bound, to castigate their progeny even in their middle teens. Yet, these absolute guidelines are tempered by love and affection, and many a time parental pride will forestall physical punishment if the offense is not too serious. It is agreed that children do not always understand what they do, and while parents do not acknowledge it in front of the children, they are ready to do so later after the child has been reprimanded. The younger parents, it seemed to us, particularly those who appeared upwardly mobile in society, seldom used corporal punishment, possibly because they had smaller families to tend. The education of boys and girls emphasizes their obligation to obey parents, elders, and those in positions of authority, notably their teachers and the parish priest. Authority is viewed as an absolute value, and in this parallels somewhat the conception of law as viewed in the Italian codes. Males and females are, however, expected to react differently and one notices a greater tolerance and flexibility vis-à-vis the male. Rebellion and the verbal refusal to obey orders are anticipated among boys. It is expected a boy will be proud and difficult because he is a little man, *un ometto*; at times an occasion for anguish, particularly when the boys are teenagers, it is also a source of pride to have a hard-headed fellow. The expression of resistance is a sure sign the young man will succeed since he is capable of demonstrating his manliness. A very different picture prevails for girls whose tantrums are far less tolerated than boys'. Discipline and obedience are viewed as the foundations of modesty: the parents' word is an absolute to which the young girl must submit.

Children are brought up with a strong sense of the social hierarchy and their role and place in society. Obedience and respect are due not only to parents but also to elder brothers and sisters who play a major role in the education of the child. Grandparents are seen to be capable of spoiling children rather than teaching them. Godparents are in the same category as parents and their desires are interpreted as orders. Children are taught the social hierarchy of their community at an early age: the social ladder is a living and concrete reality. Children always respectfully refer to and address the archpriest as Don Arturo and his chaplain as Don Remo, though all know the latter is slightly mentally deranged. Parents will have their children repeat, until the formula is properly pronounced, the greeting to the mayor, "Signor Sindaco," not always an easy task for those with a lisp. Teachers, doctors, and the municipal secretary are always addressed by their title. In the village where most address each other by first names, no particular emphasis is given to old age—in fact the older members of the community are seldom viewed as important—unless it is combined with some position of eminence. Thus deference is expressed to la Signorina Fortuna, who is custodian of the poet's house, or to Alfredo Valeri, "il Signor Valeri," who was the last fascist Podestà in Santa Maria. Parents drill into their children's minds from a very early age whom they must respect, making the social structure probably more rigid than it is in reality. Men are recognized by their positions and titles rather than for their intrinsic worth. A title of Dottore, Ingegnere, Ragioniere or Professore seems to be a rather safe guarantee of success at election time.

The emphasis on deportment is also part of the child's education in obedience, while for parents it is a search for status and an important reputational factor. In their dress children are to look nice, not necessarily to be comfortable. This is most evident on Sundays when some sons accompany their fathers to Mass and to the bar, where their fine appearance is commented upon and their good behavior rewarded with a sip of wine or a sweet, or when daughters sit with their mothers in the back of the church then go home without stopping but letting people glance at their best clothes. Good and appropriate dress applies at all times of the week. Children are not supposed to get dirty and particular care must be taken of the overalls worn to school. Coming home dirty courts punishment.

In sum, the values inculcated into the young people stress obedience and respect for forms which would tend to make them rather passive citizens, hardly likely to revolt or protest. Two elements, however, counterbalance this tendency: honor and pride. Complementary and reinforcing, they are stressed in early childhood and adolescence and become an integral part of the child's personality. With adulthood honor becomes ". . . the conciliatory nexus . . . between the individual and society, and between systems of ideology and systems of action."[10] Honor (and shame indirectly) stems from natural in-born qualities, particularly for the male, as well as acquired ones. Because the male is surely born with honor he is considered superior and ranked above the female. Essential to his image is manliness, the willingness to defend his reputation in spite of the costs, and his refusal to submit to humiliation. In adulthood this will be the essential symbol of his authority over his family and of his place in society. To accept humiliation is tantamount to dishonor.

Yet honor is tempered by another characteristic which is essential to village, and Italian, life: *furbizia*. The word is best translated by shrewdness and astuteness rather than maliciousness or conceit. Developed through experience it is a quality that is more characteristic of the male than the female. Because of it accusations or challenges are seldom cast publicly, which makes the defense of one's reputation all the more difficult. This reinforces the necessity of practicing honesty (lying and cheating are seldom tolerated by parents) though not necessarily straightforwardness. The community is the essential element in maintaining honor. Personally chosen commitments or those imposed or directly verifiable by the local society are subject to honor because one's reputation is based upon it; but those commitments imposed by outside elements or that involve outside elements are guided by *furbizia*. Thus Livorno would have no hesitation in cheating on a business deal with an outsider but, though striking a hard bargain, would use different parameters with one of his co-citizens. Yet he is not an honorable citizen of the community, though he is one of its most hard-working men, because he cheated his brother on his legitimate share of his inheritance. Pretending to be at the extremes of death he asked his brother to give up all his claims on him that derived from their parents' succession, so he could die an honorable man, without debts. Promptly recovering once the promise was made, he held his brother to his word! But *furbizia* used against an outsider is accepted. Nobody thought of blaming Gianni Pittoni when he convinced the tax collector to buy rushes by weight rather than by volume, and then soaked them overnight. *Furbizia* produces the "sly" citizen who feels no compunction in cheating the State, avoiding taxes, and even switching his vote if he is certain this will not affect his reputation locally. Thus thirty members of the Tioli clan endorsed one of their own so he could present himself as a Republican candidate in the local elections; however the list only received 11 votes. Double standards apply when they do not affect one's position in Santa Maria.

A second element counterbalances the passive effects of early education: pride. The individual's first frame of reference is his family of which he is immensely proud, whatever its social position. Its status is not questioned, no more than its integrity is doubted. The individual may well recognize that some of its elements are not without peccadillos, but as a collective being the family remains a source of pride. It is said the Occibei are far from honest, but the most one of them would admit is that they are *furbi*, and hence praiseworthy. Thus the individual assumes rigid positions, rejects conciliatory moves, and is led to family feuds that force people into positions that at heart they do not subscribe to. Today the Menato avoid the Fortuna, following an accusation of thievery thirty years old; the Bardini and the Tiberto who have a boundary dispute are yet to be found on the same electoral lists. As the carabinieri put it, "They are like wolves."

Pride in the community itself is very much present in Santa Maria, and the world is judged in relation to the latter rather than the converse. Santa Maria forgets its shortcomings to become a mythical community. "You can tell me whatever you want, there is nothing like Santa Maria anywhere in the world" is a commonly used phrase when talking to outsiders. Custodian of Petrarch's remains, it is one of the most important centers of Italy; the produce of its soil, its wines and olive oil, are considered equal to the best the world can produce. The weather, far superior to that of the plains, makes it a new Riviera waiting to be discovered; its medieval buildings make it the best preserved city in Italy. These mythical values are shared by most and may simply be considered as *campanilismo* or parochialism; but this is translated into an attachment to "antiquated" and slowly changing communal values predicated on hierarchy and authority that characterize the closed society of the past.

These values are shared in common by males and females. But certain values and roles are the product of the sexual dichotomy that orders social life. The young male is constantly reminded of his superiority over females. The worst insult to the growing boy is to call him a *femminuccia*, a little girl, and leads to fighting and kicking to prove the contrary. Boys soon learn to order their sisters around, including older ones, expecting and receiving obedience from them. Parents side with sons rather than daughters in the case of disagreements. The young man is viewed as the defender of family honor, is expected to cut a fine figure and protect his sister's virtue. Above all he is to be macho, a true man, and sexual matters play an important role in his education. Double standards are important here. To prove his manliness he is expected to demonstrate sexual prowess and yet honor requires he respect the purity of the village girls. This creates tension in adolescents who seek their sexual experiences outside the community, often having recourse to prostitutes. Sex is thus subject to considerable verbalization among the younger men: their reputation becomes ever greater but reality may be ever more sour. Marriage comes to be viewed not only as a choice but as a necessity. Man's preeminent physical role is emphasized. Not only is he taught the virtues of labor and toil, he is also cast as the major figure in society.

In the female's education restraint and discretion are the most strongly emphasized natural qualities. Sexual purity holds more of a religious connotation, but from the community point of view is more akin to modesty, which flows from discretion and restraint. In the early ages however, purity, restraint and discretion are confused and girls are conditioned to avoid *vergogna*—shame—that is, to be modest. These elements complement the qualities they learn through family training: honesty and loyalty to the family. Thus accepting humiliation in the family is equated with obedience: only humiliation in society is shameful and calls for defense, and because *furbizia* is not a female quality, the defense is often more violent than the male's, at least verbally. In their early teens girls are cast in the role of mother, caring for younger siblings, cleaning the house, cooking and embroidering. In the poorer peasant families girls often accept domestic work. Thus very early the female is taught to take on an active role in the family but a passive role in the community, where modesty calls for her to refrain from showing her more visible qualities or talents.

To the degree that childhood affects political socialization it appears that while men are cast in an active and visible role moderated by *furbizia,* females are expected to remain passive and nonparticipant citizens. A survey of the adolescent years confirms this judgment.

From all accounts available adolescence, in the past, was a period that hardly existed.[11] The children seldom attended primary school regularly and few completed the full cycle of studies. Rather, one went to work in the fields or, for the more fortunate, to be an apprentice in town. The female helped her mother in the house and shared in the agricultural work until marriage. For the male, the pre-adult years were often a search for escape from the local environment. Military service was thus a well accepted duty, often the first occasion to leave the region. Its effects included nicknames that are derived from the garrison where the soldier was stationed.[12] In the village the young sought to assert their virility as required, and at the same time prohibited, by the social norms, often escaping through wine and "dreaming of riches and another life."[13]

Adolescence today is a reality. Whenever a child leaves school, at 14 or 17, true and serious work is not expected of boys until they have performed their military duties, though girls have to work and save money towards their dowry. In the intervening time boys might work, though seldom in the fields, and they expect to enjoy themselves. The village offers a few opportunities: several soccer teams sponsored by the local bars compete quite regularly; the parish shows movies (in the late 1940s it forced a local operator to close down his cinema and dance hall, though one doubts if "immoral" films were projected); the Circolo di Lettura attempts to provide a club-like atmosphere for adolescents where they debate topics of their choice (e.g., sexual education); the town hall maintains a small library, and several plays are given every year by visiting performers. Above all the young have become mobile. Those who work are salaried, liberated from the farm, and soon purchase a small motor-bike. Thus the distractions of Padua or the dances in surrounding villages are no longer out of reach, and a few go as far as Verona to listen to operas in the summer. New patterns of education (co-education is becoming a reality in the middle school) and new values that have entered the village with television combine to encourage new attitudes among the younger generations. The less rigid division of the sexes has led to a greater respect for women. They are viewed, it seemed to us, less as objects and more as persons. Double standards have not vanished, but education has made men more conscious of women as their equals. Education and the right to play and enjoy themselves have given men a new attitude toward work. They now see their careers as a choice rather than an imposition. In school and with their peers they have learned to discuss, and this they continue in the home. Rather than obedience and blind respect for authority, reason now seems to play a part in family relations. Finally, economic prosperity and the right to keep a good share of their earnings has made the young people somewhat independent. Adolescence, as we observed it in Santa Maria, leads, among the boys, to a new self-centered concept of their person. More and more their decisions are predicated upon individual rather than family or communal interests. The "new" man thus appears far less conditioned by the patterns of his early education than his forefathers. He sees himself as more independent and able to decide his own future. In a sense youth today in the village is inspired by optimism. While some of this may be dashed when the young man enters married life, enough remains to have consequences for his political perceptions: he believes and knows change is possible.

Adult Life and Marriage

The proverb states that "wives and oxen should come from your own village," and a nineteenth-century observer noted that Mariani ". . . oblige their women, and it is unfortunate for them, to marry into the village in all circumstances, or die spinsters."[14] If a girl had not found a man by age 18, "she turned nasty."[15] The isolation of the community until the mid-twentieth century makes such assertions credible, though the patterns described were imposed more by necessity than by choice. The present situation is not radically different: 56 percent of the men married local women, and 88 percent of the women chose local men. In fact 84 percent of the non-native-born Marian wives are from the province of Padua. The population is very homogeneous and, consequently, shares a common value system which reinforces the mores of local society. In 1969, 2 out of 5 marriages involved two native-born Mariani, with non-native-born citizens tending to marry outside the community. The average age of marriage for a male is 21.2 and for the female 20.2; however 64 percent of the males marry at the average age of 25.5, while 66 percent of the females do so at 21. If marriage takes place outside the village, the average age is higher, as it is also the further away from the village proper that one resides.

Marriage makes the individual a full-fledged member of the community, obliging him to assume responsibilities he had so far been able to ignore. It also frees him from the tutelage of his parents and renders him fully independent. Thus spinsterhood or prolonged bachelorhood are considered abnormal since "single, one would not be comfortable, even in paradise." Those unfortunate enough to be in this stage are chided and derided by the young who, under the influence of wine, delight in serenading old maids.

Patterns of courtship and marriage have changed considerably

Waiting for the bell

A local wedding

Old women shredding corn

Final rites

during the past ten years under the impact of greater prosperity, new values encountered by the more mobile workers, and values reinforced by the media, notably television. Traditionally "three feasts," or religious celebrations, had to elapse (encompassing almost a full year) before the young suitor could enter his future wife's house. This did not prevent the young people from meeting openly and freely before the engagement became official. Young men and women were expected to work in the fields and only a minimum of surveillance was exercised. The local sayings recognize this situation, noting that "when girls are in love it is useless to lock the door" and that "even trees bow when a young virgin goes to the altar." Premarital sex, though frowned upon, was not infrequent, though community norms called for reparative marriages.[16] Some changes have taken place. From the very fragmentary data we were able to gather there was a clear trend toward an increasing number of abortions among nonmarried women[17] between 1961 and 1969. While most brides come from Santa Maria, in recent years many have been from Fantolon and Padua, rather than from Mirón and Beolco, which are nearer and where Mariani traditionally sought their companions. Above all, we noted that the young people were very open in discussing their futures and did not shy away from rational discussions of sex. For the male it was no longer an occasion to emphasize his *gallismo* and boast of his conquests. The female, within the limits of modesty, no longer feared to discuss what, for her parents, was considered a taboo. In brief, the reserve of the past has been substituted by more open relationships between the sexes. Today, couples decide to get engaged and inform their parents. The decision-making process is based on the individual's views of his future and not constrained by family considerations. Thus we were told that while elopements have become rare, more children marry against their parents' will.

Most weddings take place during winter or spring, with May receiving the preference, a reminder of the agricultural past of the community. None are celebrated on Tuesdays, Wednesdays, and Fridays because these days are considered to be augurs of bad luck. The ceremony is held in the parish church on the lower square, and an early morning wedding in the smaller sanctuary is considered as a sure indication of "anticipation." The pattern will endure as long as Don Arturo, the archpriest, can dictate the rules or choose the exceptions.

The bride, who is not allowed to sew her own dress, leaves home escorted by her father and a cortege following a well established route (if she lives in the upper part of the village) that avoids via Guido di Santa Maria, which is reserved for funerals. The wedding party, including the groom, is preceded by two young pages carrying the rings on a silk cushion.

Following the ceremony, Mass is celebrated by the archpriest who also gives the homily. Two themes dominated on the occasions we witnessed: the obligation for the woman to be faithful, to respect and obey her husband, and a denunciation of the legislation on divorce and its ills. While the older people did not object, the young couples to whom we talked thought these words out of place.[18] Accompanied by a salvo of gunshots the young couple leaves to have their pictures taken and guests retire to the *osterie* to celebrate before the nuptial lunch. The latter is one of the greatest occasions to assert status, and the young couples, who cover the expenses with their parents, often go heavily into debt to entertain their friends. The wedding party seldom numbers less than a hundred guests, while the menu calls for hors d'oeuvres, three *minestre* (two types of pasta and a *risotto*), three boiled meats, three vegetables, three roasts, cheese, fruit, and the wedding cake accompanied by abundant wine. Of the dozen weddings we witnessed, only one couple who had not been able to secure the bride's parents' approval to the ceremony had a small party of fifteen people.

The economic aspects of weddings are nevertheless changing. Our friends in the restaurant trade lamented that people were less willing to spend than in the past and sought to cut down on the quantities of food. A dowry is no longer required and seldom provided by the bride's parents. The future bride brings her trousseau and her (often considerable) savings. Only rarely does she have property; that is generally reserved for her brothers.[19] The linens are bought a few weeks before the ceremony, sometimes on credit. According to custom the bride furnishes the bedroom, today with a showy and expensive "suite," while the groom equips the kitchen and provides the house.[20] The habit of displaying the trousseau has now disappeared.[21] As if to symbolize their independence the young couple send out marriage announcements in their own name and the wedding meal is no longer held in the bride's parents' house but in a restaurant. One pregnant bride did not hesitate to wear pink rather than the traditional white, and insisted on getting married in the parish church, head high.

The new couples no longer wish for large families, and in spite of the strong Catholic tradition, birth control is widely practiced. The pharmacy stocks no contraceptive devices and interruption is considered the only natural method of birth control. The data we have on abortion are hardly conclusive, and we came to know only three couples that used the pill. More significant is the assertion of the chaplain who acknowledged that "if confessors applied the laws of the Church relating to sexual behavior, two thirds of the population would not take the sacraments."

The new values lead to a different set of societal norms among the younger generations. Intensive use of manpower is no longer necessary on the farms; people recognize that children have the right to an education and that deprived of this opportunity they will be condemned to menial jobs; a more hedonistic view of life and the right to enjoy oneself has become an accepted value of the young; all these elements require that families be kept small. Fifty-one percent of the population is under thirty and has been brought up and founded families with new expectations. Decisions appear less dictated by tradition. The satisfaction of the individual nuclear family takes precedence over that of the clan or the community. Economic development has brought with it forms of materialism that are oriented to self-satisfaction and no longer to survival as was the case one generation ago. While the impact of these changes on the political perceptions and orientations of the people is hard to gauge—the influence of traditional ties and parental affiliations cannot be ignored—it is possible to assert they are transforming the relations between individuals, leading to a less status and more egalitarian oriented society where opposition is viewed as legitimate. But a few words are necessary with respect to old age in Santa Maria: here traditional values still appear dominant.

Old Age in Santa Maria

In 1969 10 percent of the population was over sixty-five.[22] In the past old age had a visible economic effect on families, and a man who could not work was simply an extra mouth to feed. Much of this burden has been removed by the state pension fund and free medical care, notably since the middle sixties when the mayor pushed numerous requests through a reticent bureaucracy. Two hundred and sixty-one people received a pension when we lived in the village, and 78 percent of these were over sixty-five. This is the equivalent of $13,000 a month in income for the community, an average of $50 per month per individual. While the amounts are modest, they have nevertheless had an impact on the prevailing attitudes towards the old. They are no longer viewed as wards of their children. Also, the younger generations can now look toward old age with more serenity than before.

The utilitarian view has not disappeared, however. The older generations are expected to work as long as they are physically capable. Thus Sergio's mother, bent and broken at eighty-two, finds it normal to trudge up the hill to hoe her son's vineyards; while Lucia Pugina, after having taken care of her vineyards and her hogs, helps her daughter and son-in-law run the new restaurant. At the very least, old men and women are expected to help in the house and the garden and take care of the younger children. This should not be interpreted negatively. Strong bonds of affection exist between the children and their parents and no one would think that a son is exploiting his father. The older generations who lived through the years of limited good cannot visualize not spending their last energies for the family. Work and life go together and they are resigned to that fate. The image of the State providing for all fails to convince them entirely, if for no other reason than they realize their meager pensions are insufficient to insure their survival.

Slightly more than half of the families in Santa Maria share their houses with at least one of their parents. The lingering of the extended family combines with filial affection, sense of duty and economic necessities to keep the old in the household. A very peculiar type of respect is paid to them: "At seven they are children and at seventy they are children again." Thus, they are often chided, having lost their strength, their beauty or their manliness, and many seek solace in wine. (According to our estimates, 43 percent of those who receive a pension are either heavy drinkers or alcoholics.) Complaining about his age and the decline of his sexual powers, the old Beghin once retorted to those who were teasing him, "If God existed and was good, he would rather have cut off my little finger."

The death of a loved one (life expectancy is sixty-four) is accepted with calm resignation by those who continue to live. Sentiments, like the wake, are contained: life continues. The coffin is carried by the children and pall-bearers, and when the bells toll all the village shutters are drawn. The body is laid to rest in the modest and rather well-kept tombs of the local cemetery. Men gather briefly at the *osterie* to eulogize their departed companion; women return home to their chores. Children are taught that death is the most natural of all phenomena. A few women among the older generations will wear black for their relatives, as widows do for their husbands, but men seldom go into mourning.

Change is manifest in the patterns of inheritance. In the past, the sharing of property was an occasion of bitterness and recrimination leading to feuds and quarrels. We heard two brothers who twenty years later were still arguing over whom had property rights to the fig-tree in the family garden. Often, the property was not divided and all lived together in one household. When emigration became common, rights were retained by a *livello*: an extremely long lease for a symbolic amount such as a liter of oil, which made property rights extremely complex. The situation has been transformed by the wave of emigration of the 1950s and by prosperity acquired from factory work. It is common for one son to inherit the land and pay his brothers for their share. Long drawn out payments have led to recriminations but none have the intensity of those of the past. The feuds that survive today result from long past disagreements between the weakened clans of Santa Maria.

Kinship and Clans

Until the 1940s Santa Maria lived as a physically isolated community and many inhabitants had not travelled further than the provincial capital of Padua. This isolation explains the existence and strength of extended kinship groups. Ten family names embrace over one half of the population. Before the onslaught of emigration the proportion reached, we were told, as high as seventy-five percent. In 1969 three families numbered more than one hundred individuals (Tosi, 143; Buzzacchi, 123; Marangoni, 102), while six others had more than fifty.

The problems of distinguishing between people who carry the same patronym is alleviated by a careful search for given names to avoid duplication and by an extensive use of nicknames, some of which can be traced back several centuries in the same family. Many are derivations of trades practiced by the families in the past such as *sacchi* (flour mill for the Fortuna), *pittore* (painter, now carried by the tailor), *marangón*, *piola* (carpenter), *sarolo* (salt-merchant), etc. Others indicate the original location of the family in the *comune* as delle Marlunghe, Vicco, Baiocche, Galeni, while some families carry the nickname of long-gone ancestors: the Bardini are Zanellato, a colonel who fought with Napoleon's Italian army, the Pittoni are Solfarin, an ancestor having distinguished himself at the battle of Solferino. Many nicknames derive from long forgotten physical traits: a branch of the Gallo are *occibei* (beautiful eyes), of the Fortuna, *teta* (fine breasts), and people who have no resemblance with their nicknames still go as *bigio* (albino) or *rana* (frog). For evident reasons some disparaging nicknames only go with the individual, such as *ficcanaso* (curious) or *samauro* (donkey). Women who marry into a clan usually become known by their husband's nicknames and allegiance to their acquired family is expected.

Originally the clans were reinforced by geographical divisions of the community into *corte*, which corresponded to the traditional household of a *pater familias,* divided into several residences built around a courtyard that served as a threshing-floor. The *corte* is the peasant house separated from the village, located on the hills, though physical proximity led to the inclusion of a few *corte* (Menato, Fortuna) when the village expanded in the fifteenth century. Their origin dates to the eleventh century,[23] but in Santa Maria they only go back to 1443 following the establishment of Venetian rule and a return to more peaceful conditions after 1405.

A topographic map of the beginning of the century indicated a dozen *corte* in the territory of Santa Maria. Unfortunately, there is no precise data prior to the 1951 census (163 inhabitants). In 1961 the population had declined to 144 and in 1969 to 117. Before the war *corte* Beghin contained about two hundred people but in 1969 only had sixty-five. Most of the *corte* are abandoned (Tosi) or lived in by one or two families (Tioli, Zancanaro), their inhabitants having either emigrated or come to the village, bringing with them their own attitudes.

The inhabitant of the *corte* considers himself different from the villager. He is more independent and does not feel constrained by the obligations that derive from life in an urban society. He declares he lives "where the air is good," which was no doubt true before sewers were laid in the village, but above all expresses the fact he lives free and separated from the village. This freedom has old roots: at the end of the eighteenth century more men from the *corte* worked their own fields than men in the village; they were *coloni* while the others were *operai,* laborers. In spite of easier communication the *cortigiano* still seems to enjoy his voluntary segregation, a different way of life based on stronger family ties, and a stronger attachment to the fields he owns.

Corte and clan reinforce each other, and though emigration and population decline have affected their importance, the inhabitants still continue feuds and controversies of the past. In turn, this influences the patterns of socialization of the *cortigiani* and clan members, weakening the impact of the ethnic homogeneity of the population, creating tensions that extend to the political realm in a community that is hardly large enough to support them. In 1969 the Fortuna (Sacchi) were still at odds with the Fortuna (Teta) who had enthusiastically embraced fascism, while the first supported the *popolari.* Since 1945 the Fortuna had been arguing with the Menato following a theft of gravel from the Fortuna family by a Menato who, to add insult to injury, defecated on the doorstep of a Fortuna household.[24] Members of these clans are yet to be found on the same electoral lists, and the Bardini and the Tiberto are in the same situation because of a boundary dispute that dates from 1911. No group in the village would think of trusting the Beghin. They are said to have long hands and be thieves. The same label is applied to a branch of the Merlo, the *occibei.* As a consequence of this community infighting, outsiders have been able to exercise more influence in local politics than their number warrants.

The atmosphere of distrust which characterized certain groups has as its counterpart mutual support among members of a clan. These bonds speak rather strongly against the existence of so-called amoral familism in Santa Maria.[25] Here people support each other and recognize special allegiances to their group. This is visible, for instance, in local elections, and was true in the case of Mayor Tiberto before the 1900s. Similarly, the Fortuna (Sacchi) constituted the majority of those who signed an electoral petition headed by one of their own in 1960, and the same applied to the Tioli in 1956, leading to the official recognition of the lists. The allegiance to one's family has led to several cases of nepotism, visible in the post office and the town hall, and the streetsweeper has been a Perrazolo since 1870.

Nevertheless, clans and *corte* are remnants of the past and we did not find many people among the post-war generations who gave much importance to the old feuds: feuding is now on a personal basis. Antonio Tiberto and Vincenzo the restaurant owner have been at odds since 1968. Antonio accuses Vincenzo of not having served the entire leg of deer he had brought him to cook, but to have kept half for his own purposes. If Vincenzo is *furbo* and dishonest, Antonio says he is even more *furbo*. Whenever possible he avoids him and no longer patronizes his restaurant. The considerable emigration Santa Maria experienced removed many of the clan links as entire generations deserted the village. The greater mobility of the Mariani, and the new values of the peasant-worker make the feuds far less important; changing patterns of marriage and a greater mixing of the population weaken the clan. Above all individualism and the nuclear family spell the end of the clan's influence, leading to a more open society.[26] One element that has contributed to this new perspective is the school.

Education

Schooling, a critical element in the socialization process, has a well documented impact on political socialization and the acquisition of values. Its influence is second only to that of the family. It is possible to assert that "a person's level of education affects his way of understanding the world of politics."[27] In Santa Maria we can assume that the less educated groups will be prone to apathy and willing to accept the arguments of those in whom they have confidence, such as their elders or the parish priest, who tend to favor more conservative positions.

New perspectives and hopes have opened up for the young people in the community. In 1872, 73 pupils gathered in a one-room elementary school,[28] while from 1914 to 1954 three rooms constituted the entire school system. In 1960 the elementary school taught 246 pupils; and in 1964 a kindergarten had 75 children. In 1967 a middle school was opened in the community and has been housed in a brand-new building since 1972. The new elementary school had 11 classrooms, 10 teachers and 220 students in 1970. One can speak of a revolution in education, visible in the statistics.[29] (See Table 4.3.)

As the old generations pass away the level of illiteracy declines. The younger age groups are putting pressure on the educational system, with slightly over 25 percent of the total population being of school age, a percentage double that of 1951 and nearly triple the 1961 figure. The middle school has replaced elementary school as the finishing point for a majority of those of school age,[30] and the lyceum and even the university are becoming an aim attainable by a few.

The changes are obvious if one considers age groups and education. Table 4.4 indicates that 75 percent of the illiterates and 85 percent of the semi-illiterates are in the age groups older than 45; in the post-war generations illiteracy has been practically eradicated, and 71 percent of the population that has gone to middle school is between age 15 and 25. This group may be large enough to counterbalance the more

4.3 LEVELS OF EDUCATION

	1951		*1961*		*1969*	
	number	*%*	*number*	*%*	*number*	*%*
Illiterate	268	10.5	128	6.0	24	1.18
Semi-illiterate	418	16.4	312	14.7	177	8.68
Elementary School	476	58.1	1,409	66.5	1,121	54.95
Middle School	50	1.9	57	2.6	135	6.62
Lyceum	n.a.		n.a.		20	.98
University	n.a.		n.a.		14	.69
Under Age 6	332	13	219	10.3	539	26.42

4.4 EDUCATION BY AGE GROUPS (IN PERCENTAGES)

	15–20	*21–25*	*26–30*	*30–45*	*Over 45*	
Illiterate	0	4	8.5	12.5	75	100
Semi-illiterate	1.1	1.6	0.3	12	85	100
Elementary School	10	13	11	29	37	100
Middle School	58	13	8	11	10	100
Lyceum	5	25	5	40	25	100
University	14	7	7	43	29	100

conservative or apathetic attitudes of its elders. However, a higher percentage of the university educated are among the older generations since university education leads to emigration among the younger people; for them there is little inducement to remain in Santa Maria.

An examination of the levels of education within age groups indicates (Table 4.5) that 28 percent of adults over 45 are either illiterate or semi-illiterate, while 41 percent of children aged 15 to 20 have gone through middle school as opposed to 2 percent of the over-45 population. Again, considering that most inhabitants have no more than an elementary education (55%—Table 4.3), the fact that 41 percent of the younger generation has gone to middle school is an indication of the impact this group can have on attitudes in the community.

Finally, if we examine education and sex divisions it is clear,

4.5 LEVELS OF EDUCATION WITHIN AGE GROUPS (IN PERCENTAGES)

	15–20	*21–25*	*26–30*	*30–45*	*Over 45*
n=	*187*	*163*	*128*	*382*	*596*
Illiterate	0.0	0.5	1.55	0.78	3.0
Semi-Illiterate	1.0	2.0	0.0	5.49	25.3
Elementary School	56.0	84.0	90.6	86.6	67.9
Middle School	41.0	10.0	6.25	3.4	2.1
Lyceum	0.5	3.0	0.78	2.0	0.8
University	1.0	0.5	0.78	1.57	0.67

females being more numerous than males in the total population, that the male has had more opportunities for education (see Table 4.6). More significant than these arid statistics are the values emphasized by the school system in Santa Maria, values that are transmitted by the curriculum and the schoolteacher.

The priest and the teacher are the repositories of knowledge in Santa Maria. They are also the first models of political authority the child encounters on a regular basis outside of his family.[31] Religious education is compulsory in the Italian school and its teaching is entrusted to the clergy, the defender of conservatism. Furthermore, the priest's position is reinforced in the school by certain images: a large statue of a madonna adorns the entrance of the elementary school; a crucifix is placed above the blackboard in every room; and several elementary school teachers start the day with a collective prayer. In the middle school civics is taught in conjunction with religion by the chaplain. In sum, and naturally so in an area where Catholicism is strong, religious values have direct access to the major socialization agent, the school.

The attachment to the formal practice of religion and respect for religious values as taught to the young by their mothers is thus reinforced, notably in elementary school during the weekly hour of catechism. However, the school as we saw it in 1969 tended to espouse values that were different from those of other agents of socialization, the family in particular. Much of this can be related to the origins and the number of the teachers. For each of the first five elementary grades the children have only one teacher, after which they are exposed to different people for different subjects. Only two of the eleven teachers in Santa Maria were born there. The others came from surrounding

4.6 EDUCATION BY SEX

	Illiterate		*Semi-Illiterate*		*Elementary School*		*Middle School*		*Lyceum*		*University*	
	N	*%*	*N*	*%*	*N*	*%*	*N*	*%*	*N*	*%*	*N*	*%*
Male	15	62.5	76	43	572	51	83	61	13	65	10	71
Female	9	37.5	101	57	549	49	52	39	7	35	7	29

cities, Este and Padua, that have a more urban value system. Eight were women, but they appeared more emancipated than village women, providing a different image of womanhood from that which the children encountered at home. They drove cars, dressed differently, and believed in the intellectual equality of men and women. Though they only spent a half a day in school (Italian schools meet from eight to one), they set an example for the younger generations who, most agreed, respected their teachers. Kindergarten provided a different image, as it is operated by a religious order that maintains three sisters in Santa Maria. They take care of their charges from 9 a.m. to 4 p.m. Their reinforcing of values espoused by the Church can be illustrated by a poem the children recited to the new mayor in 1964, lauding the Mariano who had been smart enough to ignore the "wooing of imbeciles and had trounced the atheistic PCI."

Though changes are in the offing, the school system of Santa Maria follows authoritarian methods and defends elitism rather than emphasizing participation and democracy. This is more visible in the elementary school than in the middle school. In our talks with teachers and children of the elementary grades we found that the teacher is envisioned as the person who is always right. Not only is she the source of knowledge but also the strict enforcer of rules. A dress code (light colored pinafores for girls, dark uniforms for boys) must be respected and parents must make sure their children are properly attired. Order, silence, the proper forms of address, and sitting still are very much part of the child's daily school life. Penmanship is emphasized from the first grade through the fifth. Ball-point pens, pencils, and fountain pens are unacceptable, and the neatness required in daily (two hours) homework would startle many American teachers. Collective punishments were not rare and many a class was deprived of its half-hour recess or not allowed to eat its mid-morning snack. For single offenders physical punishment was more common than the imposition of additional homework.

The contrast between elementary and middle school was remarkable. First of all the basic ground rules of discipline, silence, and order were well established by the time the children entered middle school. These children were the brighter ones who might go on to the lyceum, and the curriculum was more open and dialogue became possible. In contrast to Signorina Paola of the first grade, who chose to be the

First day of school

Carrying crates old-style

The veterans

1915–1918 veterans

rigid, unchallengeable, unbending teacher, the *maestro* who taught sixth grade Italian or the chemistry *professoressa* in the seventh were always willing to talk with their pupils in and out of class. They encouraged rather than chided, led the children to learning rather than force-fed them. All agreed they were a different breed of teacher who made learning interesting, if not fun, and were ready to recognize that all could not learn at the same speed.

In general, the basic rule remained that fast and bright children (those who could learn at the speed the teacher taught) were rewarded and promoted while the others were considered desperate cases who were hardly worth the effort. Until the new middle school came into existence in 1962 the profile of the 1914 graduating class (fifth elementary) was quite typical: of 37 students, 22 were repeating. On the average 27 attended and 14 of these were promoted, while 13 had to repeat.[32] As the schoolboys of Barbiana wrote, "Dear Miss . . . you flunk us right out into the fields and factories and there you forget us."[33] Before the law of 1962 made eight rather than five years of schooling compulsory, elementary school meant the brightest triumphed while all the others were held back—*bocciati*. From our observation the filtering now extends over the eight years of schooling and is less rigid in the elementary schools. But old patterns and habits die hard in the village.[34] For instance, Paolo Ficcanaso withdrew from school at fourteen: he had been *bocciato* three times. He was bright and alert, "*un diavolo*," a devil, his teachers said. They declared he simply did not want to learn; above all he had not been taught how to learn. Though he appeared resigned to his fate he had also been frustrated by the system. The son of alcoholics, he was no "Pierino."[35]

With attendance at middle school near compulsory a new attitude towards schooling is developing among the young Mariani. If they do not like school they at least accept it. School is not necessarily a place to be avoided at all costs, and fewer and fewer parents depend upon their children for agricultural work. Few children want to go to work at fourteen. A majority of boys want to go to technical schools to get training for a job and are supported by their parents. One said, "Without training you can't get anywhere today, if not to work in the fields. And even then, if you can't repair your tractor you'll get taken by a mechanic. After school I want to go into the tank corps and later open a garage." Every day with his friends he bikes five miles to school. The girls, with a few exceptions who study accounting, seem more concerned to join the workers in the doll factories, earn some money and get married. Thus, only a minority who finish middle school will go on to the lyceum: then, their road is set—they will go to the university. They realize the difficulties but are ambitious and supported by their parents who tend to be among the most well-off in the village.

However, in Santa Maria today, status is playing less of a role than in the past. The society, though social divisions are apparent, is more egalitarian. Certainly Giuseppe, the son of the journalist, was being promoted undeservedly but even he was *bocciato* once. Children can hope they will go through their eight grades without having to experience the trauma of being held back. If they are reasonably bright they will be urged to go to the lyceum. This is the case of Silvano "Terron," whose father is a day laborer. He did reasonably well in middle school, well at the lyceum, and is now studying engineering in Padua.

Changes in the curriculum have made school more accessible to children from the lower classes. Though the dreaded *interrogazione*, literally an interrogatory in front of the class, has not disappeared, learning emphasizes reasoning rather than rote repetition. Since 1965 new math is taught in Santa Maria, though the teachers despise it, and Latin is no longer compulsory in the middle school. English and French have become part of a more practically oriented curriculum. Nevertheless, literary disciplines dominate scientific ones and twice as much time is devoted to Italian than to scientific topics. Petrarch and Dante are "deified"; and modern history stops before 1922 and fascism. Only the sixth grade maestro took pains to teach civics but more often than not what he said and even practiced was contradicted by the actions his students witnessed in daily life.[36] Thus he promoted the Circolo di Lettura where open communication, free discussion and majority decisions were the rule. But its leaders soon realized in their dealings with the town hall that success depended on authoritarian methods. Similarly, no dialogue appeared possible with the parish on delicate subjects such as sex once the young chaplain, who was willing to discuss these problems, had been removed.

Basically, political learning in the classroom is biased in favor of conservative values, and with few exceptions the educational system hardly reinforces the democratic tenets it advocates. Obedience and discipline in school may well induce passive attitudes that lead to avoidance of controversy and refusal of involvement beyond voting. However, greater literacy leads to greater expectations and capacity of problem solving. This fact has already been demonstrated in the first generation that is a product of the new middle school. The younger generations have refused the passive attitudes of their parents and are no longer content to trust their elders with respect to the election booths. They have infused new life into the opposition at the municipal level and pushed their own candidates. Communication, discussion and proselytizing have become part of the daily life of those who join in the Circolo di Lettura, the largest peer group the community has ever known, in which critical decisions, such as refusing parish sponsorship, are reached democratically. But more education means the community must offer better employment opportunities, hardly a plausible development.

The Community

The community, providing the overall environment in which the citizens live, is itself an agent of socialization. Its norms and mores are influential in determining the values that dictate individual life styles. These life styles have a direct bearing on the acquisition and transformation of political attitudes.

Mariani are extremely proud of and loyal to their village. They have only abandoned it under the duress of economic pressures, and this is most often temporary. As soon as a little capital has been accumulated the villager returns to the home land. Subsequent developments may prevent this, though it is safe to say that at least half of the males over fifty who live in Santa Maria have emigrated and returned. For those who do not come back, a yearly pilgrimage during their vacations is an established pattern. In August the observer notes an influx of new faces who bear the familiar names of the Marian clans.

Typical of this is Guido Burlon. This is his story. "We were four brothers. I was the youngest and also the strongest but I had nothing to do on the farm. In 1953, 1954, and 1955, I went to France, first to hoe beets and then harvest grapes. It kept me going for four or five months and paid well. I saved and sent money home and my father bought a field on the Sasso. The last year I got a job on a farm near Lille but the sun never shined, the people preferred to drink beer, the girls didn't talk to us, so at Christmas I quit and came home. At the end of 1956 I got a job at the cement factory. A lousy job, but at home and I'd rather be poor at home than rich with the bean-eaters" (i.e. the French).

A recurrent theme of many a conversation in the community was that people would commute and live in Santa Maria rather than be nearer to their jobs. This reaction was not dictated by the fear of an unknown environment—many have been working in Padua for the last ten years—or economic considerations. One is simply better off in Santa Maria where life is easier, where the pace is slower, and where one is recognized for what he and his family are worth. The personal aspects of life in the village outweigh the material advantages of life in the city. Similarly, a majority of the young men and women still prefer to marry within the community. Despite all appearances to the contrary, for the Mariani his village represents beauty, comfort and abundance. The historical setting, the cadre, the climate, the exquisite wines, however relative they may be, are absolutes for the locals. Santa Maria is *la patria*. Allegiance is due and paid to it. Though Italy is no object of scorn neither does it elicit strong attachment or pride. Thus, the primary loyalty is to the community rather than to the State. To maintain status in the former calls for loyalty and honesty; similar values hardly apply to the latter; one is friend, the other is foe. There is little pride in the nation but a near morbid attachment to the community.[37]

Maintaining appearances is all important and few would think of deviating from the local mores. A facade must be established if one wishes to remain an honorable man. *Furbizia*, the critical element of honor we have already mentioned (see p. 114), is a recognized and valuable social quality. Status and *furbizia* combined allow one to enhance one's position in society. From the point of view of open communication such an attitude is detrimental to political life. The refusal to commit oneself to values or positions, the necessity of not letting people know where one stands, allows for political dissimulation. The switching of allegiances can take place rapidly and defies prediction.[38] This is well reflected in the discussions that take place in the *osterie* and bars.

The community supports ten drinking establishments where the men congregate, play cards, and drink *ombrette* (little shadows) of the local red and white wines. The *osteria* serves as the community club house where all can interact, where individual status is maintained, defended and at times destroyed. In Santa Maria *osterie* are not "the agora of politics."[39] Conversations seldom reach a personal level, as if a conscious effort were made to avoid references to people in the community or to those present. When such references are made the speaker's companions attempt to make him cease. When they fail most leave or pretend not to listen. In bars conversations revolve around the weather, work, sports, and above all the quality of wines served. One may reminisce about the past, but rarely about its politics. The only exceptions we noted were among the members of the municipal council (government or opposition), who at times engaged others in their discussions, though their interlocutors did not take a stand in their answers. The same holds true for the younger people who belonged to the Circolo di Lettura, though they seldom had a large audience. When at all possible one avoids taking a stand on any matter that has a connection with community life: to remain honorable one must not be compromised.[40]

Thus, much lip service is given to appearances. Except in the case of feuds, one pays respect to the influential citizens and patrons, and whenever possible attempts to impress fellow citizens by cutting a fine figure. This accounts for a large part of what may be considered generosity but is, more often than not, prompted by a desire to be indebted to no one. In bars all will attempt to pay for each round of drinks; the gesture is essential. At home guests are served bottled wines, and whatever the quality, the highest compliments are to be paid. The fiction that everybody's wines are the best is accepted by all. The killing of the pig is followed by a dinner that takes on the proportions of a wedding feast to which friends, neighbors and patrons are invited. No pork is served, since this would indicate a lack of economic resources. At most, salami from the preceding year can be provided, becoming a signal of richness, of "capital accumulation." Invariably, in the early hours of the morning, the host thanks his guests with the phrase "Excuse me if you have not been well taken care of; we provided so little."

Mariani are gregarious, but their more intimate motivations make it difficult to talk of a "mensatic" culture, where all meet around a table, at home and in bars.[41] Too much of their lives revolves around status and the preservation of appearances. The values of a traditional rural society are still very evident, albeit attenuated by a newly discovered prosperity. The society is well integrated and the lack of strong social divisions makes for harmony. However, the underlying values and the considerable attachment to formal behavior patterns, the necessity to conform, the respect for appearances, all reinforce a passive attitude with regards to commitment—"If you don't want to be ruined you'd better shut up" (*se non vuoi che ti sputtanino . . .*), says old Umberto Merlo—and cynicism vis-à-vis power and the political system, however democratic they may be.

The people of Santa Maria are tolerant as long as their honor is not put in jeopardy. But this tolerance may only be a form of disinterest on the part of the community for the few deviants and the many alcoholics.

Deviants are objects of the local folklore but because they are also alcoholics they are less visible. Enzo Bazzi inveighs against the Church but still goes to Mass; however, he never works. Danilo Brigato criticizes the local administrators but is willing to accept a glass of wine from the mayor. Giovanni Grossi the farmer prefers dogs to people but harms neither as long as they let him drink in peace. These people have lost their honor and are tolerated, but not respected. They are alcoholics, *senza dignità*—they have no shame.

Alcoholism is a serious social problem, seldom acknowledged in a community that in the past derived much of its income from wine. The local dialect has nine different expressions corresponding to various degrees of drunkenness.[42] The problem is hardly new, since Petrarch remarked, "[He would adapt] to drink a little wine, not because it is useful, but because it is proper to act in such a way among drunkards, for whom life is not in their blood but in their wine."[43] The doctor in 1914 advocated signs in the schools proclaiming "Mothers who drink poison their children's milk! Alcoholic fathers mean mad sons." We were told that as many as twenty-eight people were "in collegio," in school, the euphemism for institutes for disintoxication, at one time.

In 1969, 7 percent of the total population was classified as alcoholic and 21 percent were considered heavy drinkers.[44] Men accounted for 94 percent of all alcoholism and women 15 percent of all heavy drinkers. Fifty-one percent of the alcoholics and 45 percent of the heavy drinkers were among the retired population, as if to confirm the proverb that "Wine is the old man's milk." Among peasants 43 percent were alcoholics or heavy drinkers in contrast to 20 percent of the secondarily employed population and 9 percent of the tertiary workers. Education is the key variable: 25 percent of all alcoholics and heavy drinkers are illiterate or semi-illiterate, and 72 percent have only gone through elementary school.

Changes in the economic structure (the decline of the peasantry) and increased opportunities for education are changing the situation. Many factory workers consider it more distinguished to drink a commercial aperitif rather than several glasses of wine, and while the young have not rejected wine consumption as a symbol of virility, they are turning more and more to soft drinks.

A progressive change in communal values is taking place. The traditional patterns of interaction resting basically on status and physical location are breaking down. The social system is no longer exclusively inwardly oriented now that the community finds most of its resources outside its boundaries. Employment and work schedules are no longer dictated by the weather and the seasons but by the needs of industry. The increase in individual wealth makes the villager less dependent on visits to the bar to assert or maintain his status. Outsiders, who were once the exception, have now become a common sight with the development of the tourist trade. Only on Sundays does the *osteria* regain its traditional place in the social fabric of the village.

In the past, communication was almost exclusively oral. Until 1972 Santa Maria had no newspaper stand. Five families received a paper through the mail; two bars put one at their clients' disposal. The main source of information was then, as it is now, gossip and the pulpit, where one can learn about a milk sale to be held in the square, the progress of divorce legislation in parliament, war in Biafra, or landings on the moon. Nowadays, the newspaper stand has most newspapers available though papers of the left are not in prominent view. (The pornographic *Playmen* sells much better!) Above all, television has been present since 1966 in practically every household, and while it favors the Christian Democratic viewpoint it nevertheless espouses values which were long alien to Santa Maria. The national view has clearly broken Santa Maria's isolation and the written word is becoming acceptable as more of the people come to rely upon the daily press.

Change is also visible in the new patterns of entertainment. Traditionally Sunday Mass and drinking provided the main opportunity for social gatherings. The major occasions for celebration remain religious and culminate in the feasts of the Holy Trinity and the Assumption. But with progress have come the first steps of cultural development. The village squares are now the settings for concerts and plays in Venetian, especially the comedies by Ruzzante, which provide a different dimension from the exclusively religious celebrations.

In a society that was not characterized by relationships based on trust, new patterns of friendship appear to be evolving. The system of patronage established ties that were seldom spontaneous and implied long-term obligations that had to be honored. To the degree Santa Maria still retains aspects of the peasant culture of the nineteenth century it provides examples of such attitudes among the older generations. It is still the accepted norm not to thank people for gifts received as they are considered obligations or the payment of services rendered. But a more open and prosperous society has to come to exist. Peer groups, spontaneous *compagnie* congregate and ties of friendship develop among the young who are less passionately attached to the earth and to the community they seek to leave on week-ends. Less self-centered orientations can be detected: not only do people believe in the possibility of a prosperous village, they have come around to express an interest in the community *as* community. The Circolo di Lettura is a good example of this as are the *compagnie* around Ugo Masiero or the younger Bardini. Since the individual is less concerned with his material well being and conflicts of interest are less evident, he can now focus more on friendship.

The progressive changes in communal values, and the optimism that characterizes the local society, indicate an evolution toward a more open value system. Because of the weight of the older generations, conservative values have not disappeared. Nevertheless, there are indications that the younger generations are being socialized to more democratic and responsive norms of citizenship.

Parents, the crucial elements in the socialization process, are less conservatively oriented than they may appear and can hardly isolate themselves from the changing values of the community. Fifty-one percent of the population never experienced fascism directly; only 24 percent of the present inhabitants grew up under Mussolini. Ninety percent support the Republican parties, notably the Christian Democratic party, but a majority of men incline more to the left. Such a radical change must, perforce, have consequences on the younger generations.

Teachers, who can be seen as defenders of the status quo, are nevertheless essential transmitters of change. New pedagogical methods and educational programs they have had to accept since 1962 and the urban values to which most were exposed make them conveyors of values far more advanced than those of the society in which they find themselves. These new values are reinforced by daily exposure to television.

The community itself, out of economic necessity, has opened to the world and a newly acquired physical mobility has enlarged the Marian horizon, exposing them to opinions and situations they long ignored. However, the change is gradual. While visible in the socialization agents we have examined so far, it is less evident in the organized groups that dominate community politics.

5. *Political Socialization, Organized Groups and Political Participation*

POLITICAL SOCIALIZATION IS THE SOCIAL-PSYCHOLOGICAL process through which the citizen acquires his own view of the political world. At a collective level it is basic to the creation, maintenance or transformation of the political culture in society. Essentially, it is a product of the diverse experiences of individuals exposed to the political beliefs of their families, to events which they themselves interpret, and to organizations which search to inculcate particular political values. The process is complex, and as we mentioned previously the role of the family in socializing the individual is critical, and can lead to discontinuities when the values advanced by parents do not coincide with those suggested by the other elements of the system. While some of these elements, such as political parties, serve an exclusively political purpose, others, such as churches or cultural organizations, are more general; though they too advance political values. When the values conveyed by these groups coincide with those encountered during the early stage of socialization, they are reinforced and become particularly effective in maintaining the political culture of the society.[1] Such is the case in Santa Maria.

In the preceding chapter we noted that Mariani are socialized to accept and respect those sources of authority to which they are directly exposed and which have an immediate effect on their daily lives. Beyond this the people see virtue in remaining noncommittal. Little emphasis has been placed upon values conducive to democratic principles. The people have always been skeptical of government under whatever form it has taken: the Venetian heritage, the Austrian interlude, the Italian monarchy, the fascist experience and finally the Republican administration. Regimes are considered transitional. The old Buzzachi expressed the feelings of many when he noted "they are all the same, all out to get you, all bad; one or the other makes no difference; taxes always go up." In the past people passively accepted the government and the local authorities. The concepts of authority that predominated in the village, as well as the established patterns of societal life, discouraged active participation and development of the individual in the life of the collectivity.

Only one institution has constantly held the people's allegiance. As the major social organization the Church dominates community life and the parish priest's word is still taken to be final, whether the topic be divorce or transubstantiation, skirt lengths or building codes. Because of its historical force and its presence in the culture, the Church's influence can hardly be contested at the local level by the State without leading to serious and divisive conflicts among the inhabitants. In a society unified around the campanile, a society where trust is absent, most organizations revolve around the Church and the parish priest. The values stressed by these organizations lead the individual to a passive attitude towards political involvement, make him shun an active role in local affairs, leave him content when he has cast his vote at election time. We shall examine this assertion by considering the role of the Church in society, the organizations it controls or opposes, and the attitudes of individuals in their political roles.

The Church

To all appearances Marian society is highly religious and this impression is confirmed when more rigorous methods of measurement are applied. To obtain a profile of the parish we used the method proposed by Burgalassi[2] which combines simplicity with precision. It uses the average attendance at Sunday Mass for the obligated entire population (67%), for men only (70%), the general and male percentage of Easter communions (87% and 90%), the percentage of devout Catholics (10%), of initiated Catholics (12%), of indifferent (19%). Based on these figures the index of religiosity, K′ is .568 which classifies Santa Maria as unanimously religious. Eighty percent of the males and 82 percent of the females practice their religion, and though only 40 percent of the obligated males (over 8 and under 75) go to church regularly, 90 percent receive Easter communion. The practice of religion, while no absolute index of faith, can certainly be interpreted as an index of the influence of the parish priest on the population. Santa Maria is no exception among rural communities where the religious motivations fall essentially into the categories of cosmic-biologic with some popular or spontaneous sociocultural orientations.[3] The function of the gods is not to change the moral existence of those who pray to them but rather to provide an answer to their daily needs. Similarly, as Don Arturo put it when talking about the Church and death, "Souls will take care of themselves; in the interest of the Church we must take care of testaments." This religious motivation does not lead to a group bond with the priest but to individual relationships where the priest serves as a simple intermediary. The relationship is one of mediation, and patronage is often the consequence. The village exists as a community, a group, but the priest himself, in his religious function, does not reinforce the spirit of community. The villagers' perceptions of most religious rituals and their motivation to attend Mass are dictated by a desire to conform to local customs, indicating the unity of the community more than its religiosity. The faithful have a direct link with the priest as man rather than to the priest as representative of God. The same holds for those aspects of religion that take on shades of magic, such as the exorcism against hail; the relationship is exclusively of the patron-client type.

In the village the Church remains the basic frame of reference, and the immensely able parish priest dictates the norms of society. The Church represents stability: physical, moral and social. Preserver of the traditional values, it still inveighs against liberalism and socialism as it did a century ago. All social events that deviate from the traditional patterns are attributed to these doctrines, or to atheism, prompting the priest to caution against work in the factories and to point out the stability and moral value of an agricultural civilization. Don Arturo preaches regularly against blasphemy, though cursing is such common practice it might reflect religiosity rather than the contrary; he also chastises the lack of modesty, especially among women (mini-skirts were fashionable at the time of this study). In his thundering sermons there were also references to "the deicide Jerusalem" and one of his arguments against divorce was that "animals don't divorce, so why should men?" "In the factories, and also in the cities," says Don Arturo, one meets "those communists who have no God . . . and lead the sheep astray from the Father's flock." It is here that women "forget the modesty their mothers taught them . . . and lose their honor which is so precious in motherhood."

It is through the conservative Don Arturo that one establishes his position in the village society. One rises or falls in the social hierarchy according to the degree of obedience and respect for the Church. If total acceptance of Church dogma is not always necessary, formal adhesion is imperative: one misses neither Mass nor a procession, and life is still regulated by the ringing of the bells. Few can afford to deviate, certainly no one who aspires to a political role, because in the final analysis success depends upon the priest. Any candidate who hopes to win must at least tacitly acknowledge his superiority.

As an institution the Church plays a dual role. It is essentially religious, but has social and economic functions in reality. From the religious point of view it offers hope and consolation, and performs this service well, though for the individual it often takes on aspects of fatalism based upon acceptance and resignation to one's ills. Emphasis on the more formal aspects of religion such as church attendance, catechism, etc., leaves little room for virtues such as charity and forgiveness. As if to compensate, Don Arturo in his sermons reserves his strongest words to preach against blasphemy which, in this fundamentally Catholic society, is very much a common form of speech. But in the lingering cosmological peasant society where to use the Marian expression "one shouldn't mistake bread for holy wafers," the external practice of religion is often considered a good form of insurance; one accepts rather than protests. One might hope to placate the elements, but never to dominate them. There is a bond created between man and God, with the Church as an intermediary. However, it is more personal and material than spiritual. It assumes the form of being between man and the Church with the priest as an intermediary. Both parties derive benefits from this link that are conceived to be spiritual when they are in great part material.

Charity is a major activity of the Church, and in Santa Maria the parish has always offered relief to the poor, distributing alms and food whenever possible. Since 1945 the parish has been the employment office.[4] The priest has played an essential role in this function because he is well known in the province. He contacts or is contacted by those who have employment to provide. During the 1950s prior to the economic boom, the parish priest, Don Arturo, found means of livelihood for at least three hundred people. The price to be paid in return is allegiance to and support for the Church. As if to transcend the new prosperity and capitalistic era, the priest in this small village also wears the hat of the banker. The peasant is still reluctant to trust the anonymous banking institutions and feels that the parish offers far better guarantees. The system is simple; when in need of money one contacts Don Arturo, describes his needs and puts down a guarantee in the form of a house or a field equivalent at least to the amount he wishes to borrow. Don Arturo turns to those he knows to have the necessary means. The borrower pays 7 percent, the lender gets 5 or 6 percent, with the difference remaining for the broker, who in the case of default of payment can either pay the balance and take over the guarantee or pass it over to the lender, whichever might be more convenient. In view of his intimate knowledge of the territory the priest takes little risk but reaps substantial benefits. Not only does he perform a service, it is also well remunerated. This service, however, is offered only to "good" Christians, people who can be counted upon, and not only to repay their debt. It is also to the benefit of borrower and lender who get better terms than those granted by commercial banks.

This role of broker has made the parish hall the only real estate agency in town. Other *mediatori* are available for selling products and animals, but everyone must pass through the parish priest for more important transactions. The prices set by the priest are accepted by the seller who has learned to trust Don Arturo's business acumen. Little room is left for bargaining. The power is such that outsiders who wish to purchase property in the village are in fact screened by the parish. The intermediary role has been traditional for authority figures, but seldom has it taken on so commercial an aspect. In the mid-fifties a cement company started buying the Monte Ricco as a source of materials: Don Arturo covered the transaction for some fifty families. His major coup—that classified him once and for all as *furbo*—was to buy the old school building from the state, sell it back to another state agency for three times the original amount paid, and then obtain state support to build a parish hall.

In the village one's social position is very much a function of one's formal acceptance of and by the Church, independent of wealth. To be near the parish hall brings greater status and to be snubbed by the priest can make one's position quite uncomfortable. It can mean difficulties in finding a job, obtaining a loan, selling property, and being considered as a serious person, *una persona per bene*.

Social pressures and superstition combine to reinforce the priest's role of broker and patron. In Santa Maria religious processions are very much a part of social life, coinciding with major religious celebrations. The feasts of the Trinity, Assumption, Palm Sunday, Good Friday and the Ascension see half of the village join in the trek from the church to the *castello* and back. The men come first, followed by women and children, with the parish priest standing on the side and directing the singing through a portable microphone, noting the present and the absent. It is a subtle form of pressure, and few avoid this religious and social duty.

The priest's power is reinforced by the intermediary role he plays between the people and the elements—many believe he has the power to control rain and hail. This comes from *triduos* and *novenas* calling for rain or for sunshine, but even more so from the prayer offered on the feast of the Trinity, cursing the demons that bring bad weather and ordering them to retreat. If hail has not fallen by then, the popular belief is that it is exorcised until the harvest is over.

The mysteriousness of the priestly office also strengthens the grip on the people, and some still see the priest as a sorcerer, able to *gettare il malocchio,* to curse his enemies. Such would be the power of Don Remo, one of the chaplains. In the fall of 1969 when a demonstration was being organized against the mayor, Don Remo simply told the leaders he would curse them if they attempted to have the church bells ring to convene the people. The bells did not ring and no gathering took place.

Today Don Arturo's power is absolute and irresistible, and little can be done without his blessing, particularly in the town hall. Patron, mediator, intercessor with God and the elements, not to mention the Christian Democratic party, Don Arturo, who has been in the village since 1937, is a fact of life with which one must contend. Like other natural elements little can be done to resist him—and only passive opposition is socially permissible. For many Mariani Don Arturo *is* the Catholic Church. One goes to church "because one goes there; otherwise Don Arturo gets angry." He comes before the other world and his values are those a successful Mariano must adhere to if he wishes to live in the community. Tommaso Begossi states flatly: "If he wants to screw you, he will. I believe in God but don't often go to church because I don't like Don Arturo's ways of thinking or behaving. He wouldn't endorse me when I joined the opposition, though he helped Bardini, our leader. Last year he never put in a good word for me when I tried to sell off my piece of land for the parking lot and again I lost out. If it hadn't been for my own friends and the mayor I doubt I would ever have got the building permit for my new house and the gas station. Heck! He'd rather go to Fantolon to get gas. Now look how he helped Menato [the leader of Catholic Action] get his job, or Bruno Beghin [Christian Democratic municipal councillor]. He spent more time in Venice for him than he did for half of the village. And I won't go into the details that aren't that clean."

Running a one-man show, preaching values that reinforce the authoritarian aspects of the society, interpreting all social, political and economic events for his parishioners makes the priest the universal guide to village life, an essential line of communication with the outside, and *the* communication line in the village. He tends to inhibit active participation by providing very few chances for effective participation. The Mariano has few opportunities to be an independent citizen: the social organization he joins and the society he lives in are permeated by the Church. The self-image of the citizen, the way in which he perceives his role in the system and his place in politics are dependent upon the Church and Don Arturo's good will. In brief his choices are limited to the organizations present in the system, a majority of which are Church oriented or controlled.

Organized Groups and the Church

Church-Controlled

Catholic Action is the lay organization of Christian militants whose aim is to foster the development of an ever greater and more intense

Don Arturo Ferlini

Assumption day procession

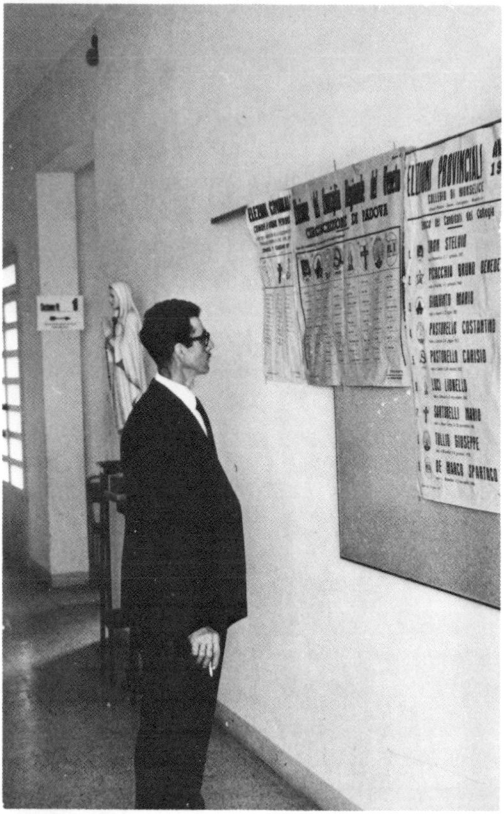

Seeking inspiration before voting

Veterans day in church

faith in the village, preaching through example and word. Organized at the local, provincial and national levels, it is run at the parish level by a "responsible" supervised by the clergy. In 1969, 25 men and 32 women belonged to the adult groups, with 20 young men and 22 young women (age 15-20), 30 boys and 20 girls (age 10-15), and 40 younger boys and 25 girls (age 7-10) belonging to other junior groups. It is complemented by a purely religious organization of men, the Holy Congregation of Franciscan Tertiaries, officially distinct, yet sharing the same male clientele. Its only official appearances are during religious processions; the Tertiaries and Catholic Action young men bear the large candles, carry the dais, flags and religious statues; the women follow behind the flag of their association. By statute Catholic Action is not political, but in its activities it is. The first mayor after fascism was its president; the present vice-mayor is its president. Recruiting among devout Catholics, its purpose is to set examples of living Christianity. Unofficially, however, it insures the DC a solid bloc of votes and a core of uncompromising militants and propagandists. Its lay leader appointed by the parish is also leader of the local DC when it comes out of lethargy at election time. Because in Santa Maria the DC organization exists only on paper, Catholic Action becomes the DC, and as such the DC is directly controlled by the parish. The first elected mayor since fascism was removed in 1947 more by the parish priest than by the municipal council when Don Arturo withdrew his support, and the present vice-mayor remains on the ticket in spite of the mayor's wishes because the priest continues to back him. The religious motivation predominates, yet members of Catholic Action acquiesce in its political role. Importantly enough, it provides the DC and the local administration with a solid core of supporters and as many as one hundred assured votes.

Don Arturo appointed Ottorino Menato leader of Catholic Action in 1952 and has maintained him in the position though his work keeps him away from Santa Maria except during week-ends. He is a devout Catholic, has six children and can rely on the support of most of the Menato clan for whom he serves as a channel of access to the favors of the provincial DC organization. Local leader of the DC and Catholic Action, an evasive man, he says there is no connection between the religious and political. All the DC "notables" in the village, essentially municipal councillors, acknowledge he is a good recruiter and vote-getter who keeps the priest well informed about what goes on, and that his opinion cannot be ignored when drawing up electoral lists. One of his colleagues says that "if he wants to juggle the lists, remove or bring somebody in, he can; if he doesn't, it means Don Arturo doesn't want him to."

The only union existent in Santa Maria, the *Coltivatori Diretti* or farmer's association, is for all practical purposes the only association in the Veneto to organize farmers. Membership is not individual but by families. In Santa Maria it is led by Gilberto Bettola, a small farmer who according to many is more interested in his job as a full-time trade unionist than in his constituents. A persuasive man now in his sixties, he started the first local group in the late 1940s, the Catholic Action group providing him with the first nucleus of members. The association is perceived by all as serving a purely utilitarian function. Through it seeds and fertilizers can be purchased at prices cheaper than commercial ones, though delivery delays often counterbalance this asset. Still it has lobbied successfully to get the farmers a pension scheme, it backs guaranteed prices and supports, it processes most requests for damages due to the weather, and it lobbies for parity between the agricultural and industrial sectors. In Santa Maria over two hundred families belong to the association.

Like other large associations it is intensely bureaucratized. The local council submits to a regional federation in Fantolon which processes demands and transmits them to the regional federation in Padua. Then they are forwarded to the various ministries for action. The process is a long and harrowing one, often incomprehensible to the peasant. Here Bettola plays his role: as president of the local council and member of the regional council he is up to date on all developments and relays them to his clientele. He explains what can be obtained, and above all fills out the endless forms that are necessary. This secretarial task creates a bond, reinforced by success in obtaining benefits. The relationship is very personal and the local council is merely a rubber stamp that meets once or twice a year. Bettola translates into dialect a federation letter on what has been accomplished and what remains to be done, and concludes by dispatching telegrams to the government to request more help. When in need, one consults with Bettola who contacts Fantolon, Padua and Rome if necessary. Bettola, Cavaliere della Repubblica, has become a patron. Some murmur that his services are not free, but based on what we could see, presents were freely given as a gesture of thanks, never expected, and only accepted with reticence. Services performed can be compensated for in other ways, particularly at election time, insuring Bettola's representation on the regional council of the union as well as on the municipal council and the *giunta* where decisions are made. In the men and women who support him Bettola has a strong clientele that makes him the second best vote getter (after the mayor). Bettola and Don Arturo work hand in hand; their philosophies and basic aims are the same, to watch over the people on the earth and to avoid the premature death of the peasant class. No conflict appears to have arisen between them. Bettola is one of the most devout members of Catholic Action and his career has been supported by Don Arturo. In turn Bettola has always sided with his protector and thus been able to establish his own base of support. In local politics he is perennial and irremovable.

To what degree the association has pursued a socializing function is difficult to establish. It has taught the peasants to organize and manifest their needs more peacefully than in the mid-twenties, but its essential function is self-interest and not general. No efforts have been made to encourage or to create a cooperative movement in spite of offers from a wine cooperative in Vo to establish a branch in Santa Maria. Little energy has been spent on pointing out the merits of the VDQS wine label, and restructuring properties is out of question. More evident is the uninspiring picture of the State presented to the peasants. All benefits must be wrested from it through the strenuous efforts of the association. While the State is not bad—it, too, is controlled by the DC—it is at best neutral toward the peasants, who must continually solicit and challenge it if they want to survive. And this takes place at a time when the peasant class is disappearing from Santa Maria, to such a point that one is tempted to see self-perpetuation as the major function of the association rather than the defense of its clientele's interests. Furthermore, the association is exclusive and Bettola tolerates no opposition, which is hardly conducive to the development of faith in the democratic process.

The oldest social organization in Santa Maria is the Società Filarmonica Francesco Petrarca founded in June 1888 with the financial help of the municipality.[5] It is the municipal band and the pride of the village. It plays at all civil and religious functions and has come to be dependent on the parish. In shambles at the end of the war, it was brought back into existence in 1964. Today it derives its income from several sources. On January 1 the band serenades the village households and collects most of its money (212,000 lire [$342] in 1969), to which the town hall adds a contribution of 50,000 lire ($80) while the State contributes the salary of the band director. The parish adds another "extraordinary" 50,000 lire. The income is spent on rental and repair of instruments and "administering" wine and food to the players who receive no other compensation.

The band has no formal leadership structure; its director and musical instructor is hired by the parish and his authority extends no further than rehearsals and scores. Communications are dealt with by the parish and all announcements made in church. This public relations function, the special financial contribution, and a lack of enthusiasm on the part of the town government (no contribution was paid from 1967 to 1969) makes Don Arturo the formal patron of the association, even though the municipality is the official sponsor. An example of their respective roles took place at a plenary meeting which provides an annual occasion for a huge dinner and abundant libations. In 1969, with Don Arturo presiding, the point was raised whether to continue to rent or to purchase the instruments. Was the band really there to stay? The priest introduced the discussion, made his points, and then reverted to private conversation, leaving the mayor to expound his point of view, and allowing him to summarize and conclude so that both played a role of some importance.

The band in Santa Maria is the only institution where the young and the old meet and come together on equal terms, the players varying in age from ten to seventy. In 1971 the first female was admitted to the band. This could be an excellent occasion for the exchange of ideas between generations. Unfortunately, the group aged fifteen to twenty-five is hardly represented, the young men seeking pleasures other than music and refusing to submit to schedules and discipline. Also the band is perceived as a creation of the parish and one has the distinct impression that membership excludes anyone who does not sympathize with the parish priest. Although recreational in its aims, it can easily appear to be an arm of the dominating elite.

This elite controls the parties and politics in Santa Maria. To an extent "party" is a misnomer, since none maintains any formal organization in the village. Politics are based on personalities and personal followings; a few patrons with the proper political connections take care of the needs of the community. In fact they serve their function well. The priest has direct access to the DC in Padua and the Honorable Gui, its representative, as does the village mayor.

The DC has always done well in Santa Maria, gaining a minimum of 70 percent and a maximum of 85 percent of the votes. Its card holders are limited to the men in Catholic Action, the mayor and a few members of the municipal council. At most it numbers thirty members many of whom take out a card through the Catholic Action group. The secretary, Angio Testoni, who is head of Catholic Action and vice-mayor, lives in Padua. Bettola, at one time DC representative, lives in Fantolon, and the mayor, who also lives in Padua and ran on the DC ticket, proclaimed himself an independent until 1970. The connecting link is Don Arturo. In 1945 the Church provided the DC with its grass-roots organization. In Santa Maria the situation is the same today. Alternatively, the DC is seen as being Catholic Action, occasionally *Coltivatori Diretti* or mayor, but above all Don Arturo. Parish and party at the local level are one in the minds of most. Election lists for municipal elections are elaborated in the parish house more than in the town hall, and cement an alliance between the two major patrons, the priest and the mayor, the latter becoming the electoral creation of the former. They are the party and neither feels the need nor has the room for any formal party organization.

Organizations Not Committed to the Church

Under these conditions opposition groups find survival difficult. Political parties are content at the time of national elections to make a formal appearance in Santa Maria. They set up their posters in the spaces reserved for this purpose and hold one meeting in the village square. At least this was the case in 1970 and 1972 when the PCI (Italian Communist Party) and the MSI (Italian Social Movement) made token appearances.[6] The PCI draws much of its support from Mandonego which lies outside the parish limits; the MSI garners a melancholy vote from the older people who still have nostalgia for Baratella. The other parties have neither the time nor the strength to bother about a village where the DC dominates so clearly: the votes they receive are solicited at the place of work outside the village.

Local politics provide for an opposition that is not formally connected to any party, though its leaders incline towards the PSI (Italian Socialist Party). Since 1964 its name and symbol has been the Bilancia (the scales of Justice). While it does not espouse the narrow views endorsed by the parish it is tolerated and even welcomed by the DC list since it reaps a sufficient number of votes to prevent others, the left and the PCI in particular, from reaching the municipal council. In 1970 and 1975 its leaders sought informally Don Arturo's and the mayor's advice before setting up their slate.

For practical purposes, outside of the *Coltivatori Diretti* no unions exist in Santa Maria, not even the Christian Democratic CISL, which caters to industrial workers. Individual members of the CGIL (PCI inclined) and of the CISL exist in Santa Maria but they are organized according to their place of employment. The Mariano is reluctant to proclaim his union membership. It is only revealed in the case of a conflict with his employer. Our informers, Don Arturo in particular, indicated that from 10 to 12 percent of those who worked outside of Santa Maria belonged to a union, and for the major part to CISL. People see the unions as an instrument of defense in the case of a grievance rather than an instrument of pressure that could play a local political role. Thus the mayor had no qualms in advising Antonio Tiberto, who had been laid off following a disagreement with his foreman, to seek counsel and defense through the CGIL which is far more aggressive than its DC counterpart. All in all opposition parties and unions in Santa Maria find it extremely difficult to act as agents of political socialization because they are perceived as evil.

Mariani have a low opinion of national politicians, even the Christian Democrats. One of their strong supporters expressed the feelings of many Mariani when he said, "Sure, they try to help and sometimes do. But that's just because they want your vote. First they have to line their own pocket and you can be sure they'll never die hungry. Look at Rumor and all the farms he's bought since he's in the government. Now, where does the money come from? The fascists were no better and the communists will be worse—they have no law. Nobody cares in Rome. You can change the conductor but the music is always the same. The decent guys? They never get anywhere. If they do, they've been corrupted on the way."

The situation is hardly different with regard to the unions that most view as instruments of the parties "which for their own reasons oblige you to strike and lose your pay." Only for the Mariani who work outside the village and in particular in factories are attitudes slightly different. The union defends the workers against the owner, but as a 31-year-old cement factory laborer told us: "They don't do it for you. It's to bug the other groups and show they are stronger. They want our votes in the committees so they help you get benefits—not because it's good for you but because it's good for them. I vote for the CISL to keep the reds out, but if I have a grievance I'll go to the CGIL: they're more efficient. The owners are afraid of the PCI and are quicker to bargain with them rather than with their own in the CSIL. Union leaders are all ass-holes."

The two other groups worthy of mention in Santa Maria, the Veterans and the hunting circles, perform at best a social function and have almost no effect on the political life of the community. The Veterans' Association (World War I) provides flag and pall bearers at its members' funerals, a far cry from its days under Baratella. The two hunting circles, one of which leans towards the local administration while the other favors the Bilancia, are social groupings that organize hunting parties to Yugoslavia (practically no game is left in Santa Maria). Their membership is unstructured and an increase in the costs of Yugoslav game hunting spells their demise.

A Struggle for Influence: the Circolo di Lettura

The organizations controlled by the Church are not committed to change; and the others have few occasions to influence the conservative values of the society. When the Church organizations see their influence menaced they band together and face the challenge. This was the case when the Circolo di Lettura was founded. In the fall of 1968 the young people of the middle school supported by a few university students approached the young and eager chaplain, Don Lorenzo, and a teacher in the elementary school with the idea of sponsoring and creating a club that would belong to and be run by the young while admitting all those who would wish to join, including the older people. Officially the aim was to create a cultural center more than a recreational one, so that financial support could be obtained from the State, which in effect provided the group with the use of two rooms in the basement of the school and agreed to pay a teacher to chaperone the group three times a week. More simply the young wanted a place where they could meet, talk, enjoy themselves, a center for entertainment which appeared so necessary in Santa Maria. In a short period of time, nearly spontaneously, a youth group, open to all, had been created by the young people themselves, with the help of the teacher and the parish chaplain, and the support of the local doctor and the pharmacists, ex-members of the *FUCI* (Italian Federation of Catholic University Students), but without much or any consultation or support from the establishment. In spite of a strong Christian orientation, the group sought above all to be independent. While open to advice it still wanted to make its own decisions and learn through trial and error. When asked why the initiative had not been taken earlier, the answer was that "nobody seemed interested or was ready to give up free time," that "Don Arturo was too old to understand what interested young people"—but that Don Lorenzo was ready to go along with their ideas and they didn't have to buy his.

On November 10, 1968, the Circolo di Lettura officially opened its doors and met with tremendous success. Over one hundred young people, ages fifteen to twenty, gathered in the school building, and for the first time in an "official" function, boys and girls were free to mingle and discuss problems, between themselves, with Don Lorenzo and the teacher. The same week Don Lorenzo bought a projector on credit and in church asked people to give generously to the young who would come around to collect money to pay off the debt. This request was put forth against the wish of Don Arturo, who did not announce it when he preached the sermon. The center started a successful series of movies, a cine-club with good quality films, such as Pasolini's *Gospel according to Saint Matthew,* which were introduced and commented on by outsiders, a series of conferences and debates varying from "contestazione" to religiosity among the young, from Vietnam to Italian politics. For the more mature, sexual education classes were provided by the local doctor and pharmacist; for the girls, lessons in make-up were proposed. At least once and more often twice a week something was going on at the Circolo.

Such activity was revolutionary in Santa Maria. What appeared normal to the university students, the young chaplain and the young people, often seemed to be verging on revolt and sin to their elders. In the debates and discussions, criticisms were freely aired on all topics, and in particular on the international, national and local political situation. The young, expressing themselves collectively, made it clear they did not feel represented, heard or listened to in the town hall, and that while respecting the parish priest they wished for a little more dynamism in religious leadership, less concern for the forms and more for the substance of religion.

Neither the parish priest nor the mayor visited the Circolo di Lettura though they had been invited: the official attitude was to wait and see—this could be a temporary blaze that would rapidly extinguish itself. The contrary soon became clear. Don Lorenzo was becoming more popular—and the older young people took to calling him Lorenzo as if he were a brother. The group of founders was holding tight; the young were looking for worthwhile projects in the village and criticizing the administration; and in church Don Lorenzo celebrated Mass accompanied by guitars.

In January a campaign of uncertain origins was started to discredit the Circolo and Don Lorenzo. It was murmured that more than casual discussions took place at the Circolo and that feminine underwear had been found after meetings. Don Lorenzo asked Don Arturo to squelch such rumors as was in his power, but nothing was done. A week later a new rumor started: one of the girls was said to be pregnant by the chaplain. In early March Don Lorenzo was transferred to another parish, and Don Arturo in self-defense felt the need to tell his parishioners he had done all he could to prevent this: "I can say with Saint Paul, 'I do not lie.' "

The young received support from the maestro, the doctor and the pharmacists. Writing in their mimeographed news sheet they declared "how sad it is to feel the wind blow away our hopes," and concluded:

> . . . in spite of all the indifference and abulia expressed towards the problems of youth by many, [Don Lorenzo] gave life to an experience that was unique. Now that he has left, we have decided to continue the action already begun and wish that those who follow our efforts from near or far away desist from killing

> the enthusiasm of the members of this center, and instead help us seriously and concretely to continue, inspired by the maturity of our intentions that has characterized all our initiatives.[7]

The indirect criticism was addressed to the parish and to the municipality alike. Facing the challenge, the establishment felt it necessary to attempt a take-over, to coopt the Circolo di Lettura. The school administration no longer granted it space. The parish decided on a long postponed project of building a parish hall that could accommodate and control youth activities. The town hall interceded with the EPT (Italian Tourist Agency) so that the temporary use of a house it owned be given to the young until they could find other quarters large enough. Electoral lists were written up with the young in mind and three members of the Circolo joined the municipal council. However, the Circolo has continued its activities and remained independent. It has attracted a few men in their late twenties and early thirties. With Don Lorenzo gone the Church has less influence than ever, and an offer to use the new parish hall was turned down by the center. The municipality soon came to realize that the young councillors refused to endorse every proposal automatically and intended to propose their own policies. In brief the establishment was being challenged by the young. Because neither priest nor mayor considered the Circolo as a valid experiment but instead a subversive movement, it has produced a conflict between the generations.

Joining in Santa Maria

In Santa Maria there is a fear and distrust of formal associations. Those who join, including the young, do so for utilitarian reasons. Political parties and social organizations that attempt to promote rapid change are usually received with a sneer. First of all there is a suspicion of all formal associations. Preaching for a cause is rather hard to comprehend and hidden motives are always suspected. The individual has been conditioned to fight and strive for himself and suspects that all associations wish to exploit him for their own and often secret aims. Hence there is a preference for informal types of associations, for bonds between individuals that constitute a group, but a fluctuating and seldom formalized group. It resembles more a clique bound by common interest—as, for example, the political groups in the village that cluster around the mayor, the members of the *giunta*, and the leader of the opposition. No formal commitment is required. An unwritten agreement of support exists, but it is broad enough to allow one to withdraw without losing face. In this situation a person cannot be labeled a follower; at most he can be called a sympathizer. Such a relationship is a product of the general mistrust for leadership in Italian society and a mistrust in the human individual. In the village this type of relationship also has another advantage: one can avoid associating with those with whom feuds exist or linger on.

While Santa Maria derived benefits from joining and committing itself to an organization such as the Veterans', the latter had one exclusive aim: to give the land to the peasants. When its task was accomplished it lost its raison d'être, though many continued to support its leader in his political designs out of loyalty or opportunism. In reality there exists a fear of joining and of militancy. The Italian parties and their abstract ideals to transform society, including the DC, make little sense to the Mariani, who prefer to deal in concrete terms. Economic associations that call for a commitment that goes beyond formal association, such as a cooperative, represent an aberration. They would force the Mariano to compromise himself, to join in with others he feels he can only mistrust.

Only the Church is broad enough to escape this attitude. One is born into it and does not join; it is a universal point of reference for the entire society. The respect for its forms is shared by all and hardly calls for a commitment to substance. Its rituals do not demand great sacrifice, while benefits can be reaped. Membership in an association might lead to a new and better social status, but it can also make one distrusted in the village. To affirm one's position it is much easier and less dangerous to advance in the most respected group, the Church. Influence in the parish hall provides a certain social leverage—but with no obligation to use it. The Church's ultimate goals being extraterrestrial, the member need not act in society unless it is to his direct benefit, which in turn can always be justified in terms of the Church's social efforts. The existence of formally structured associations weakens the intermediary function of brokerage and patronage played by the elite. These roles are perceived to be essential mechanisms for everyday village life. They operate in place of organizations, except when they also control the association. Such is the case of Bettola and the *Coltivatori Diretti,* Testoni and the DC, and above all Don Arturo. Patronage is a better source of direct benefits than purpose oriented associations—and in all cases direct benefits are the only ones worth considering. While the value of social benefits is not denied, they are not the responsibility of individuals, but rather of the anonymous State, which in any case cannot be trusted.

The development of associations rests upon concepts and patterns of authority as they exist locally, combined with a distrust for the authority of the State. Authority is viewed in its more absolute dimensions, implying submission. Only one font of authority exists that combines spiritual and temporal values: the Church, or more precisely, Don Arturo. All the visible as well as informal patterns of decision-making are linked to the rectory. In the self-contained unit that Santa Maria has been for so long, all activity revolves around the campanile which, while it rings for Mass, also rings to inform people that taxes are due. Even when doubts are felt in this society, it is easier for a majority not to express them rather than damage their social status. The young, however, have presented a challenge and might well succeed in making their generation active participants in the political process.

Political Socialization

The organizations that inculcate political attitudes reinforce the value system acquired by the individual in the early stages of socialization. Emphasis is on obedience to the local Church, passive acceptance of orders, avoidance of commitments whenever possible, predominance of communal over national values and skepticism vis-à-vis the State. Under these conditions political participation tends to be formal and passive.

Several factors compound this situation. Many people are afraid to challenge the existing structures because this would antagonize the elite in power and would cast doubt on the role of the parish priest in the temporal realm. Active participation and social engagement could lead to a type of socialization that the Church is reluctant to accept nationally and even more so locally. In the Veneto—White Italy—the DC and the government would reap no advantage from supporting this line.

Equally important is the role played by the family and the clan. To participate successfully in politics one needs the active support or at least the implicit consent of the clan. However, to avoid feuds or the resumption of antagonisms most families find it easier to avoid all-out support for their brethren. This provides greater opportunities for those outsiders who enjoy the confidence of the parish and to keep this position they avoid any action that may change the existing arrangements.

The size of the village and the scarcity of local leaders is important in this connection. Politically antagonistic groups can hardly be supported without creating tensions in the village's social structure.

The older local elites are hurt by their past association with or continued commitment to fascism. This is true for Alfio Martelli who led the Black Shirts in Santa Maria and is now the local correspondent for a newspaper in Rovigo. The elders of the Fortuna (Teta) family are jealous of the success of their cousins Fortuna (Sacchi) in municipal affairs and stayed out of local politics; only recently have the younger members of the family become active through the Circolo di Lettura. Others have been discouraged by the lack of support they received from the villagers when they sat in the municipal council. Luigi Gaddoni, a farmer turned archeologist and past member of the council who has good connections at the University of Padua, feels that "belonging to the Council only creates problems and that in any case nobody listens to what you have to say." Consequently, a good man has simply withdrawn into his shell.

The lack of autonomy of local government does not explain why few people are ready to participate in the local political process. It is true that a small community does not provide a sufficient base for a regional or national political career. But within the local society, membership in the local government and the rectory's support offers prestige and makes running for office worthwhile. Notwithstanding these factors, passive participation satisfies most villagers' needs, notably in the case of national elections.

Electoral Participation

Practically all who reside in Santa Maria vote, including several mentally retarded persons whose vote is cast by their fathers or mothers, faithful supporters of the DC. Table 5.1 summarizes the situation for all post-war elections to the lower House of Parliament.

5.1 NATIONAL ELECTIONS 1946–1972

	Electors	*Voted*		*Did Not Vote*		*Valid Votes*		*Nonvalid Votes*	
	N	*N*	*%*	*N*	*%*	*N*	*%*	*N*	*%*
1946	1,338	1,252	93.6	86	6.4	1,174	93.8	78	6.2
1948	1,395	1,325	95.0	70	5	1,315	99.2	10	.8
1953	1,426	1,313	92.0	113	8	1,251	95.2	62	4.8
1958	1,380	1,256	91.0	124	9	1,204	95.8	52	4.2
1963	1,277	1,208	94.5	69	5.5	1,170	96.8	38	3.2
1968	1,220	1,150	94.2	70	5.8	1,117	97.1	33	2.9
1972	1,227	1,187	96.7	40	3.3	1,138	95.9	49	4.1

The high percentage of the voters (high, 96.7%, low, 91%) is a function of effective residence in the community. The consequences of the war (all prisoners had not returned in 1946) and emigration (many emigrants failed to return in 1953 and 1958) explain the relatively low percentage of votes during those years. The percentage of valid votes, with the exception of 1946, has always been above 95 percent, averaging 96.2 percent and peaking in 1948 at 99.2, when very explicit instructions on how to vote were given from the pulpit. The decline in illiteracy does not seem to have had any major effects on the percentage of nonvalid votes (the higher percentage in 1946 can be explained by the novelty of voting) which are divided equally between purposely spoiled ballots and blank votes. The first are cast in protest, the second in ignorance rather than from a desire to abstain. The reasons for such heavy turnouts have been explained in many ways: the rediscovery of democracy, a sense of duty, indirect sanctions of the law. The latter case no longer applies, if it ever did. Abstention is no longer noted on the certificates of good conduct necessary to seek employment, and the list of nonparticipants is no longer affixed on the municipal bulletin boards, and the percentage of abstentions has not changed. The duty and right to vote are certainly motivational factors as we shall see later, yet they do not appear very important. More important, particularly in a small community such as this, is the social pressure exercised by the community itself (the parish explicitly instructs the faithful to vote) and the party responsible (DC in national elections, DC and Bilancia in local cases). Polls are open all day Sunday and Monday morning, and party representatives, usually members of Catholic Action or the municipal council, keep tally of those who have not voted. At the end of the first day and during the second they provide transportation and put pressure on the faithful and the citizens ("Sétú ti, ghe ti te devi votar' cossi," "Now, you know, you must vote this way"), driving them to the polling station, and occasionally even bringing them from their sick beds. The DC displays considerable dilligence and even transports in the name of democracy those it considers doubtful supporters, recommending, "Varda, non andar votar' per qu'ei là" ("Now, look, don't vote for those nogoods"), and mentioning all the good things the mayor has done for the village.

Informally we had occasion to query the voters about why they voted. Those who appeared actively involved or interested in the political situation had two sets of answers—"it is a duty" and "so the others [PCI] will not win." Answers were seldom elaborated upon; the idea of making a choice and determining one's future was rarely expressed except in the case of municipal elections, where "they are the best" was the most frequent answer. But a majority of those questioned answered "bisogna," a fatalistic "one must,"—"è cosi," "that's the way,"—"tutti fanno cosi," "all do it,"—"mi portano," "they take me there." An openly passive attitude seemed to be expressed in casting a ballot, and it did not appear that one can in any way, in this rural environment, consider formal participation as an index of involvement or true political participation, but only as a passive recognition and acceptance of a duty, the implications of which may not be fully understood. Exceptions are found when issues are strongly polarized, and when the Church takes sides openly as in 1948 when 99.2 percent of all votes cast were validated (though the talliers could also have helped).

Electoral Opposition

Returns for the national elections are presented in Table 5.2.

In national elections the DC is clearly the dominant party, having always received nearly 70 percent or better of the total vote, peaking at 85.3 percent in 1948 and increasing its percentage in 1968 (6.1%, in relation to 1963) when doubts were being cast on the future of the center-left. In both cases the parish explicitly recommended voting DC. The government party scored 14 and 17 points higher than its regional average and 27 and 28 points more than its national average in 1958 and 1972.[7] The nongovernmental left, after its success in 1946 (19.6%), has been unable to boost its position beyond 11 percent. In 1972 the PCI in alliance with the PSIUP recouped its losses following the switch of the PSI to the government camp in 1963, polling 11

5.2 NATIONAL ELECTION RETURNS*

	1946	*1948*	*1953*	*1958*	*1963*	*1968*	*1972*
PCI	43		47	41	85	67	105
PSIUP		88				47	21
PSI	187		73	91	122	67	30
PSDI		55	24	25	29		29
PdA	14						
Other Left			19				6
PRI	11	2	2	10	1	2	13
DC	833	1,123	961	839	818	849	797
PLI	60	15	8	7	23	18	23
UQ/PDIUM/ PNM	26		19	123	15	4	
MSI		22	92	68	75	63	115
Others		10	6		3		
Totals	1,174	1,315	1,251	1,204	1,170	1,117	1,139

*In 1948 PSI and PCI ran on a single ticket.

The initials stand for the following: PCI, Italian Communist Party; PSIUP, Italian Socialist Party of Proletarian Unity, a splinter group of PSI often more to the left than the PCI; PSI, Italian Socialist Party; DC, Christian Democratic Party; PLI, Italian Liberal Party; UQ, Common Man, ran in 1946 only; PDIUM, Italian Democratic Party for Monarchical Unity; PNM, National Monarchist Party; MSI, Italian Social Movement, neo-fascist.

Figures provided by the Mayor's office.

5.3 NATIONAL ELECTION RETURNS IN PERCENTAGES

	1946	*1948*	*1953*	*1958*	*1963*	*1968*	*1972*
DC	70.9	85.3	76.8	69.7	69.9	76.0	68.8
Nongovern-mental Left	19.6	6.6	9.6	11.0	7.2	10.2	11.0
All Groups Perceived as Left*	21.7	11.0	13.2	13.9	20.3	16.3	17.8

*In Santa Maria all groups except DC, PLI and extreme right are considered as left, including the PRI. For 1946 we have counted PCI and PSI as nongovernmental though they were in fact in the government. The locals never considered them as worthy partners.

percent, while in alliance with the PSI it had received 10.9 percent in 1958. If we consider all groups perceived to be left of center (PRI to PCI), and with the exception of 1963 when the PSI was presented as a legitimate government partner, the left has regularly increased from 11 percent in 1948 to nearly 18 percent in 1972. The extreme right is in decline after experiencing relative success in 1958 when Baratella returned to active politics (17%) and in 1972 (10%), riding on the national wave.

Considering the influence of the parish priest and the fact that the local administration has always been controlled by the DC it is possible to hypothesize that those who do not vote for the DC, even if they vote for its governmental allies, are expressing opposition proclivities and are more likely to be active participants in politics. Under these conditions 30 percent of the electoral body reaches its decisions independently from the major sources of power and authority as shown in Table 5.4. This was confirmed by the returns of the May 1974 referendum where, in spite of strenuous efforts by the DC, the parish and Catholic Action groups, 29.59 percent voted in favor of divorce, 68.3 percent against and 2.07 percent cast spoiled ballots.

The situation is different in local elections, the returns of which are given in Table 5.5. The electoral body is considerably smaller, representing in 1960 at the peak of emigration 67 percent of the electoral body of 1958, and 86 percent of the electoral body of 1968 in 1970.

5.4 GOVERNMENT AND OPPOSITION PARTIES IN PERCENTAGE

	1946	*1948*	*1953*	*1958*	*1963*	*1968*	*1972*
DC	70.9	85.3	76.8	69.7	69.9	76.0	69.9
Government	92.6	90.9	79.5	73.1	74.4	82.1	78.8
Difference Government–DC	21.7	5.6	2.7	3.4	4.5	6.1	8.9
Opposition	7.4	9.1	21.5	26.9	25.6	17.9	21.2
Difference + Opposition	29.4	14.7	24.2	30.3	30.1	24.0	30.1

Emigrés seldom bother and are not encouraged to return and cast their ballots although their names figure on the electoral rolls. Campaigns are animated because politics are personalized (this is discussed in chapter 6). They suffer, however, from the fact that the outcome is never in doubt: the DC receives a majority of the votes, four-fifths of the seats on the municipal council, and the mayorality. There is little interest in a two-way race (1951, 1960) where the choice is between the PCI and the DC, though the outcome seriously complicated running the municipal council where the left was assured three of the fifteen seats. Three-way races with an independent list sponsored by local personalities (1956, 1964, 1970, 1975) provided more animation and gave the people an opportunity to express opposition to the party in power. However, this third list is in fact encouraged by the DC which, in such a way, eliminates the left from the municipal council. Nevertheless, between 1964 and 1970, the left increased its electoral strength by 42 percent due to the fact that more Mariani work in industries beyond the village limits. If we combine both opposition lists, in 1970, 33.5 percent of the people voted against the "official" list, down from 38.9 percent in 1964. While an indication of the success of the local administration, it is still true that in local and national elections one-third of the people can be categorized as opposition.

This was confirmed in the 1975 local elections. The PCI concentrated all its efforts on the regional contest which was held at the same time, and, rather than presenting its own slate of candidates for the local election in Santa Maria, advised its electorate to vote for the

5.5 LOCAL ELECTION RETURNS

	1951		*1956*		*1960*		*1964*		*1970*		*1975*	
	N	%	*N*	%	*N*	%	*N*	%	*N*	%	*N*	%
List 1 (DC)	743	83.7	642	61.5	701	86.7	534	61.1	641	66.5	590	66.36
List 2 (Left)	144	16.3	44	4.2	107	13.3	38	4.3	71	7.4	77*	8.66
List 3 (Ind.)			357	34.3			302	34.6	252	26.1	222	24.98
Totals	887	100	1,043	100	808	100	874	100	964	100		

*In 1975 List 2 was neo-fascist.

independent list rather than for the MSI. In spite of its national difficulties, which were compounded by local quarrels, the DC in Santa Maria, led by a successful though not overly popular mayor, garnered 66.37 percent of the vote with 33.6 percent going to the combined opposition. In the regional elections, however, the reversal against the DC was clear: compared to 1972 it lost 7.57 percent in Santa Maria while the PCI increased its share of the electorate by 7 percent, reaching an all-time high of 16.76 percent.

We now turn to a consideration of the electoral variables as they existed in 1969.

Electoral Variables

The information provided is based on the data we gathered in the community in 1968 and 1969; all tables are derived from this source.[8] Sex provides a critical line of division in Santa Maria voting patterns. Among the certain DC supporters, women provide the party with 61.7 percent of its strength (56.34% if certain and probable are combined). In this case 91.9 percent of all women would vote for the DC while only 67.8 percent of the men would do so. There is less indecision among females (16.8%) than among males (31.8%). The male is more prone to change his allegiance and more inclined to be among the opposition.

Ten percent of the adult male population votes for the left, and 20 percent gives it their support if one combines certain and probable

5.6 SEX AND ELECTORAL CHOICE

	Male		*Female*		*Total*	
	N	*%*	*N*	*%*	*N*	*%*
Left	65	10.01	9	1.45	74	5.84
DC	300	46.23	485	78.48	785	61.96
Right	26	4.00	.7	1.14	33	2.60
Probable Left	64	9.86	18	2.91	82	6.47
Probable DC	140	21.58	83	13.44	233	17.61
Probable Right	2	0.30	3	0.48	5	0.39
Unknown	52	8.02	13	2.10	65	5.13
Totals	649	100	618	100	1,267	100

votes. In spite of Church interdiction one Marian male out of five expresses leftist leanings. On the contrary, only 1 percent and 5 percent of the female population is a certain or probable leftist voter. Males provide the left with 82.7 percent of its total strength. Similarly the right receives 73.6 percent of its votes from the men. Politics and extremes are reserved for males, while women are content to accept Church instructions and vote for the DC, the only party that has any real electoral strength in Santa Maria, the only party recognized as acceptable for a Catholic.

All devout Catholics but one support the DC, while 85 percent of those who practice their religion support the party. Devout and practicing Catholics provide the party with 89 percent of its strength. On the other hand, 53.6 percent of the indifferents support other parties, and 55 percent of the leftist vote is from indifferent and contrary.

Combining religion and sex, practically all devout males support the DC (95%, one exception), as do the females (100%). Among practicing males 67 percent certainly support the DC and the figure increases to 86 percent if the certain and probable categories are taken together, though many of the latter might well support other parties of the government coalition. Ninety-seven percent of all practicing females support the DC. Indifferent males split their support equally between DC and left. Conversely 76 percent of the males who

5.7 POLITICS AND RELIGIOUS PRACTICE*

	Devout	*Practicing*	*Indifferent*	*Contrary*	*Total*
Left	1	17	48	1	67
DC	181	542	54	0	777
Right	–	11	18	1	30
Probable Left	–	48	30	3	81
Probable DC	3	161	53	1	218
Probable Right	–	2	2	–	4
Unknown	–	38	26	1	65
Totals	185	819	231	7	1,242

*Those who go to Church, belong to Catholic Action and/or receive communion once a week were classified as devout (14.9%); those who attend Church regularly on Sundays and receive Easter communion were considered practicing Catholics (65.9%); indifferent were those who seldom come to Church (18.6%), and contrary those who never come to Church and actively oppose it (0.56%).

5.8 POLITICS AND INCOME IN PERCENTAGE

		N	*Over $3,000*	*Over $1,350*	*Over $775*	*Under $775*
N=792						
Certain	Left	66	3	33	41	23
	DC	476	3	28.5	29.5	39
	Right	30	20	37	16	27
Probable	Left	61	3	56	23	18
	DC	156	6	37	29	27
	Right	3	–	–	33	66
All	Left	127	3	44	32	21
	DC	632	3	31	29	36
	Right	33	18	33	18	30

certainly support the left are indifferent to religion while only 9 percent of the male DC supporters are. Overall, slightly more indifferents (55%) support the left, but 82 percent of these are males.

With respect to income and voting, on the left only 3 percent of its strength is from the upper income brackets, 76 percent from the middle income level, and 21 percent from the lowest income group. The poverty bracket is not the left's main source of votes, but rather the middle range made up of the secondary workers whose occupations take them out of Santa Maria.

The DC receives 3 percent of its support from the upper level income groups (89% of which vote DC), 60 percent from the middle group and 36 percent from the lowest salaried group. Poverty does not affect DC support. The party does particularly well among the agricultural workers, 80 percent of whom vote DC, while 79 percent are in the lowest income group.

The education variable reveals surprisingly few differences between the electorates of the DC and the left if we combine certain and probable leanings: 18.8 percent of the leftist strength versus 15.5 percent of the DC strength is illiterate or semi-illiterate, while 77.4 percent of the left and 78.3 percent of the DC have received elementary education (Table 5.9). However 83 percent of all illiterates and 92 percent of those who have gone to secondary school vote DC.

5.9 POLITICS AND EDUCATION IN PERCENTAGE

		N	*Illiterate or Semi-illiterate*	*Elementary School*	*Middle School*	*Lyceum*	*University*
n=1,192							
Certain	Left	73	31.5	64.3	2.8	–	1.4
	DC	776	14.6	78.7	4.1	1.3	1.3
	Right	33	15.1	51.5	18.2	9.1	6.1
Probable	Left	82	7.3	89.1	1.2	2.4	–
	Center	223	18.8	76.7	3.6	0.9	–
	Right	5	–	60	40	–	–
All	Left	155	18.8	77.4	1.9	1.3	0.6
	Center	999	15.5	78.3	4	1.2	1.0
	Right	38	13.2	52.6	21	7.9	5.3

The right does particularly well among those who have received advanced education. If we consider only certain votes the illiterate group provides the left with 31.5 percent of its strength but only constitutes 14.6 percent of the DC forces.

Several other factors should be noted: employment outside the village and geographical location in the community are significant variables in politics. This can be briefly stated by noting that the farther away the Mariano finds himself from the center of local power the more likely he is to manifest his independence. The relationship between politics and geographical location is visible in Table 5.10 which indicates the preference given to the left in the hills and the nuclei where communication with the village and its sources of power is the lowest. This characteristic is particularly clear in the case of the nuclei, 75 percent of which is constituted by the population of *corte* Beghin, which is outside of the parish limits.

The influence of the left is also clear among the commuters (Table 5.11), collectively the most prosperous group in the community (76 percent are in the middle income brackets compared to 60 percent of the primary and 68 percent of the tertiary groups). Outside employment is an important source of leftist strength, considering that 62.4

5.10 POLITICS AND GEOGRAPHICAL LOCATION IN PERCENTAGE

	DC Center	*PCI Left*
n=1,251		
Total Community	80	12.3
Village	80.4	8.6
Plains	82	9.4
Hills	79.4	14.8
Nuclei	70.5	22.5

5.11 EMPLOYMENT AND POLITICAL ORIENTATION IN PERCENTAGE

	DC Center	*PC Left*
n=492		
Locally Employed	83.7	9.1
Commuters	69.5	23.

percent of the work force is employed outside the village: 23 percent of the commuters vote for the left while only 9.1 percent of those who work in the community do so.

Three out of four leftist voters were born in Santa Maria, while only two out of three DC electors were. The homogeneity of the province of Padua, where most of the electorate born outside of the village originates, explains why not being born in Santa Maria has less importance for the left than the DC.

We also checked the relation between housing and voting, because housing turned out to be one of the most sensitive issues during our stay in Santa Maria. The relationship is far from clear. Poor quality housing is not a deterrent to voting for the DC party and provides only a slight inducement to vote left. Proportionately there are more good houses among the left than among the DC. However, twice as many DC voters are satisfied with their houses than are leftist voters. Unfortunately, we do not have a breakdown of housing and voting patterns in local elections. We can only suspect that the variable carries considerable weight in explaining the opposition.

To summarize, in terms of political participation understood as the act of casting a vote, people vote either out of a sense of duty or because social conventions and pressures require it. The pattern is well enough established to believe it will continue.

With regard to the choice of parties, in Santa Maria as in most of the Veneto, findings made elsewhere are confirmed and accentuated.[9] The critical variables for the DC are the women's vote and religious practice. Other variables appear less critical though not devoid of importance, in particular the combination low income and peasantry, and location in the community.

To vote left is essentially a male phenomenon and is accentuated by indifference to religious matters. The lowest income brackets tend not to vote left. Instead, the left recruits among the secondary categories of employment that fall into the average or better than average income brackets and are less susceptible to social pressures of the community. Considering voting for the DC as the norm, those who choose to do otherwise have received slightly less schooling than their DC counterparts if they vote left, more schooling if they vote right, are better off financially, not religiously oriented and are nearly exclusively male.

The overwhelming advantage of the DC in regional and local elections, however, makes politics an item of little importance in daily life—the DC is a given fact—and polarization and ideology play a limited role in the village. Furthermore, considering the division that exists between national and local politics, the way the town is run will not induce people to participate actively in the political process. Why there is little effective participation in the community can thus be understood. There are few rewards to stimulate the opposition. Power is concentrated in one single source, the rectory, which accepts no exceptions. The choice is between acceptance of the social norms or deviancy. To openly oppose, especially in national elections, is equivalent to cutting oneself from the mainstream of social life. This position can be acceptable only for the individual who is either not a village inhabitant or who works outside the village circle. Furthermore at the local level there are few chances to win and successfully administer a small community when one party dominates the province, even if it has to share its power on the national level. The electoral law permits the DC to eliminate all leftist opposition by encouraging an independent list, while the semi-official endorsement it receives from the parish priest reduces its effectiveness as opposition.

The rather passive attitude of the population can be attributed to a lack of commitment to societal values, to the predominance of religiously oriented organizations and a refusal to openly take a political position that deviates from the norm. What transformation has taken place must be attributed to increases in education and a greater prosperity, particularly among the young who have sought to organize and have succeeded in making themselves heard. The towering personality of the parish priest and his critical role of patron and broker make it difficult to challenge his rule. Furthermore, the size of the village unit, the importance of family links and clans, and the possibility of feuds do not encourage active participation. Currently, an active opposition could only be directed against the Church, the source of authority, and could tear the community asunder. Change will take place only with the disappearance of the man who runs the parish. The village is preparing for this change. An increase in the levels of education might create an elite and a larger number of interested participants enabling the community to enjoy a participatory democratic system.

6. *Administration and Politics in Santa Maria*

ADMINISTRATION AND POLITICS IN SANTA MARIA ARE influenced by the size of the community, its past isolation from the mainstream of Italian political life, patterns of socialization that seldom encourage active participation in politics, a value system that is not democratically oriented, and the ". . . persistent, clerically defined hegemony"[1] that characterizes the Veneto. In this chapter we will examine some elements that have a bearing on administration, the attributes of the local administrators, the local elections of 1964 and 1970, and several examples of decision-making in the community.

Administration in Santa Maria

The issue of administrative power was put in scathing words by Luigi Einaudi, first president of the Italian Republic:

> In countries where democracy is more than a vain word people manage their own local affairs without awaiting the suggestion or the permission of the central government. . . . A political class cannot be formed if the person elected to manage the municipal . . . affairs is not fully responsible for his own actions. If someone can give him orders and countermand his acts the elected official has no responsibility and does not learn how to administer. He merely learns how to obey, to intrigue, to recommend and to seek influence.[2]

Every five years or so in communities of less than five thousand inhabitants the population elects a municipal council of fifteen members, twelve of whom belong to the winning list.[3] In turn, the council selects by a majority vote the mayor and two advisors who form the municipal *giunta*. The mayor heads the municipality and directs the *giunta*. He represents the community, deals with third parties, signs and is responsible for all communal acts. Preparatory work is done in the *giunta* while the council meets only three or four times a year, allowing the mayor considerable latitude in decision-making and far more extensive powers than statutes indicate. In fact the size of the majority in the municipal councils of small communities often makes them rubber stamps for the mayor's desires and policies.

There are two other officials with legal, administrative and political power. One is the municipal secretary, who is dependent upon the mayor and paid by the *comune,* and yet is appointed by the government. His responsibility is to insure the legality of local government activities, provide legal counsel, maintain records and serve as head of personnel. The second is the prefect, the government's representative in the province, who has the power to reverse municipal decisions. He is duty bound to pass judgment on the legality of municipal acts, but can also refuse to approve them on the grounds that they lack merit. His ultimate power enables him to dissolve the municipal council and remove the mayor.

Financial limitations are an obstacle to effective local administration. Santa Maria prides itself on maintaining balanced budgets, but a small village has few opportunities to practice deficit financing in large amounts. With a $220,000 budget in 1970 the possibility of floating bonds is reduced to minimal amounts. Major (and even minor) projects depend upon the good will of the State, its representative, the prefect, the Christian Democratic party or the party that controls a special ministry from which funds might be obtained. Thus, the municipality and the mayor depend on outside organizations for financial support, and these relationships rest on interest or patronage, on *clientela* and *parentela*,[34] where influence is more important than merit.

In Christian Democratic Veneto the prefect acts more as an administrator than a politician, notably when dealing with the smaller centers. Yet the municipalities perceive him to be a political figure. A subtle link develops between prefects and mayors who reinforce each other's power.[5] To influence the prefect, local leaders must submit to and engage in intrigue and be capable of exploiting the electoral support they give to their DC parliamentary representatives,[6] as well as the special links they maintain with the Catholic hierarchy. It is to the mayor's advantage if he can appear as the social equal of the prefect, a qualification not easily achieved in rural communities but one that can be facilitated by the election of outsiders. The mayor of Santa Maria makes it a point to frequent the same circles as the prefect, is closely associated with the local parliamentarian whose district encompasses Padua and Santa Maria, and has his entries to the bishopric where he serves as an expert for the ecclesiastical tribunal on marriages.

While local administrators give considerable weight to personality in their dealings with provincial and regional authorities, the same holds true in their relations with the national political system. Particularly in small communities, interest comes first and ideology second. Patrons, real and imagined, are important in local politics. In Santa Maria, the mayor was able to get political mileage from the visits of Prime Minister Moro in 1967 and Minister Gui in 1969 when plans were drawn for the promotion of tourism and the establishment of a Center for Petrarch Studies. Similarly, Bruno Beghin, the municipal assessor and restaurant owner, is able to exploit his position of regular host to the Honorable Bisaglia, Prime Minister Rumor's secretary. Having important friends creates an image of power, though it may also nourish the illusion that local requests will be favored over others. The importance attached to personalities was revealed in an incident that took place during a meeting of the municipal council in 1969. Since 1964 eighty million lire were dormant in Santa Maria's account in Rome, originally designated to pay for the paving of the village streets. Through the Honorable Gui alternative sources of funds had been located before the original ones were made available. But Santa Maria has not given up on getting both. The mayor declared in the council that positive action would be taken as soon as the socialists were dislodged from the ministry of public works.

Dario Zibordi has been mayor of Santa Maria since 1964 when he was elected at age thirty-eight. He was born in Venice where his father was in the hotel trade and by all criteria he is a true Venetian. He has the braggadocio of the characters of Goldoni and the cunningness of some of Ruzzante. Talkative, he is an excellent storyteller and imitator. A heavy eater and a good drinker (can one beat tripe for breakfast?), his waistline tends to suffer from these excesses. He is a thoroughly congenial person.

Educated at the Lyceum in Venice, he turned his energies to medical studies, specializing in legal medicine with the intent of following a university career. The system thwarted his ambitions and forced him to turn to private practice, where he has encountered considerable success, specializing in "road-traffic medicine," alcoholism and road accidents, fields in which he has published widely. He is a prominent member of the high society of Padua, where he maintains his practice and his residence and is well known in the province. His marriage is apparently successful, though the couple disagrees on the education of their daughters, on how much he eats and above all about Santa Maria, "his new mistress."

Zibordi is an egocentrist who in all circumstances wishes to be the best and the *deus ex machina*. He loves "to do." In fact his efforts have brought much good and happiness to Santa Maria, from electricity in the distant houses of Mandonego to pensions to those entitled to them. The favorite and often quoted citation, proferred with a rather barbaric French accent—"Il ne faut jamais parler de soi-même, pas même pour en dire mal"—is somewhat of an understatement, and "il professore" loves to hear his entourage sing his lauds. He is enthralled by his job where, according to his wife, "he sees himself as the center of the universe for his co-citizens." Maybe one can, in his own words, characterize him as a pleasant demagogue "who speaks to his people with his heart in his hand . . . inspired by a sincere desire to do well and help . . . with the help of the State, the Province, the Prefect and DC ministers." With regard to politics, as he puts it, "he is a little Communist, some Socialist, a good part Christian Democrat, loves Republicans and finds some good points in the Fascists." In sum, an independent Christian Democrat.

In the late fifties Zibordi purchased a small house in the hills overlooking Santa Maria, where he could escape from Padua. In 1963 the parish priest in search of a mayoral candidate approached him, promising that if he would agree to run "they would carry the heavy burden together." He promptly accepted the offer and was appointed as an expert to the ecclesiastical tribunal in Padua. The bishop and the DC voiced no objections and his election became a matter of course. In Santa Maria the mayor lives with an image of absolute power he finds gratifying and fulfilling, which serves as an escape valve from the pressures of his career and a compensatory mechanism for his university failure. The local bureaucracy implements his orders, the opposition is easily dominated, and the people seek out his company. The position has opened the doors of the prefecture and provided for an ever larger circle of acquaintances and friends. Only the priest ranks higher than the mayor in the community,[7] but one of the priest's greatest qualities is his capacity for self-effacement, flattery and ego-building, which makes the mayorality appear to be the supreme source of authority.

The last fifteen years have witnessed considerable changes in the composition of the municipal council. The average age of the Christian Democratic majority dropped from 47 in 1964 to 38 in 1970, while that of the opposition went from 62 to 37. For the first time four men under 25 were elected, indicating the weight of the youthful supporters of the Circolo di Lettura. The number of outsiders (neither born, living, nor working in the village) has declined from 7 to 4. The professional composition has also changed. In 1956 there were ten men in primary occupations, three employed in the secondary sector and two in the tertiary. The corresponding figures in 1970 were three (one peasant, two peasant workers), five and seven, illustrating the appearance of a local elite.

Nevertheless, the way in which the town hall is run has not changed substantially, in spite of the efforts and frustrations of the younger members in the municipal council. The mayor, today as in the past, runs a one-man show. The young were included in order to be silenced and neutralized, not to play a role. It is not by accident that one hears rumors of "Duce, Pope, SS-Gruppenführer." While discussions are relatively free, we did not witness one case where the mayor's point of view was not accepted. It is our understanding that the election of a young councillor to the *giunta* in 1970 has not changed the situation. Its decisions, when warranted, are transmitted to the council for the final vote. However, seldom is there any defection from the majority party since all councilmen agree to support a common position before the formal council meeting. The question that many of the young and not so young have often asked is why participate when their opinions are not heeded? A councillor of the Christian Democratic majority seemed to present the opinion of most of his colleagues when he mentioned, "It's a sacrifice we have to make, and you don't make friends while serving on the council. But somebody has to be active to help the village. Sure, we don't do very much. If Zibordi wasn't there. . . . He does a lot. He goes right and left, to Venice, to Rome. You would think all his time is for Santa Maria. And all because he wants to. We're poor guys, but he knows how to get around." The minority did not air a substantially different view. "It's not right that he should do everything, even if he does it well. He knows the village well, but there are certain things he just can't understand. It's fine for him to act in Venice or Rome, but here, we ought to be able to do and decide on things by ourselves. He shouldn't decide for us." When the views of the mayor and the parish priest coincide, the opposition, and the young in particular, have to overcome a powerful foe.

Elections in Santa Maria, 1964-1970

The election of 1964 was as ardently fought as the one of 1913 that divided the village. The opposition, many believed, had a better than token chance of winning. For the first time jobs were available in the immediate surroundings of Santa Maria. Young people in their twenties and thirties were no longer leaving the village. They could, if they organized and found a leader, offer alternatives to the DC administration.

The administration was led by Mario Fortuna, a professor of letters born in Santa Maria who wished to retire. His twelve-year tenure was marked by some impressive achievements as well as conspicuous faults. The town hall, destroyed in 1943, had been rebuilt, a new school put into service, electricity and water brought to most houses, the streets that had been rivers of mud during the winter were being repaved, the old earth-beaten roads asphalted, the State had been solicited to help the farmers who were near ruin. But the record was not enough. Many felt that Fortuna was *superiore*, haughty, that he wished to administer the town single-handedly, without debating questions with the members of the municipal council. Success not

PCI election meeting

Church and state reconciled

Neo-fascist MSI speaker

The mayor speaking for the local administration and the DC

only breeds success but also jealousy, and the mayor was accused of being anti-democratic. Many thought he should live in Santa Maria rather than Padua where he taught, and pointed out he was seldom available to the public. He lived in a world of ideas and ideals while his citizens had to live with the hard facts of life. To replace him the DC presented a list headed by the outsider Zibordi, the personal choice of Don Arturo, with several new names around those of a few stalwarts of the parish. Of the thirty sponsors of the list seven were directly linked to the rectory through family ties and eleven indirectly through Sergio Fortuna, the DC recruiter, whose brother was the local chaplain.

The opposition chose the scales of Justice, *la Bilancia*, as its symbol. The driving force in the group was made up of four young men, Ugo Masiero and Bardini, who worked in Padua, Frasson and Prandi, who earned their living in Santa Maria. They were in their late twenties or early thirties, held good jobs, inclined toward socialism and thought that mayor Fortuna did not devote enough time to Santa Maria. They chose Bardini, a traditional name in local politics since 1870, as their leader in spite of his limited experience and age. He was 27, the only member of the group who had finished secondary school, and was a dispatching clerk in Padua. This original group that believed in constructive opposition was obliged to coopt various groups of opponents of the DC, which did little to enhance the Bilancia's image. Several members came from the old fascist group, including Aggio, who had been jailed at the liberation. One came from the left carrying with him the nickname of Armando the Red. The rest was made up of traditional DC opponents such as Francesco Menato, who had been accused and convicted of stealing municipal property. They ran as a nonpolitical list, though it soon became known that the parish was not adverse to their efforts. (Bardini had consulted with Don Arturo.) The priest wanted to prevent the extreme left, sponsored by the PSIUP, from winning seats on the municipal council. Beyond the candidates' lack of luster, the list had another shortcoming. It was composed exclusively of men who lived in the village, neglecting the representation of the *corte* and the countryside.

Lack of experience, youthful ardor, unfortunate associations, unjustified and poorly stated criticism, and faulty strategy combined to make the Bilancia's efforts a campaign of slander and lies. That some were ready to accept this reflects the intense dislike Fortuna had accumulated by slighting individual citizens while serving the community. On November 1 Bardini launched his major attack. He accused the mayor of personally benefitting from his position and insinuated Zibordi would take his orders from Fortuna. The mayor was accused of centralizing all power in his own hands, of succumbing to the cult of personality, of having reduced the council to an assembly of "mute, inert, humiliated and shrivelled" men. His administration was described as "inert" and accused of not defending the peasants with sufficient energy. Bardini attempted to project an image of energy and dynamism that would make him the antithesis of his opponents, mayor Fortuna and Zibordi. The Bilancia offered no program, and asked the citizens to trust in its "competence, dynamism, efficiency," asserting it would save rural Santa Maria, a Santa Maria that was no longer rural. Its major broadsides were reserved for the PSIUP list (led by the first DC mayor, deposed by the council after the war when Don Arturo withdrew his support), which it accused of communism, atheism, opportunism, and practically all the village's and the world's ills.

On November 8 Mario Fortuna answered the charges, moderately yet caustically, "to dissipate from the minds of the honest people those eventual doubts and suspicions created by facile disseminators of lies." In a town hall of Santa Maria's size, he pointed out, "one cannot 'eat' but only lose one's appetite" on a ten dollar monthly indemnity. Here, one does not govern but collaborates with all who are ready to collaborate. All of the mayor's energies had been devoted to helping the peasants, and with reference to the hail-storm damages, he noted, "one should not forget that a government cannot cover all expenses." The mayor, with the consent of the prefect, had made municipal funds available to cover payments due to the rural family insurance fund. One should not forget, Fortuna added, that "those who clamor the most forgot many years ago the shape of a hoe" referring to the fact that the leaders of the Bilancia were employed in activities unconnected with farming. His record was easy to present. During his tenure Santa Maria had received more monies from the State than in the previous century. His opponents presented "no program, no idea that can illuminate or reassure the electorate."

Zibordi had no need and no desire to answer criticism. In Santa

Maria he had found "people with a generous heart, with a charge of genuine humanity, sensitive to all manifestations of sympathy, ready to return affection." These were the people who convinced him to run and those for whom he and his colleagues would "contribute all their energies . . . to develop the village, providing for individual and collective well-being, for schooling and public health." Roads would be improved, electricity brought to those fourteen houses still not served, a new middle school would be built, tourism promoted, the municipal band resurrected. The mayor would be available to the public two days every week "to listen and act on every single proposal, difficulty and question."

The insidious campaign of sotto voce lies backed by the Bilancia appeared nevertheless to carry some weight and the out-going administrators were far from confident in victory. Only Don Arturo predicted the outcome, giving the winner 532 of 874 votes. He was off by two, but the DC list, though reaping 60 percent of the votes, lost some 170 votes compared to 1960. However, by splitting their votes the DC elected the three men in the Bilancia best known for their honesty and their nonassociation with either left or right.

In 1970 the Bilancia was ready to campaign once again, this time avoiding slander but unable to present a new list of candidates. The record it had to fight against was impressive: the streets had been paved, the village had a new lighting system, all houses had enough electric power, a pharmacy had been opened, the middle school was being built, many had received their pensions. Zibordi had kept and gone beyond his promises. He had commissioned a town plan (which technically and legally was not required) and had seen it unanimously adopted by the municipal council. He had published a municipal ordinance aimed at maintaining the architectural harmony of the community. These were, in fact, sore points. The town plan foresaw the village expanding in the surrounding hills, while most Mariani preferred the plains where it was cheaper to build; the ordinance prevented disorderly building patterns and changes the owners wished to make.

Since Bardini had gone along with most of Zibordi's proposals between 1964 and 1969, his opposition could hardly be termed effective. He had accepted the town plan and voiced few criticisms. Thus, in the summer he proposed to switch to the DC with his entire group, if he received the assurance that he and his friends would receive three seats on the municipal council. The proposal was promptly turned down. In the fall Bardini sought to gain the support of the young people of the Circolo di Lettura in which his brother was active. His wooing of the Circolo's leader, Carlo Fortuna, proved unsuccessful when Don Arturo and Zibordi offered Fortuna a place on the DC list and a seat in the municipal *giunta*. The Circolo chose to fight the battle in the DC and the Bilancia appeared isolated. In March Don Arturo was afraid they would not run and pressured Bardini and Ugo Masiero to keep the 1964 list alive, to prevent the left from gaining access to the municipal council.

The Bilancia had little to offer against the DC record, and it could not even campaign on its role as an opposition. It held one electoral meeting which it followed up with a letter to all family heads. The Bilancia proposed to become "the new governing class," and "promised a democratic, honest and dynamic administration," to establish "civic committees for every street, . . . to provide an administration sensitive to all problems," and to enlarge four communal roads. It was soon noted they served property belonging to Bardini's immediate family. The only hope for the opposition was to exploit the dissatisfaction that reigned in the village over the town plan, but the Bilancia could not use the argument with any vigor as it had endorsed the plan a year before.

Zibordi had little difficulty in deriding the Bilancia's program. His promises of 1964 had been maintained and his colleagues had no ambition to become the "governing class." He did not intend to request the paving of the road leading to his farm. He maintained that the DC was there to serve. More sources of financial support would be sought and assured by a DC success in the provincial and regional elections. The young people would be constantly associated in decision-making to insure the future of Santa Maria. Zibordi headed a list that contained four persons in their twenties. The party had behind it strength in parliament and in government: it requested a vote of confidence.

To insure a resounding victory, a few tricks were pulled. The Bilancia had not respected electoral spaces when putting up the manifestoes. As a result after a few days of campaigning the mayor ordered they be taken down, creating a considerable loss of face for the Bilancia. On Sunday, May 31, the Bilancia was obliged to delay its electoral meeting, the mayor having scheduled a "brief" ceremony for the heroes of World War I. On the same day Don Arturo, convalescing in the hospital, had a letter distributed to all villagers in which he stressed that contrary to the rumor espoused by some (i.e., the Bilancia) "it was false [that in early May] he had discussed politics on the main square at 2 a.m." Taken seriously ill, only now could he confidently say he would be back among his flock ready to devote "his energy and the remaining days of his life to the well-being of the parish." Exhorting his flock "to set aside all feelings of hatred, rancor and division" the priest "request[ed] that all faithfully accomplish their duty. Do not abstain. Do not vote blank. Do not betray your civic sense. You have always loved God, Country and Family. I am sure that under these circumstances you will be wise."

On June 8 the extent of Zibordi's triumph became evident; the Bilancia was defeated 641 to 252, the DC list carried 65 percent of the total vote. One problem remained: uncertain of victory the DC supporters had not split their votes to insure the election of their "preferred" opponents, but now found it difficult to stomach the third and fourth men on the Bilancia preferential list. It was soon pointed out informally to these candidates they were ineligible, the first because of his condemnation for fascist activities, the second because he was a felon. They both withdrew leaving room for the fifth candidate, who was far more congenial to Zibordi.

In Santa Maria the electorate was interested in good administration bringing material benefits rather than in politics. With an intimate knowledge of the candidates there existed few problems in selecting the more appropriate ones, as a survey of the preferential votes cast for the individuals on the two lists indicates (DC 243, Bilancia 109). Over 10 percent of the electorate used this possibility to indicate its desires in an election where the DC had recommended not to split the vote. Personalities turned out to be far more important than programs, and the latter had little or no ideological content: Zibordi towered above Bardini and it was recognized that to govern the mayor needed authority over the council.

The most disturbing aspect of electoral campaigns was the intervention of the clergy in the selection of candidates and the pressure it exercised, indirectly or directly, upon the electorate. In this rural,

Catholic and conservative society where the DC as a party is nonexistent outside of the parish, it is normal (though deplorable) for the priest to play such a role, particularly when his tenure has been long and successful. With an increased political conscience among the electorate one might anticipate, at best, a decline in blatant interventionism.

In 1970, four men under twenty-five were elected to the council: two schoolteachers, one draughtsman, and one horticulturist. The young people who had received education beyond the primary degree had organized and, though their aim was not political in origin, they had managed to insure their representation in municipal politics. Rather than join a weak opposition they entered the DC to provide internal opposition perpetuating the rule of a near one-party system. However, for the first time outside the direct control of the parish, an associational group had provided a structure for an orderly renewal of the elites.

In a small and relatively united community the alternation of government and opposition in the democratic tradition as called for by the Bilancia is almost impossible. The size of the unit, the homogeneity of the community, the scarcity of elites cannot support it. In the present framework, internal opposition is the only possibility and its efficacy depends on the quality of the educational system. Since 1970 the majority in the municipal council of Santa Maria is no longer silently unanimous: the mayor must bargain with the young men who have been able to play a role in the decision-making process. This, however, produces serious tensions and calls for flexibility on the part of the mayor; a flexibility which is not always evident and might, unfortunately, discourage those who are genuinely working for what they perceive to be the future well-being of their community.

Only the left can offer a challenge, but it is a challenge that remains symbolic. In national elections it has been able to increase its share of the local electorate from 11 percent in 1948 to 18 percent in 1972, but in local elections its representation in council has remained dependent upon the absence of an independent or noncommunist list. Even under these more favorable circumstances it garnered only 18 percent of the vote in 1951 and 15 percent in 1960. The left has never been able to field a list of twelve candidates and those lists it does present contain only one or two Mariani, apparently the instruments of outside leaders. At election time the PCI is hardly visible. In 1970, the three candidates it ran (only one was a Mariano), received 7 percent of the votes. Only one speaker from Padua gave a speech, unaccompanied by the very men whose names were on the list, never referring to the local political situation but addressing only the issue of the failure of the center-left.

In terms of electoral returns in Santa Maria the PCI can serve as a release for frustration. It has no hopes and makes no pretense of winning. Correctly assessing the situation, the left seeks to sensitize the population to broader political issues and then to engage them in a dialogue, which is no easy task. During our sojourn only once did we see and hear a communist propaganda car in the village calling the people to demonstrate against the situation in the stone quarries. The PCI accepts its isolation and avoids projecting an image of fanatical militancy. What impact it may have is on the Marian workers employed in the factories of Fantolon, Battaglia and Padua. In the village there is little hope for a dialogue: the parish priest is uncompromising and the young chaplain who might have accepted the challenge has been removed. Santa Maria retains the image of a united community where exclusive values are shared, where personalities and not ideologies are the subjects of discussion, where national politics carry only little weight.

Decision-making

The formal political and administrative bodies in the village involved in decision-making are the *giunta* led by the mayor, the municipal council where he is the *primus inter pares*, and the municipal secretary. Do these bodies effectively play the role they are assigned? Which other elements enter the decision-making process? At bottom, who effectively wields power in the community?

In 1969 we asked twenty-five villagers to name the most influential persons in Santa Maria. The following profile emerged:

1. Don Arturo Ferlini: archpriest; in the community since 1937.
2. Dario Zibordi: elected mayor in 1964; professor of legal medicine.
3. Gilberto Bettola: head of *Coltivatori Diretti; assessore anziano* of the *giunta*.

4. Bruno Beghin: restaurant owner; assessor for public works; member of the *giunta*.

5. Angio Testoni: vice-mayor, head of Catholic Action; resident of Padua since 1965.

6. Pasquale Raminella: municipal secretary.

7. Sergio Fortuna: town clerk since 1943; DC recruiter.

8. Ferro Fortuna: broker, member of the town council 1919-1923.

These may be considered the men of power in the village, who, in varying degrees are its policymakers,[8] though other elements may well come into the process.

Four people are connected directly with the Church: the priest, Don Arturo; Bettola, a member of Catholic Action and leader of the *Coltivatori Diretti*; Testoni, the head of Catholic Action; Sergio Fortuna, the town clerk whose brother is part-time chaplain in the village. Four men are members of the municipal council, and three of these also constitute the *giunta*. They are also connected with the Church: Bettola and Testoni lead Church-sponsored organizations; Zibordi and Bruno Beghin were selected by the parish to run for municipal office. Two on the list hold administrative positions: the municipal secretary and the town clerk. Only one person, Ferro, the broker, is not associated with the town hall or the church. In brief, the five most influential people are tied in one way or another to Don Arturo. The opposition is not represented among those who we anticipate will play leading roles in the decision-making process.

We will examine three types of decisions we had occasion to witness in 1968 and 1969. Some were uncontroversial and the formal decision-making bodies participated in full. Others, where agreement on principle but disagreement on the means of implementation were visible, led to a combination of formal and informal mechanisms of decision-making. A few, where disagreements were strong, bear witness to the importance of informal decision-making channels and the role of influential actors in averting the development of acute conflicts and crisis situations.

General Agreement

Fascism exploited the Italian custom of giving presents to children on the Epiphany. Tradition holds that an old and ugly woman, the

Befana, delivers the toys. In poverty-stricken Santa Maria the Befana Fascista was an occasion for great rejoicing when Baratella distributed toys, food and clothing to the population. In 1965 Zibordi, seeking to emulate his ever popular predecessor, revived the tradition using the local name of Striga for the old witch. To provide more excitement she travelled each year by different means: an ox-driven cart, a truck, an antique stagecoach, a helicopter. In 1969 the choice had been set on a team of mules, an alternative that appealed little to the mayor who was to lead them, and who felt that too many inferences might be drawn. The Sunday preceding the feast I suggested that a camel, inhabitant of a near-by zoo, would create a greater effect and the idea was adopted enthusiastically by the mayor. A flurry of phone calls secured the services of the animal. The following Wednesday Zibordi informed the *giunta* of his decision and no objections were raised. It was properly assumed that the mayor would cover all expenses incurred by the change of plans. The impact of the camel's arrival was considerable; unfortunately the animal threatened to charge when the municipal band struck up and it was brought to a stop with the mayor desperately hanging around its neck. In a brief speech the mayor reviewed the accomplishments of his administration and was heartily applauded while national television covered the festivities. A decision made on the spur of the moment, contrary to all previous plans, met with everyone's approval. There was no controversy, and all expenses were paid by the mayor, who obtained excellent publicity for his initiative. The Striga was pronounced his personal accomplishment, though the municipality bore the major expense of purchasing the toys.

In March, Antonio Tiberto, a member of the town council, requested a license to open the first souvenir store in Santa Maria. Sergio, the town clerk, informed him that his chances were slim because an application had already been filed by Don Remo, the chaplain and Sergio's brother. When the mayor, at Antonio's behest, inquired into the matter, the falsity of the clerk's assertion was revealed. The Commission of Artisans, delegated by the council, speedily granted the permit to Antonio. In June the situation was rendered more complex when Antonio asked for authorization to sell wine in his store; a similar request from an outsider, Gianni Rossi, had been turned down at the March meeting of the commission. This body, after long discussion, now took a middle course, granting Antonio a permit to sell bottled wine only, from whatever origin, while Rossi, the outsider, was allowed to sell only wines he produced locally. The object was to avoid damaging the barowners' trade, which Antonio would have damaged had he sold wine by the glass. The decision also appeared not to discriminate against Rossi, yet it limited his activities because he could produce very limited quantities of wine on his property. Since there were no good reasons to deny the permits, the commission acted wisely and independently without offending or favoring anyone too visibly. There were few doubts that Antonio would obtain a permit because he was one of the mayor's closest confidants; Rossi, who was on poor terms with the mayor, was certain to have a bad time.

The Commission of Artisans had other uses, notably in the case of Tagliazucchi, the butcher, who sold meat of such poor quality that some claimed it was unfit for their dogs. When an outsider applied for a butcher's license Tagliazucchi was informed it would be granted, though the village could hardly support two butcher shops, unless the quality of his meat improved. When it did, the outsider's request was rejected. Everyone agreed that local commerce had to be protected against competition.

A third example of an easily reached decision is the choosing of individuals to sit on the tax commission. At the mayor's suggestion the *giunta* nominates a candidate who is unanimously endorsed by the municipal council. Raising taxes is an unenviable privilege, but all agree that turning down a unanimous offer would entail considerable loss of face for the individual selected.

In these minor cases, where no financial expenditure is involved, decisions are reached easily and unanimously. There is no need to consult with the parish or the influentials in the village on routine matters. The situation is different when local funds are involved.

Partial Agreement

When the mayor and the *giunta*, at the suggestion of the town planners, agreed that a parking lot had become a necessity to accommodate the influx of tourists, two options were considered. If cars could park on a piece of land belonging to Tommaso Begossi, all traffic would be diverted from the village square; however, the location of the parking lot on a slope would necessitate considerable expenditure for masonry work. The mayor had approached Tommaso, who was willing to sell provided the council granted him the right to open a gas station nearby. The total cost for the project was estimated at the not insubstantial figure of twenty million lire ($32,000), to be financed by a long-term loan. The second alternative called for cars to cross the main square. Costs were estimated at ten million lire but there was no assurance the owner would sell his land. In private the *giunta* agreed the second alternative was the best, but agreed to push the first in public so the second owner would not become too greedy. It was also necessary to avoid offending Tommaso because preliminary negotiations had already begun. A founding member of the Bilancia group, he was also an excellent source of information on the opposition's plans.

In council the mayor presented the issue as "a matter of life or death for the village." The lot was necessary to attract more tourists and to protect the village's image of peace and tranquility from traffic jams, the noise of motors and their harmful fumes. "How could a tourist enjoy walking through the narrow streets while constantly dodging cars?" Bruno Beghin, the assessor for public works, indicated that Tommaso (who was present among the public) was willing to sell his property. The Bilancia, with Bardini as its spokesman, recognized the need for a parking lot, but subscribed to the view it would only benefit tourists and that the money could be more wisely spent paving the rural roads used by the peasants going to work in their fields. Zibordi then proposed a vote on the principle of the parking lot, while the *giunta* would be delegated the task of seeking appropriate means to purchase the necessary property. The motion was adopted unanimously. Bardini had recognized the need for a parking lot and did not wish to antagonize his friend on whose land it was to be located. Accepting the mayor's proposal meant the opposition also surrendered the ultimate disposition to the *giunta*.

In January 1970 the *giunta* purchased for seven million lire ($11,300) the piece of land that always had been its first choice. The owner was convinced to sell on the assurance that he would receive a coveted building permit to modernize his house. The opposition was never informed about what went on and, since the less costly solution was adopted, the decision was unassailable. Bardini, to whom it had been inferred that Tommaso was betraying the Bilancia's secrets, was not saddened to see him lose out. Tommaso was placated by a permit to build a gas station on another piece of land he owned and his earth-moving company was given the contract to level the ground for the parking lot. The location of the facility was less than optimal but the people had little reason to object because the costs were half the original estimate. The role of the mayor, the source of the initiative, was critical. He obtained a parking lot without offending Tommaso and at the same time the municipal council was maneuvered into giving him a free hand. All the negotiations took place on an *ad hoc* basis, between the mayor and the concerned parties.

The same session of the municipal council, the second of four held in 1969, also dealt with the question of the football field. The opposition took the initiative, proposing the enlargement and reseeding of the existing field, so that professional pre-season games could be held there to provide additional income for the community. The young people wanted a glamorous field "appropriate to the beauty of the community," and the Bilancia wanted to get their votes. Tommaso had informed the mayor of the proposal beforehand and the *giunta* adopted a tactic it felt would be beneficial to the DC. The mayor recognized and welcomed the initiative of the opposition. He immediately continued and noted, leaving little time for Bardini to develop his arguments, that the majority had always sided with the young people, which was patently false because the mayor had refused to visit or support the Circolo di Lettura. He had no doubts the necessary funds could be located through the DC for such a worthy task. Bardini proposed that the young people be put in charge of the task, and suggested his brother would be an excellent candidate. The council led by Zibordi approved. The mayor then pointed out that a permit from the Fine Arts commission in Venice would be necessary before any work could be started, because enlarging the field involved cutting into a calcareous hill that bordered it on one side. Sensing the difficulty, Bardini proposed the project be undertaken *alla chetichella*, in secret. The council did not take sides and the proposal was not written down in the minutes. Informally the mayor agreed Bardini's brother would take the responsibility for enlarging the field. The young worked diligently and in six weeks all was ready. The initiative was the Bilancia's but the DC received benefits without sharing the risks. Thanks to its informants it had anticipated the move and prepared itself accordingly, forcing the Bilancia to assume the responsibility of violating the law. The mayor, by his role in council, increased his prestige, appeared as a compromiser, maneuvered the show and defused the opposition's initiative.

These two cases appear anecdotal, but in small communities minor decisions are important. They point out the mere formalism of the discussions in the municipal council. Decisions are reached beforehand by the mayor and the *giunta*. The minority attempts to play a role but is constantly out-maneuvered by the skillful tactics or the duplicity of the mayor. When no fundamental opposition on principles is involved, and the population at large is not interested, the municipal council serves as a rubber stamp for the *giunta* and the mayor. Sessions are formally opened in the name of the Republic and democracy is practiced to the degree that the opposition is recognized, but the majority, led by Zibordi, conducts the meetings at its will.

Opposition

In reality the opposition's view is expressed by the people or by a few influential citizens but not by the representatives of the Bilancia. This fact is demonstrated by what is known in Santa Maria as the *crisi edilizia*, the building crisis. Because it is closely connected to the elaboration of the town plan, we will consider the planning controversy first and Zibordi's ordinance on building second.

In 1968 Professor Zibordi commissioned a Paduan architect to prepare a town plan. In spite of the expense involved ($5,000), the issue was decided by the *giunta*. Such a plan was not legally required and a zoning scheme, far less costly and rigid, would have sufficed. In support of his idea the mayor invoked several overriding considerations. Among them was the fact that the physical integrity of the village was protected by a series of laws that made it a national monument where no changes could be brought without the assent of the Commission of Fine Arts in Venice. Consequently, a town plan would involve no more limitations than the existing ones while providing guidelines for an orderly expansion of the village and the preservation of its integrity. Maintaining the medieval character of Santa

Maria would attract more tourists and make it the main contender for the administrative seat of a national park to be established in the Euganean region. Preservation and planning were the only ways to attain these aims. Not mentioned was the fact that Zibordi's Santa Maria would be the first community of its size in the province to have a town plan and a reputation for foresight.

The planners set to their task with energy and enthusiasm. All the buildings were surveyed in considerable detail, a history of the physical development of the community was gathered, a demographic study and the projected expansion for the next thirty years elaborated, all family heads were questioned as to their needs and the physical condition of their dwellings was assessed. In the plan two desires had to be reconciled: preservation and expansion.

In January 1969 the planners met with the *ad hoc* town planning commission, where the minority was represented, to discuss the preliminary outlines of the plan. The critical issues were the size of the green zone where no further building would be allowed, the location of the zone of expansion in the hills rather than in the plains, and the building of a new road to direct the traffic flow to parking lots by-passing the center of town. The arguments justifying the size of the green zone were overriding. Much of the village's charm comes from its trees and open spaces. Channeling cars to strategic points would allow more people to wander in the village in peace, while the cost of the road would be borne by the province. Critical in the planners' view was the zone of expansion. The village's location in a conch precluded building in the plains because the new houses would either dissimulate or overshadow the main core of medieval buildings. Developing the zone on the hills would insure that the abundant trees would provide a cover for the houses that were not to exceed two stories. In response to the commissioner's objections the planners agreed to set aside a second expansion zone to the west of the village, near the modern school building, where popular housing in the form of three-story apartment buildings would be located.

The same day the planners paid a courtesy call on the parish priest, who had collaborated in gathering material for the plan, to discuss their tentative plans. Again the main criticism concerned the location of the expansion zone. Unfortunately, not enough attention was paid to these remarks. The planners felt supported by the town commissioners and had assurance from the mayor that expropriation could and would be used if necessary to create the zone of expansion. Another meeting was held in February with the planning commission to report on the minimal changes that had been made to the plan. The commissioners and the mayor agreed wholeheartedly to the plan.

On March 5, 1969, Zibordi officially presented the plan to the council and the public in attendance. He backed its recommendations, stating his conviction it would be advantageous for the community whose needs the planners had well understood. The plan respected the law but allowed for orderly expansion. The mayor concluded he was certain all would appreciate and support the initiative of the Christian Democratic administration. Bardini, in his response, stressed that administrators had to serve the people and not dictate their own desires. One had to see the local needs "with one's heart in hand" and not only in function of the law. "The village is beautiful but the inhabitants need toilets and the plan must make room for them. . . . The villagers wish to live more comfortably and must be able to improve the inside of their houses." After having been reassured there would be no restraints on building toilets inside the houses, that even volumes could be modified if proportions were respected, Bardini endorsed the general lines of the plan and commended its architects. Council adopted the plan unanimously and made it available to the public. Very soon criticisms started flowing, though none had been expressed by the public at the council meeting.

The first and most violent objections came from those whose property had been included in the green zone. This was land on which they could no longer build. Soon the population at large started grumbling, noting that building in the hills was more expensive than in the plains (which was true), that they would not be allowed to follow their tastes (which was partially true), and that the plan was more restrictive than the existing laws (which was false). Only a handful took the trouble to check the plan in the town hall.

At this same time the mayor was in the midst of the building crisis. Rather than confront the opposition on both issues, Zibordi decided to shelve the plan and allow tempers to cool. In June 1970 he was re-elected and by then most thought the plan was dead. After discussing the issue with Don Arturo, and without informing the council, which probably would have applauded his decision, the mayor shelved the plan indefinitely.

The planners, who envisaged their work as a model of what could be done to preserve medieval communities, pointed out that once a plan had been approved by the council the mayor was bound by law to present it to the provincial authorities for review or to request a modification. The mayor suggested the people would prefer a zoning scheme rather than a town plan and that he was consulting with various architects to elaborate such a scheme. All communication had broken down and the Fine Arts commission in Venice, influenced by the planners, let it be known it would not issue any building permits for Santa Maria until the plan was submitted for review.

In June of 1973, in what can be termed a *compromesso italico*, the mayor and the municipal council bowed to the pressure of the State and, according to law, requested the planners modify the original plan. They indicated that the expansion zone had to be in the plains. The architects agreed and were assured of being entrusted with particularized plans that would consider every building in the community. The revised document preserved the major core of medieval buildings; the modifications suggested corresponded to the desires of a majority of the population.

In summary, once again, the Bilancia which originally had opposed the idea of a plan was led, with the entire council, to accept the mayor's initiative. However, when opposition developed among the people who were tacitly supported by the parish, the mayor, seeking re-election, was forced to gain time and shelve the plan. In a case where the people felt directly affected they were able to influence the decision-making process. Even after the major decision had been made they had it reversed. The State, through the Commission of Fine Arts and prodded by the planners, forced the issue. The resulting compromise met with the approval of everyone concerned. Had the planners been more attentive to the needs of the people and less enthralled with ideal criteria much time could have been saved. This, however, is only one facet of the question because tensions were created by the concurrent building crisis.

On November 4, 1968, during the celebrations of the fiftieth anniversary of the armistice of World War I, the town planner noticed the ungainly structure of a house which seemed to have originated above the main square overnight. A check of the records in the town hall revealed that blueprints had never been submitted to the building commission, that the drawings available in the town hall called for two floors while the structure had already reached four, and that the Fine Arts commission had never authorized the building. Yet, the town hall had granted a building permit. The mayor immediately issued an injunction ordering all building activity on the house to stop and the carabinieri were requested to enforce it pending an inquiry.

On November 7, the municipal council voted the following order of the day:

> The council notes the existence of building laws. It asserts its intention to enforce them, and delegates full powers to the mayor for such purpose. The council also requests the mayor solicit the Commission on Fine Arts to act with greater speed on projects submitted for its opinion. The council has appointed a new building commission that will include the town planner and a representative of the Commission on Fine Arts.

Within a week, following a series of telephone calls by the mayor and the assessor for public works, the building of a large containment wall and a battery of dog kennels was stopped. In both cases the projects had been initiated by outsiders.

On the eighteenth the newly appointed building commission refused to endorse the plans for a house proposed by Umberto Merlo. It had good reason. The house had already been built, and without the required permit. However, the house was completed, Merlo was popular and had invested all his savings in it, and, above all, he had been encouraged by Don Arturo to build the house and sneak the project through the commission. Zibordi's furor knew no limits. After visiting the priest, he wrote and signed a municipal ordinance on building activities. It declared:

> Any kind of work, including painting, reconstruction, partial destruction, the building of walls large or small, sanctuaries, etc., can be undertaken only after approval of the local building commission and the Commission of Fine Arts in Venice. THE LAW ADMITS NO EXCEPTIONS OR COMPROMISES.

The entire tradition of easy-going administration was about to collapse. The mayor appeared willing to challenge the people and they were ready to respond. Very soon rumors circulated that a demonstration against the mayor was being organized. The Bilancia declared the ordinance deprived the individual of his basic freedom of choice and that Zibordi was acting like a dictator. The DC majority which had not been consulted was far from united. Neither Bruno Beghin nor Antonio Tiberto could understand the mayor's position and considered the forthcoming elections already lost. Don Arturo suggested that one should let bygones be bygones and that only new buildings should be built in scrupulous adherence to the law. Zibordi threatened to resign.

On November 22 the mayor, Bruno and Don Arturo met secretly at the Fontanella restaurant. The mayor was confronted with a united front requesting a compromise on the Merlo house. Its destruction would mean popular revolt and defeat at the elections. Don Arturo knew his man too well to believe Zibordi would resign. On the twenty-third an attempt was made to burn the town hall. The fire was quickly contained and only the front door was damaged. The priest omitted reading the municipal ordinance from the pulpit, the normal channel for important news, though he had assured Zibordi he would do so on three different occasions. The rumored demonstration against the mayor became reality. It was said that up to seventy heads of families were ready to march on the town hall, radio Venice announced the date, and the Christian Democratic vice-mayor let his workers off early so they could join the parade to be led by Danilo Brigato, the major alcoholic-politician of the village. The mayor braced for it, decorated his office with the Italian flag, and kept his ceremonial sash on hand. The parish realized that a large confrontation would destroy the mayor's credibility, and Don Remo, the chaplain, who was rumored to possess magic powers, mentioned that the demonstrators would be cursed if they protested. Bruno, always prudent, asked the carabinieri to be available at short notice. On the thirtieth the mayor was met by eight protestors led by Danilo and five carabinieri! A majority of the people had realized the law had to be enforced in the case of blatant violations and that Don Arturo had not taken a position against the mayor. That evening, the majority convened for dinner at the rectory: the forces of evil had been defeated but Don Arturo still had no formal agreement on a compromise over the Merlo house.

Pressured by the priest and by the younger members of the council, notably Antonio Tiberto for the DC and Ugo Masiero for the Bilancia, the mayor agreed the following week to discuss his views on the building crisis with whoever cared to attend. The *giunta*, and even the mayor who was starting to have doubts as to his re-election if he did not side with Don Arturo, agreed that a face-saving compromise on the Merlo house was necessary. It was suggested that Merlo submit new plans that reflected the present state of his house and that approval would be sought for them from the Fine Arts commission in Venice; if small modifications of the facade were requested they would be taken care of; if major modifications were required they might be overlooked. For three hours the mayor then talked to the eighteen people who had come to the meeting. He defended the local building commission and pointed out that having a representative of Venice sit on it insured a speedier approval of projects; the unfortunate delays were due to the paralysis of the bureaucracy: where Zibordi and Santa Maria needed two weeks, Venice, it seemed, needed fifteen months. The mayor practically drowned the people with his oratory, before providing them with bottled wine, holding the stage for two hours until the drunken Danilo stumbled in declaring that ordinance or not he was going to build an outhouse. Zibordi finally stated that all would be done to interpret the law as humanely and generously as possible (Danilo's toilet did receive a building permit later). Bruno echoed the mayor, declaring that no building suits had been brought in Santa Maria, and that he was confident none would be. Merlo's house would remain, the other house was destroyed, the law from now on would be respected.

The opposition in council, while it disagreed totally with the mayor, had little occasion to influence events. Reason and the parish forced a compromise that favored the villager over the outsider. The compromise allowed the mayor to declare he would strictly enforce the building laws in the future. The people accepted the fact that the law had to be enforced, that it was a reality to which even the mayor had to submit, that it could not be disregarded, avoided or bent. Seeking re-election Zibordi had little choice but to compromise to be assured of Don Arturo's support.

"The more unequally the community is divided, the less likely are open political struggles to be the major expression of a clash of interest and the more likely is decision-making to be the prerogative of a cozy few."[9] In Santa Maria the *giunta* functions at best as an advisory body to the mayor who often fails to consult with its members. The council is dominated by the majority and is strongly influenced by the mayor who is the only one to have a university education. Informal channels of decision-making are far more important than formal ones, while the interplay between the two varies as a function of the intensity with which the issues are felt. In the case of basically nonconflict situations, most groups can share the decision-making process if they so desire. This was the case of the artisans' commission granting licenses, of individuals offering constructive criticism during the elaboration of the town plan, of the Bilancia when the decision was made to enlarge the football field. When serious conflicts arise, and minor incidents can be magnified out of proportion in a small community, few regulatory mechanisms are available in the local governmental structure. When an issue is divisive, however, the council majority, while it has the means to impose its decision, is in fact reluctant to do so. Its members are connected with most of the families in the village and are seldom ready to face unpopular decisions, unlike an outsider such as the mayor. Informal channels of communication lead to compromises that attenuate the original council decisions. A community of Santa Maria's size can ill afford radical divisions: politics are pragmatic, not ideological. The observation that in poor and uneducated communities "the proportion of visible leaders found in the leadership structure is low"[10] is confirmed. The priest and the mayor dominate the political and social situation, devoting a considerable part of their time to local events, often taking on aspects of full-time politicians. They make few distinctions between their official role and their other roles, which leaves considerable room for extra-official considerations to play in their decisions and amplifies their range of action.[11] The mayor and the priest are controllers and opinion leaders.[12] Although the reputational scale identified eight people of influence, in reality only two play a decisive role in the political process.

Santa Maria is a society in transition, which under political and economic pressures is rejecting the values of the society that characterized its life for generations. It has entered the twentieth century.

Changes in the political structure are the least visible. Yet, it is no longer possible to consider the structure of power to be exclusively pyramidal, dominated by the rectory acting through the mayoralty. Aspects of polylithism[13] are coming to the fore. Forces of leadership, distinct from the parish priest and the mayor, are evident among the younger townspeople who have succeeded through the Circolo di Lettura in organizing an emerging opposition, which for tactical reasons has chosen to fight its battle for power within the ranks of the majority. Following the failure of the Bilancia in 1964 the opposition has challenged the establishment in the only realistic way available in a small community, that is, from the inside. The young look with anticipation to the future and are convinced that power should not be exclusive but shared, associational rather than pyramidal. The monolithic pyramidal system culminating in the priest's veto can survive under the challenges of the mayoralty and the opposition only as long as the present occupant of the parish seat remains.

Undoubtedly, the political forces in power belong to the conservative Christian Democratic strand of thought and action. United in support of the national party, they remain divided with regard to local options and values. The "religious groups" centering around the rectory, the farmers union and Catholic Action that presently hold power see the Church and the local community as their essential frame of reference. The "lay groups" attached to the mayor and the Circolo di Lettura envisage the community in terms of its integration in the regional and national context. The future of the religious orientation is predicated on the maintenance of bonds of patronage and religious links between priest and individuals that are progressively weakening. The lay group seeks integration into the broader community, which will enhance the local power and control. However, the two groups and the community, with its customs and particular social relations, are hardly inclined to accept ideological deviants, or, more simply, those who do not believe that the village is a united community. Only moderate challenges are acceptable and radical change is rejected.

The left represents the only direct challenger. Although visible in terms of electoral returns, it has little direct political effect at the local level. However, the PCI, while viewed negatively and thus ostracized, is no longer denounced in the manner of the late forties and fifties. In the Veneto it is the only party to effectively challenge the DC, and its activity in the factories does not go unnoticed by the Marian peasant-worker.

The Church hardly favors change in Santa Maria. While preaching against materialism, the Church has done little to discourage its manifestations and provides as much financial as spiritual counsel. At the national level the physical well-being of Catholics is now emphasized. Neutral to democracy, which its overall structures and attitudes do not foster, the Church has desisted, nationally and locally, from negating its values. The political role it was forced to play in the wake of the war is now de-emphasized, providing more leeway for local autonomy. Finally, and more importantly, its new personnel —such as Don Lorenzo, the one-time chaplain of Santa Maria —espouses a different set of values that encourages change without slighting the Church's interest in the spiritual well-being of its members.

The economic developments of the sixties have led to the political and social transformation of the community just as they did in the 1920s. While the redistribution of property brought population expansion and kept the people on the farms, the Italian economic miracle and the adoption of a market economy did exactly the contrary. Emigration turned out to be a blessing in disguise. Limited resources could not support an expanding population and caused frustration, jealousies and conflict. The halving of the local labor force together with an increase in real purchasing power has led to a decline in tension.

A new social structure has been grafted on the divisions of old. The traditional peasant and his value system are in the process of disappearing. He has been replaced by peasant-workers or by a few farmers who own and rent property, sell choice products and are not content with a mediocre standard of living. The peasant-workers combine the limited security of small property ownership with the relative prosperity of factory wages. When the younger generations mature they will have to choose between factory and farm. Their attachment to the community may well lead them to become commuters rather than emigrants and some will eventually join the new class of entrepreneurs appearing in Santa Maria, especially in the tourist trade. These new groups have higher aspirations than their forefathers, aspirations supported by greater education.

The center left governments, among their few achievements, have made eight years of compulsory schooling a reality in Santa Maria. Parents, no longer attached to the farm, can afford to help their children through school and have realized the opportunities that education can provide for their offspring. The young themselves have come to believe in and aspire to a life different from that of their fathers. With more education they are willing to accept more responsibilities, including political ones. The new generations, as witnessed by their participation in the Circolo di Lettura, are becoming increasingly socialized to political participation and no longer to apathy.

Mayors Fortuna and Zibordi have provided effective and dynamic leadership. They have learned how to work with the system in spite of its shortcomings. Above all they have learned to compromise and recognize not only the needs but also the desires of the people; Zibordi, in particular, has been forced to accept the input of the new elite.

Santa Maria, under the Italian Republic, has progressively become economically and politically integrated into a broader system, breaking away from the isolation and parochial views of its past. Political participation in an active form is becoming a reality for a larger share of the people. However, the villagers, if they anticipate and want change, believe it should not be at the cost of the unity of their community which remains their most treasured value, where the quality of life is not based exclusively on material rewards but on such intangibles as a sense of contentment and belonging.

Notes

Preface

1. Edward C. Banfield, *The Moral Basis of a Backward Society* (New York: The Free Press, 1958); Charlotte G. Chapman, *Milocca, a Sicilian Village* (Cambridge: Schenkman and Co., 1971); Ann Cornelisen, *Torregreca, Life, Death and Miracles* (Boston: Little and Brown, 1969); Johan Galtung, *Members of Two Worlds, A Development Study of Three Villages in Western Sicily* (New York: Columbia University Press, 1971); Francesco Kjellberg, *Political Institutionalization, A Political Study of Two Sardinian Communities* (New York: John Wiley and Sons, 1975); Feliks Gross, *Il Paese, Values and Social Change in an Italian Village* (New York: New York University Press, 1973); A. L. Maraspini, *The Study of an Italian Village* (Paris and The Hague: Mouton, 1968); Beldon Paulson and Athos Ricci, *The Searchers* (Chicago: Quadrangle Books, 1966).

2. Alessandro Pizzorno, "Amoral Familism and Historical Marginality," *International Review of Community Development* 15 (1966): 55.

3. John Clark Adams and Paolo Barile, *The Government of Republican Italy* (Boston: Houghton and Mifflin, 1972), Chapter 1.

4. Sabino S. Acquaviva, *Bozze del terzo capitolo del rapporto sulle aspirazioni delle categorie agricole nel Veneto* (Venice: IRSEV, 1966), pp. 3-7.

5. Enzo Bandelloni and Robert Evans, *Profilo di una comunità Euganea* (Padua: Marsilio, 1971).

Chapter 1

1. Several centuries ago the village was called Santa Maria Arquata, from the name of the major church. The villagers also argue that the name comes

from the arch of the church of the Holy Trinity; the arch is said to have been the only remnant standing after Attila plundered the village in 453. While the barbarian invasion is well documented (e.g., J. Salomonio, *Inscriptiones Agri Patavini* [Padua: Seminario, 1696], p. 150, and C. Cantù, *Grande Illustrazione del Lombardo Veneto* [Milan: Corona, 1859], vol. 4, p. 285), Santa Maria is not specifically mentioned in that context. Furthermore, the church dates from the twelfth century.

2. D. E. Burchardt, "The Urban Aesthetic," *Annals of the American Academy of Political and Social Science* 314 (November 1957) 113.

3. Ibid.

4. See Boccacio, Shelley, Byron, Chateaubriand, Foscolo, Faure, etc. The best essay on Petrarch in Santa Maria is by Adolfo Callegari, *Una visita a Santa Maria* (Padua: Antoniana, 1941). See also the brilliant E. H. Wilkins, *Petrarch's Later Years* (Cambridge: Medieval Academy of America, 1959).

5. Ugo Ojetti, *Diario* (Milan: Sansoni, 1964); entry of March 4, 1918.

6. Morris Bishop, *Petrarch and His World* (Bloomington: Indiana University Press, 1963), p. 360.

7. Byron, *Childe Harold's Pilgrimage*, canto 4, stanza 32.

8. Boccacio as quoted in Faure, *Wanderings in Italy* (London: Heinemann, n.d.), p. 225.

9. Franco Vani, in *Il Resto del Carlino*, January 25, 1959, p. 7.

10. Pietro Chevalier, *Una visita a Santa Maria* (Padua: Gamba, n.d. [1831]), p. 8.

11. A. Callegari, Letter to Minister of Culture, July 8, 1939, in Bibliotecca Comunale, Este.

12. Enzo Bandelloni and Robert Evans, *Profilo di una comunità Euganea* (Padua: Marsilio, 1971), pp. 54-58. In particular villa Contarini, casa Mentasti, casa Donà, villa Rova, Palazzo Strozzi, villa Callegari.

13. F. Cordenons, *Antichità preistoriche della regione Euganea* (Padua: Prosperini, 1888), pp. 67-99. Also A. Alfonsi, "Scoperte accidentali sulle rive del laghetto della Costa," in *Notizie degli Scavi*, Padua, Fasc. 10, pp. 353-56, and A. Callegari, *Una visita*, pp. 39-40.

14. Pliny the Elder, *Natural History,* 3, 24, 2.

15. "After the downfall of Troy . . . Antenore with a multitude of Eneti expelled from Paflagony for rebellion . . . came to the innermost reaches of the Adriatic Sea, and . . . caused the Euganeans who lived . . . (there) to flee . . . ," Livy, *History,* I, 1. See also Lucano, *Fars.*, 192. Silvio Italico, *Pun*. 8,603;12,216; Martial *Epigr.*, 4,25; 10, 93; 13, 89.

16. G. Brunnacci, *Storia Ecclesiastica Padovana*, Manuscript, Padua Municipal Library, 1755, pp. 185-86.

17. Cantù, *Grande illustrazione*, p. 289.

18. L. A. Muratori, *Delle antichità Estensi ed Italiane* (Modena: Stampa Ducale, 1717), vol. 1, p. 95. S. Orsato, *Historia di Padova* (Padua: Frambotto, 1678), vol. 3, part 1, pp. 229-30.

19. A. Simoni, *Storia di Padova* (Padua: Randi, 1968), p. 340. See also B.

Scardenone, *De Antiquitatis urbis Patavii* (Basle: Nicholas Episcopus, 1560), p. 325.

20. A. Gloria, *Il territorio Padovano illustrato* (Padua: Prosperini, 1865) vol. 3, p. 175.

21. "In such a way you will enhance the quality of this beautiful country and will double the fertility of the Hills, rich in the fruits of Minerva and Bacchus but denied those of Ceres by the stagnant waters." Quoted in *Il Bosco*, June 16-30, 1943, p. 3.

22. "Ad montum sponsi astra moventur, spondent pluvias, ventus incitant, turbant maria, aerea lugubria reddunt, ingurgitant gramina campi emolientur et madent undique aspera terra." *Varia* 3.

23. *Ordini per li Mag. li Sindici ala Sp. Vicaria di Santa Maria Arquata MDLXXXII*, Manuscript, Museum, Padua. *Ordini e regole per il buon governo della Vicaria e comuni di Santa Maria Arquata*, 1672, Museum, Padua.

24. Callegari, *Una visita*, p. 43.

25. Salomonio, *Inscriptiones*, p. 150.

26. A. Portenari, *Della felicità di Padova* (Padua: Tozzi, 1623), Book 2, Ch. 9, p. 75. Scardenone in *De Antiquitatis urbis Patavii* (1560) writes, "In iisdem Collibus non longe a Titulo est Arqadom, Collis apricus, et amonenus, atque cultissimus, vino dulcissimo abundans."

27. *Miscellanea*, busta 124, Archivio di Stato, Padua.

28. *Estimi*, 1418, Tomo 307, Archivio di Stato, Padua, pp. 52-248.

29. Callegari, *Una visita*, pp. 43-44 for basic information.

30. Salomonio, *Inscriptiones*, "Inscriptiones Vici Arquade," n. 43-44.

31. Callegari, *Una visita*, pp. 44-51; also Fernando Bologna, "Contributo allo studio della pittura Veneziana del Trecento," *Arte Veneta* 5 (1950), pp. 17-20.

32. *Visitationem Diocesis*, July 1747, vol. 79. Museum, Padua.

33. C. A. Cibotto, *Proverbi del Veneto* (Milan: Martello Editore, 1966), p. 59.

34. Callegari, *Rassegna Studi Francesi* (Bari, 1934), p. 214.

35. "The Agricultural Economy of the Italian Regions," in *Italy: Notes and Documents*, vol. 15, no. 3 (May-June 1966), p. 215 provides a very convenient summary.

36. Sabino S. Acquaviva, *Bozze del terzo capitolo del rapporto sulle aspirazioni delle categorie agricole nel Veneto* (Venice: IRSEV, 1966), p. 5.

37. Joseph La Palombara, "Italy: Isolation, Alienation, Fragmentation," in *Political Culture and Political Development* (Princeton: Princeton University Press, 1965), La Palombara and Weiner, eds.

38. Callegari, "Usi e costumi degli Euganei," *Atti*, IV Congresso Arti e Tradizione Popolare (Rome 1942).

39. Acquaviva, *Bozze del terzo capitolo*, pp. 1-34 and more particularly pp. 17-19.

40. Iginio Michieli, *I Colli Euganei, Vicende economiche e sociali* (Padua: Cooperativa Tipografica, 1965), p. 150.

41.

	Temperature Cent.	*Rainfall mm.*
Spring	11.6	161
Summer	20.9	217
Fall	12.8	194
Winter	3.1	222

L. Susmel and A. Famiglietti, *Condizioni ecologiche ed attitudini colturali dei colli Euganei* (Padua: Consorzio per la Valorizzazione dei Colli Euganei, 1965).

42. See *Illustrazione Italiana*, June 1874.

43. Callegari, unsigned letter to *Il Gazzettino*, October 6, 1947. Original letter at Bibliotecca Comunale, Este.

44. Real Deputazione Provinciale, Busta 68, Padua, Archivio dello Stato.

45. M. Savonarola, "Libellus de magnificis ornamentis regie civitatis Padue," in *Rerum Italicarum Scriptores* (Città di Castello: Lapi, 1902), vol. 25, part 21, p. 29.

46. Portenari, *Della felicità di Padova*, p. 75.

47. Various authors. "Un Comune Veneto," *Comunità*, no. 29 (February 1955), pp. 8-9.

48. *Seniles*, 12, 2.

49. *Una visita*, p. 39.

50. Ibid., p. 56.

51. *Il territorio Padovano*, p. 176.

52. G. L. Cerchiari, *Santa Maria Arquata* (Padua: Rongaudio, 1902), p. 12.

53. Ibid., p. 13-14.

54. This will be dealt with in more detail in chapter 4. Here we simply wish to point out some of the critical values of a peasant society which survive in the twentieth century and are connected with Santa Maria's past isolation. It seems to us there are some differences with the value systems of other Mediterranean societies. See Julian Pitt-Rivers in Peristiany, ed., *Honour and Shame, The Values of Mediterranean Society* (Chicago: University of Chicago Press, 1966), p. 44.

55. George M. Foster, "Peasant Society and the Image of Limited Good," *American Anthropologist* 67 (April 1965), p. 295.

56. F. Mascia, *La scuola e l'igiene nella educazione delle masse del XX secolo* (Padua: Seminario, 1914), p. 22.

57. Joseph Lopreato, *Peasants No More: Social Class and Social Change in an Underdeveloped Society* (San Francisco: Chandler Publishing Co., 1967).

Chapter 2

1. Some theoretical justification for this approach can be found in particular in S. M. Lipset and S. Rokkan, *Party Systems and Voter Alignments* (New

York: The Free Press, 1967), Introduction, pp. 1-65. See also: Gil Gunderson and Jack Goldsmith, "Introduction to Comparative Local Studies," *Comparative Local Politics* (New York: Holbrook Press, 1973), and Gabriel Almond, "Determinancy—Choice, Stability, Change: Some Thoughts on a Contemporary Polemic in Political Theory," *Government and Opposition*, vol. 5, no. 1 (Winter 1969-70), pp. 22-40.

2. *Santa Maria, Prima Porzión*, in *Miscellanea*, Archivio di Stato, Padua, 1789.

3. Ibid.

4. See Denis Mack Smith, *Italy. A Modern History* (Ann Arbor: University of Michigan Press, 1959), pp. 60-70.

5. Gabinetto Prefetto, Ufficio Politico, Busta 530. Archivio di Stato, Padua. Quoted as Gab.

6. Real Deputazione Provinciale, Busta 33, 79, Archivio di Stato, Padua. Quoted as RDP.

7. *Ultime lettere di Jacopo Ortis* (Milan: Mursia, 1965), pp. 29-31.

8. Prefect to Minister of Education, May 19, 1874.

9. Unsigned letter in *Il Gazzettino*, October 6, 1947. Original Manuscript in Biblioteca Municipale, Este.

10. RDP 68.

11. RDP 5. Ufficio Pubblica Sicurezza to Prefect.

12. RDP 15.

13. RDP 68, 88.

14. RDP 59.

15. RDP 68.

16. RDP 97, Letter, July 14, 1893.

17. RDP 218.

18. RDP 103.

19. Gab. 279, 461.

20. L. Cappelletti, "Local Government in Italy," *Public Administration*, vol. 41 (Fall 1963), pp. 247-64.

21. RDP 30, 15.

22. RDP 44.

23. RDP 65, 10.

24. RDP 15.

25. RDP 30.

26. RDP 15.

27. Ibid.

28. RDP 21.

29. RDP 345.

30. RDP 65.

31. Gab. 494.

32. RDP 337.

33. *Giornale di Padova*, May 5, 1874.

34. RDP 65, 732, 354.

35. *L'Adriatico*, March 16, 1908.

36. RDP 732, 801, 345.
37. Gab. 484.
38. See Enzo Bandelloni and Robert Evans, *Profilo di una comunità Euganea* (Padua: Marsilio, 1971), p. 50.
39. RDP 15.
40. RDP 948, Real Economato ai Benefici Vacanti to Prefect, September 18, 1884.
41. RDP 58.
42. *Miscellanea*, Archivio di Stato, Padua, 1789, Anagrafi, N. 39.
43. RDP 337, Commissario to Prefect, December 31, 1874.
44. Ibid.
45. RDP 63, Comizo Agrario Distrettuale, June 16, 1885.
46. RDP 15, Commissario to Prefect, September 30, 1873.
47. RDP 50, Commissario to Prefect, July 13, 1882.
48. RDP 65, November 11, 1882.
49. RDP 95.
50. RDP 44, July 1, 1880.
51. RDP 50, Commissario to Prefect, July 20, 1882.
52. RDP 79.
53. RDP 83, December 22, 1891.
54. RDP 1104.
55. RDP 15, December 31, 1874.
56. RDP 17, 70.
57. F. Mascia, *La scuola e l'igiene nella educazione delle masse del XX secolo*, (Padua: Seminario, 1914), p. 12.
58. RDP 63, 65, 354.
59. RDP 44, 65.
60. RDP 524.
61. Bandelloni and Evans, *Profilo di una comunità Euganea*, p. 82, and RDP 15, 59, 748, 1097, 30.
62. RDP 748.
63. RDP 1097, 30.
64. RDP 95.
65. RDP 47.
66. Gab. 473.
67. Gab., Ufficio Politico, 311, 328, 366, 453, 454.
68. Gab. 328.
69. G. Mira and L. Salvatorelli, *Storia d'Italia nel periodo fascista* (Turin: Einaudi, 1964), p. 150-56.
70. Interview with the children of Mrs. Diani, Signora Margherita and Professore Giulio.
71. Mira and Salvatorelli, *Storia d' Italia,* p. 215.
72. Gab. 282, June 23, 1923.
73. Ibid., Carabinieri to Prefect, August 19, 1922.
74. Gab. 282, June 23, 1923.
75. Ibid., Report of Commissario to Prefect, July 18, 1923.

76. Gab. 311, Baratella to Prefect, April 24, 1926.
77. Gab. 311, April 21, 1926.
78. Gab. 282, Baratella to Prefect, December 1926.
79. Ibid.
80. RDP 948.
81. RDP 984, Real Eceonomato ai Benefici Vacanti, November 8, 1884.
82. RDP 70, Commissario to Prefect, August 1, 1887.
83. RDP 24, 30.
84. RDP 95, April 1, 1893. For a summary of the movement in the Province, see Letterio Briguglio, "Gli internazionalisti di Monselice e di Padova," *Movimento Operaio*, vol. 7, no. 5 (1955), pp. 728-60.
85. Today they form a good part of the communist electorate in Santa Maria. They live on the fringes of the village society; religious borders separate them from the influence of the parish priest in Santa Maria, their own parish being Qualto; administrative borders make them Mariani, and their vote carries weight there.
86. RDP 103.
87. RDP 209, Carabinieri to Prefect, April 3, 1909.
88. Ibid.
89. Ibid., Carabinieri to Prefect, November 19, 1911.
90. RDP 206.
91. RDP 209.
92. Ibid.
93. Gab. 304, Carabinieri to Prefect, June 13, 1925.
94. Ibid.
95. Gab. 311, September 15, 1925.
96. Gab. 292.
97. Gab. March 26, 1929.
98. Gab. 311, July 2, 1926.
99. Gab. 364, July 28, 1931.
100. Gab. 364.
101. Gab. 369.
102. Gab. 375, 364.
103. Gab. 323.
104. Gab. 375.
105. Gab. 409, Podestà, March 15, 1932.
106. Gab. 457, Prefect to Minister of Interior, January 26, 1934.
107. Gab. 455.
108. Gab. 473.
109. Gab. 492.
110. Gab. 536, January 17, 1940.
111. Gab. 531, 494.
112. Gab. 530.
113. Gab. 672.
114. The material that follows is taken from the municipal archives.

115. Lia Miotti, "La Resistenza nel Veneto," *Civitàs*, vol. 16, no. 12 (December 1965).

116. G. E. Fantelli, *La Resistenza dei Cattolici nel Padovano* (Padua: FIVL, 1965), pp. 63 and 228.

117. February 7, 1946.

118. June 10, 1946.

119. December 11, 1946.

120. Mattei Dogan, "Le donne italiane tra il cattolicesimo e il marxismo," in La Palombara, ed., *Elezioni e comportamento politico in Italia* (Milan: Comunità, 1963), pp. 475-94.

Chapter 3

1. G. Marcuzzi and A. Camuffo, "Prima applicazione della teoria dell'informazione allo studio dell'ecologia umana," *Rivista di Biologia* 61:5 (April-September 1968), pp. 293-313. This article applies directly to the area of the Euganean Hills.

2. Unless otherwise specified, all figures dealing with population movements are from the town hall records. Figures for 1969 were collected and elaborated by the author.

3. Remnants of the medieval *curtis*, the *corte* is a grouping of several households which originally led a life separate from the village. For a similar situation in Latium see Felix Gross *Il Paese* (New York: New York University Press, 1973), p. 35.

4. This is supported by a consideration of absolute variations, absolute annual averages and annual indexes of population variations for the periods 1952-1961, 1959-1968, 1966-1969. The natural and social balance annual index is, respectively, −1.99, −0.90, +0.10. The critical element is the social balance (emigration and immigration), the annual index of which increased as follows: −3.19, −2.00, −1.03. For methods of calculation see Umberto Frank and Antonio Matteazzi, *Previsioni di popolazione e dimensionamento delle zone insediative nei programmi di fabbricazione*, Amministrazione Provinciale di Padova, mimeographed, no date (1968).

5. For a similar situation see Laurence Wylie, *Chanzeaux, A Village in Anjou* (Cambridge: Harvard University Press, 1966), p. 139.

6. Various Authors. "Un Comune Veneto," *Comunità*, no. 29 (February 1955), p. 10.

7. *Age index by groups and years*

	0–6	*6–14*	*14–65*	*Over 65*	*Age Index*
1951	332	432	1,591	189	24.74
1961	209	369	1,350	197	34.08
1969	238	276	1,276	203	39.49

8. L. Cerchiari, *Santa Maria* (Padua: Rongaudio, 1902), p. 15.
9. Wylie coined this felicitous term; see *Chanzeaux*, p. 157.
10. See note 7.
11. George M. Foster, "Peasant Society and the Image of Limited Good," *American Anthropologist* 67 (April 1965), pp. 295-97. Emphasis in the text.
12. In a context which includes but goes beyond the Italian situation see John Duncan Powell, "Peasant Societies and Clientelistic Policies," *American Political Science Review* 64 (June 1970), pp. 411-25.
13. "Agricultural Economy of the Italian Regions," *Italy: Notes and Documents* 15, no. 3 (May-June, 1966), p. 215.
14. F. Petrarch, *Seniles* 12, 10 and 15, 5 in "Briefwechsel des Cola di Rienzo" Piur Bardach, *Von Mittelalter zur Reformation*, vol. 2, Berlin, 1928, pp. 356-58. Quoted in *Il Bosco*, June 16-30, 1943, p. 3. See also A. Malmignati, *Petrarca a Padova e Venezia* (Padua, 1874), pp. 91-96.
15. See Iginio Michieli, *I Colli Euganei*, *Vicende economiche e sociali* (Padua: Cooperativa Tipografica, 1965), p. 110. Average prices at constant value per 1000 kgs.

	Cereals	*Corn*	*Wine*	*Grapes*
1937–39	6,910	4,900	6,290	2,570
1960–62	6,690	4,250	7,820	5,260

16. Ibid., pp. 153, 296, 301, and unofficial data of the agricultural census of 1970. The total area under cultivation has declined from 1,200 hectares in 1930 to 892 in 1970.
17. Real Scuola di Agricoltura di Brusegana, *Annuario* (Padua: Penanda, 1890), p. 154.
18. Vini delimitati di qualità superiore–origine controllata. Decree of the President of the Republic, August 13, 1969, in *Gazzetta Officiale,* November 6, 1969, no. 281.
19. Michieli, *I Colli Euganei*, pp. 77 and 288-90, for figures prior to 1969; unofficial data provided by the municipality for 1970.
20. D. Agostini, *Sintesi delle principali caratteristiche e prospettive di sviluppo del settore agricolo nel comprensorio dei Colli Euganei* (Padua: Consorzio, 1967), p. 7. Also for what follows.
21. *Corriere della Sera*, October 27, 1968.
22. Data based on information collected by the author; also Tables 3.4, 3.18, 3.20.
23. Sabino S. Acquaviva, *Bozze del terzo capitolo del rapporto delle aspirazioni delle categorie agricole nel Veneto* (Venice, IRSEV, 1966), pp. 31 and following.
24. Michieli, *I Colli Euganei*, p. 128-29.
25. Ibid., p. 153.
26. See, in another context, Theron A. Nuñez, "Tourism, Tradition and Acculturation: Weekendismo in a Mexican Village," *Ethnology*, vol. 2, no. 3 (July, 1963), p. 348.

27. E. Calvino, *Le Cave dei Colli Euganei* (Padua: Consorzio, 1967), n.p.
28. *Gazzettino*, August 9, 1969; August 28, 1968; *L'Espresso*, November 3, 1968; *Corriere della Sera*, December 7, 1968; *Resto del Carlino*, November 17, December 12, 1966, February 6, 1967.
29. *Gazzetino*, November 25, 1971.
30. The local employment office states that in 1969, 18 percent of available manpower was unemployed. These figures should be considered with caution since a large number of young people ages 15 to 18 work, yet are declared unemployed so parents can collect social security benefits.
31. L. Malfi, *Situazione e prospettive del settore industriale* (Padua: Consorzio, 1966).

Chapter 4

1. These groups affect the political leanings of the citizen indirectly. We deal with the Church, certain peer groups, parties and unions, groups which seek to influence political beliefs in a more direct manner, in Chapter 5, where political participation is considered.
2. In preparation for the town plan, the municipality examined housing conditions in Santa Maria. The focus of the study was on density, hygienic, static, heating and overall conditions of the buildings, as well as the degree of satisfaction the inhabitants expressed in their residences. Questionnaires were filled out on the occasion of the yearly paschal visit by the parish priest and his chaplain. Eighty-nine percent of the parish dwellings were thus covered, equivalent to 75 percent of the total population. A higher percentage could not be obtained because of discrepancies between the religious and administrative boundaries. This explains the small over-representation of the village versus the periphery (2.92 percent).
3. In 1952 only 7 percent of all houses had an indoor bathroom. "Un Comune Veneto," *Comunità*, no. 29 (February 1955), p. 18.
4. Figures for 1951, 1961 and 1969 are derived from town hall records. For 1967 see Corrado Barberis and Camera di Commercio, Padua, *Famiglie coltivatrici e attività non-agricole* (Rome: DeLuca, n.d. [1970]), p. 43.
5. For a similar situation in the Veronese, see Giorgio M. Manzini, "Tradizione e innovazione in alcune forme di religiosità della famiglia rurale Veronese," *Sociologia Religiosa*, no. 9-10 (1963), pp. 86-101.
6. "Un Comune Veneto," p. 18.
7. Gallatin Anderson, "Il Comparaggio: The Italian God-Parent Complex," *Southwestern Journal of Anthropology*, 13:32-33 (1957), p. 46. The financial aspects of godparenthood are far more emphasized in the South. See A. L. Maraspini, *The Study of an Italian Village* (Paris and The Hague: Mouton, 1968), pp. 200-03.
8. *A gamba sopra*: little girls form a circle and must continuously go around on one leg. If they rest their leader hits them three times on the back. See

Arrigo Balladoro, "Giuochi infantili Veronesi," *Folklore Italiano*, vol. 4, no. 2 (1928), pp. 209-16. *Salta caselotto* and *pin decca* are traditional games of Venice (where they are called *pali marzi* and *massa e pandolo*). In the first the players divide into two groups: the first forms a line perpendicular to a wall with the first boy leaning against it so as to form a long "horse." The other team jumps on the horse. The aim is to get all the team on the horse. If it collapses it has to start again. If it withstands the assault the two teams change places. In *pin decca* two teams score points by hitting a small piece of wood with a stick as far as possible and guessing how many steps away the piece of wood lands. Opponents try to stop the missile as quickly as possible. If they catch it in mid-air the thrower is eliminated. See D. G. Bernoni, *Giuochi e indovinelli popolari Veneziani* (Venice: Filippi, 1968), pp. 98 and 106.

9. Adolfo Callegari, "Usi e costumi degli Euganei," *Atti,* IV Congresso Arti e Tradizione Popolare (Rome, 1942), p. 245. Also Dino Durante, Jr. *La Ciarastela* (Battaglia Terme, n.d. [1968]).

10. Julian Pitt-Rivers: "Honour and Social Status" in J. G. Peristiany, ed., *Honour and Shame, the Values of Mediterranean Society* (Chicago: University of Chicago Press, 1966), p. 73.

11. F. Mascia, *La scuola e l' igiene nella educazione delle masse del XX secolo* (Padua: Seminario, 1914).

12. The older men to whom we talked seldom mentioned that they had greatly missed their village during the years of military service, or that their time in the army constituted a great sacrifice for them. The opposite is true of southerners. See Maraspini, *Study of an Italian Village*, pp. 195-96.

13. Callegari, "Usi e costumi," p. 242.

14. Pietro Chevalier, *Una visita a Santa Maria* (Padua: Gamba, n.d. [1831], p. 56.

15. L. Cerchiari, *Santa Maria* (Padua: Rongaudio, 1902), p. 14.

16. See Callegari, "Usi e constumi," p. 244; "Un comune Veneto" p. 18; and Cleto Corrain, "Constumanze nuziali Venete," *Rivista di Etnologia*, 1964, pp. 252-64. While virginity is recognized as important from a religious point of view, in Santa Maria in particular, but also in other areas of the Veneto, social norms do not attach so much importance to it as in the South; see, for example, Maraspini, *Study of an Italian Village*, p. 153. We found no evidence in Santa Maria of the particular relation that would exist between first cousins in the South (ibid., p. 149) where "a certain amount of sexual experimenting is known to take place, and is accepted as normal."

17. However this might be due to the fact that hospitalization calls for better record keeping.

18. In 1971 the first civil wedding was performed in the town hall of Santa Maria between two outsiders: while the old people criticized, the young approved.

19. Contrary to the customs of the South, brothers do not await the marriage of their sisters before they themselves marry.

20. The regulations on building new houses in Santa Maria run counter to the desires and newly discovered financial capabilities of the young couples

and cause frustration. Many of the younger generation appear, in words at least, opposed to the present local administration, which is seen as responsible for the enforcement of the building regulations. In reality it is not.

21. See Callegari, "Usi e costumi." For an example that I believe could have been characteristic of Santa Maria prior to 1960, see Donald S. Pitkin, "Marital Property Considerations Among Peasants: An Italian Example," *Anthropological Quarterly* 33:1 (1960), pp. 36-39.

22. This represents an increase of 14 over 1951; however the age index increased from 24.74 to 39.49 (age index = $\frac{P>65}{O>P>14} \times 100$). These figures and those that follow are based on our 1969 inquiry.

23. R. Caggese, *Classi e comuni rurali nel Medioevo Italiano* (Florence: Galileiana, 1907), p. 177.

24. L. Wylie refers to the "brouillés" in Peyrane (*Village in the Vaucluse* [Cambridge: Harvard University Press, 1957], pp. 196-205). The effect in Santa Maria is probably stronger as feuds are taken up by extended families.

25. E. Banfield, *The Moral Basis of a Backward Society* (New York: The Free Press, 1958).

26. An indication of the decline in family ties are the *martoriani*, the weasels. These are past emigrants who return for the holidays. Villagers declare that like weasels they deplete the chicken coop, the stick on which salami are hung and the wine cellar. The *martoriani* believe the family ties of the past are still valid and expect room and board. While no villager who wishes to maintain his reputation would refuse to give hospitality, there is nevertheless a sharp resentment of these exploiters, even if they are cousins or brothers.

27. Richard E. Dawson and Kenneth Prewitt, *Political Socialization* (Boston: Little, Brown, 1969), p. 145. Gabriel Almond and Sidney Verba, *The Civic Culture* (Boston: Little, Brown, 1965), pp. 315-24.

28. Mascia, *La scuola*, p. 18.

29. Figures for 1951 and 1961 are from town hall records. We gathered those for 1969. This applies to the tables that follow (n.a = not available). We considered as illiterate those who could not sign their name and semi-illiterate those who could but had not finished elementary school.

30. The right to education for eight years is recognized by the 1948 Italian Constitution, art. 34. However, the new intermediate school (middle school) that makes this provision truly effective was only promulgated in 1962. Before that, a majority of children stopped their schooling experience at the end of the five elementary grades.

31. We will deal with the Church as an agent of socialization in Chapter 5.

32. Mascia, p. 18. See *Letters to a Teacher* by the Schoolboys of Barbiana (New York: Random House, 1970).

33. Ibid., p. 3.

34. The situation is different in the cities where, in 1974, over 95 percent of the candidates to the *maturità* were promoted. In this case automatic promotion would appear to be the rule.

35. The symbol of children born in well-to-do families. See *Letters to a Teacher*, p. 34.

36. See Wylie, *Village in the Vaucluse*, p. 206, for a similar situation in France.

37. See Almond and Verba, *Civic Culture*, pp. 64-68.

38. Similar attitudes are noted in Banfield, *Moral Basis*, p. 41.

39. Maurice Duverger, *Political Parties* (New York: Wiley, 1957).

40. To some extent this may be due to the fact that though each bar has its own clientele, patrons make an effort to visit several establishments to maintain their visibility and status, to avoid divisions and to maintain their relative position with the various groups. It appears that clienteles divide in terms of status and geographical location, with political beliefs appearing as a very distant third. The bar Petrarca caters to white and blue collar workers of the lower square and tends to be opposition, that is, anti-DC in municipal politics; Al Guerriero caters to blue collar workers and farmers in the lower square but inclines more to the DC; Annibale on the upper square caters to the farmers and pensioners and is opposition; Piero also on the upper square has the younger clientele and is pro-administration. For a somewhat similar situation see John D. Photaidis, "The Position of the Coffee House in the Social Structure of the Greek Village," *Sociologia Ruralis*, 5:1, 1965.

41. See Feliks Gross, *Il Paese* (New York: New York University Press, 1973), p. x.

42. Slightly unclear (*in ciarina*), ahead (*avanti*), buttered up (*unto ben*), well done (*fatto*), full (*beu*), weighing forward (*pes'avanti*), putrefied (*putrefatto*), rotten (*marcio*), only bones (*despolpà*). Only the last three categories are considered reprehensible. In a different context see John J. Honigmann, "Dynamics of Drinking in an Austrian Village," *Ethnology*, 2:2 (1963), pp. 157-69.

43. *Seniles*, 22, 2.

44. In cooperation with the local physician we considered the entire population. We classified as nondrinkers those who had a glass or two of wine with meals; normal drinkers those who consumed less than a liter and a half a day; heavy drinkers those who drank more; alcoholics those on whom the physical effects of drinking were visible. We classified a general sample of 1,201 people over age 17, and a particular sample of 889 who were gainfully employed or retired. Figures quoted come from the latter group.

Chapter 5

1. See Richard E. Dawson and Kenneth Prewitt, *Political Socialization* (Boston: Little, Brown, 1969), pp. 3-15 in particular.

2. Silvano Burgalassi, "Metodologia statistica per indagine di pratica religiosa," *Orientamenti Sociali*, vol. 10 (August 15-30, 1954), pp. 332-35. The index $K^1 = 0.0167 \times \quad P^2$ equal to the sum of the squares of the elements. $K^1 = 0.0167. (Dm^2 + Pm^2 + Du^2 + Pu^2 + d^2 + I^1)$, with Dm =

attendance at Sunday Mass; Pm = Easter communion; Du = Sunday Mass, men; Pu = Easter communion, men; d = devout Catholics; $I^1 = 100 - I$, with I = Total obligated population – separated from Church – (Sunday Mass attendance + Easter communion)/2. The differences in population sizes between parish and *comune* is 10 percent: the profile of the parish accentuates the religious practice of the *comune* by no more than 5 percent, according to Don Arturo. The two hundred Mariani who do not belong to the parish are on the eastern side of the *comune*, particularly near Mandonego which lies outside the parish boundaries and which has always inclined to the left. The basic data were gathered through the parish and *Bollettino Diocesano, Annuario 1968* (Padua: Antoniana, 1969).

3. Emile Pin, "Les motivations des conduites religieuses et le passage d'une civilisation pré-technique à une civilisation technique," *Social Compass*, vol. 13, no. 1 (1966), pp. 25-27.

4. The effects of patronage in the form of letters of recommendation might well have become imaginary by 1969 when occasions for employment were abundant. It remains that *lettere di racommandazione* are part of the Italian way of life and in a village the priest is the major dispenser. Whatever good they might do is questionable, but none in Santa Maria would think of doing without them.

5. RDP 658, June 10, 1888.

6. Circolo di Lettura, *La Voce*, no. 2, (March 1969).

7. "Analisi del voto del 28 Aprile," *Tempi Moderni,* vol. 6, no. 13 (April 1963), p. 76, and *Gazzettino*, May 9, 1972.

8. The electoral body was divided into four major categories: left (as perceived in Santa Maria, i.e., including the PRI), DC, right and unknown. The first three categories were further divided between those definitely in a group and those probably belonging to either left, DC or right, depending upon whether informants were in complete agreement or were divided. The margin of error, compared to the 1968 election, is tolerable: the DC is over-represented by 3.57 percent, the left and the right under-represented by 4 percent and 3.1 percent. For a thorough survey of Italian electoral variables, see Samuel H. Barnes, "Italy: Religion and Class in Electoral Behavior," in Richard Rose, ed., *Electoral Behavior: A Comparative Handbook* (New York: The Free Press, 1974), pp. 171-226.

9. Giorgio Galli and Alfonso Prandi, *Patterns of Political Participation in Italy* (New Haven: Yale University Press, 1970).

Chapter 6

1. Alan Stern, "Political Legitimacy in Local Politics: The Italian Communist Party in the Northeast," in S. Tarrow and D. M. Blackmer, *Communism in Italy and France* (Princeton, Princeton University Press, 1976), p. 247.

2. Luigi Einaudi, "Via il Prefetto," *Gazzetta Ticinese*, July 17, 1944. Quoted in J. C. Adams and P. Barile, *The Government of Republican Italy*, 3rd ed. (Boston: Houghton Mifflin, 1972), p. 126.

3. Ibid., pp. 120-26. See also Luigi Cappelletti, "Local Government in Italy," *Public Administration* 41 (Fall 1963), 247-264.

4. Joseph La Palombara, *Interest Groups in Italian Politics* (Princeton: Princeton University Press, 1964).

5. See the case of France in Mark Kesselman, "Over-institutionalization and Political Constraints: the Case of France," APSA, 1969, notably pp. 17-19.

6. Alan Zuckerman, "On the Institutionalization of Political Clienteles: Party Factions and Cabinet Coalitions in Italy," APSA, 1973.

7. In October 1969 we asked twenty-five people chosen at random in Santa Maria to indicate and rank the ten people they thought to be the most important and influential in the village. Few were able to indicate more than six, but twenty-three out of twenty-five ranked the priest above the mayor. (The exceptions were the priest himself and the municipal secretary.)

8. See Floyd Hunter, *Community Power Structure, A Study of Decision Makers* (New York: Anchor Books, 1963), pp. 5-7.

9. Peter H. Rossi, "Power and Community Structure," in Lewis Coser, ed., *Political Sociology* (New York: Harper and Row, 1967), p. 140.

10. Charles M. Bonjean and Lewis F. Carter, "Legitimacy and Visibility: Leadership Structures Related to Four Community Systems." *Pacific Sociological Review*, 8: Spring 1965, p. 20.

11. See Rossi on this theme, "Power and Community Structure," p. 138.

12. Robert E. Agger and Daniel Goldrich, "Community Power Structures and Partisanship," *American Sociological Review* 23 (August 1958), p. 384.

13. Rossi, "Power and Community Structure," p. 143. Polylithism: "Separate power strucures definable for major spheres of community activity."

Selected Bibliography

Books

Adams, John Clark, and Barile, Paolo. *The Government of Republican Italy*. 3rd ed. Boston: Houghton Mifflin, 1972.

Agostini, D. *Sintesi delle principali caratteristiche e prospettive di sviluppo del settore agricolo nel comprensorio dei Colli Euganei*. Padua: Consorzio, 1967.

Almond, Gabriel, and Verba, Sidney. *The Civic Culture*. Boston: Little, Brown, 1965.

Bandelloni, Enzo, and Evans, Robert H. *Profilo di una comunità Euganea*. Padua: Marsilio, 1971.

Banfield, Edward. *The Moral Basis of a Backward Society*. New York: The Free Press, 1958.

Barberis, Corrado, and Camera di Commercio, Padua. *Famiglie coltivatrici e attività non-agricole*. Rome: DeLuca, n.d. [1970].

Barnes, Samuel H. "Italy: Religion and Class in Electoral Behavior." In *Electoral Behavior: A Comparative Handbook,* edited by Richard Rose. New York: The Free Press, 1974.

Bernoni, D. G. *Giuochi e indovinelli popolari veneziani*. Venice: Filippi, 1968.

Bishop, Morris. *Petrarch and His World*. Bloomington: Indiana University Press, 1963.

Bollettino Diocesano, Annuario 1968. Padua: Antoniana, 1969.

Caggese, R. *Classi e comuni rurali nel Medioevo Italiano*. Florence: Galileiana, 1907.

Callegari, Adolfo. *Una visita a Santa Maria*. Padua: Antoniana, 1941.

Calvino, F. *Le cave dei Colli Euganei*. Padua: Consorzio, 1967.

Cantù, C. *Grande illustrazione del Lombardo Veneto*. Vol. 4. Milan: Corona, 1859.

Cerchiari, G. L. *Santa Maria*. Padua: Rongaudio, 1902.

Chevalier, Pietro. *Una visita a Santa Maria*. Padua: Gamba, n.d. [1831].

Cibotto, C. A. *Proverbi del Veneto*. Milan: Martello Editore, 1966.
Codice di Santa Maria. Padua: Zenon, 1810.
Cordenons, F. *Antichità preistoriche della regione Euganea*. Padua: Prosperini, 1888.
Coser, Lewis, ed. *Political Sociology*. New York: Harper and Row, 1967.
Dawson, Richard E., and Prewitt, Kenneth. *Political Socialization*. Boston: Little, Brown, 1969.
Dogan, Mattei. "Le donne italiane tra il cattolicesimo e il marxismo." In *Elezioni e comportamento politico in Italia*, edited by Joseph La Palombara. Milan: Comunità, 1963.
Durante, Dino, Jr. *La Ciarastela*. Battaglia Terme, n.d. [1968].
Duverger, Maurice. *Political Parties*. New York: Wiley, 1957.
Fantelli, G. E. *La Resistenza dei Cattolici nel Padovano*. Padua: FIVL, 1965.
Faure, Gabriel M. *Wanderings in Italy*. London: Heinemann, n.d. [1920?].
Foscolo, Ugo. *Ultime lettere di Jacopo Ortis*. Milan: Mursia, 1965.
Frank, Umberto, and Matteazzi, Antonio. *Previsioni di popolazione e dimensionamento delle zone insediative nei programmi di fabbricazione*. Mimeographed. Amministrazione Provinciale di Padova, n.d. [1968].
Galli, Giorgio, and Prandi, Alfonso. *Patterns of Political Participation in Italy*. New Haven: Yale University Press, 1970.
Gloria, A. *Il Territorio Padovano illustrato*. Vol. 3. Padua: Prosperini, 1865.
Gross, Feliks. *Il Paese, Values and Social Change in an Italian Village*. New York: New York University Press, 1973.
Gunderson, Gil, and Goldsmith, Jack. *Comparative Local Politics*. New York: Holbrook Press, 1973.
Kjellberg, Francesco. *Political Institutionalization*. New York: John Wiley, 1975.
La Palombara, Joseph. *Interest Groups in Italian Politics*. Princeton: Princeton University Press, 1964.
__________. "Italy: Isolation, Alienation, Fragmentation." In *Political Culture and Political Development,* edited by La Palombara and Weiner. Princeton: Princeton University Press, 1965.
Lipset, S. M. and Rokkan, S. *Party Systems and Voter Alignments*. New York: The Free Press, 1967.
Lopreato, Joseph. *Peasants No More: Social Class and Social Change in an Underdeveloped Society*. San Francisco: Chandler Publishing Company, 1967.
Mack Smith, Denis. *Italy: A Modern History*. Ann Arbor: University of Michigan Press, 1959.

Malfi, L. *Situazione e prospettive del settore industriale*. Padua: Consorzio, 1966.

Malmignati, A. *Petrarca a Padova e Venezia*. Padua: 1874.

Maraspini, A. L. *The Study of an Italian Village*. Paris and The Hague: Mouton, 1968.

Mascia, F. *La scuola e l'igiene nella educazione delle masse del XX secolo*. Padua: Seminario, 1914.

Michieli, Iginio. *I Colli Euganei, Vicende economiche e sociali*. Padua: Cooperative Tipografica, 1965.

Mira, G., and Salvatorelli, L. *Storia d'Italia nel periodo fascista*. Turin: Einaudi, 1964.

Mommsen, T. *Inscriptiones Galliae Cisalpinae Latinae (Corpus Inscriptionum Latinarum)*. Vol. 5, Part 1. Rome: Berolini, 1872.

Muratori, L. A. *Della antichità Estensi ed Italiane*. Vol. 1. Modena: Stampa Ducale, 1717.

Ojetti, Ugo. *Diario*. Milan: Sansoni, 1964.

Orsato, S. *Historia di Padova*. Padua: Frambotto, 1678.

Pitt-Rivers, Julian. "Honour and Social Status." In *Honour and Shame, the Values of Mediterranean Society*, edited by J. G. Peristiany. Chicago: University of Chicago Press, 1966.

Portenari, A. *Della felicità di Padova*. Book 2. Padua: Tozzi, 1623.

Real Scuola di Agricoltura di Brusegana. *Annuario*. Padua: Penanda, 1860.

Salomonio, J. *Inscriptiones Agri Patavini*. Padua: Seminario, 1696.

Savonarola, M. "Libellus de magnificis ornamentis regie civitatis Padue." In *Rerum Italicarum Scriptores*, edited by L. A. Muratori. Vol. 25, Part 12. Città di Castello: Lapi, 1902.

Scardenone, B. *De Antiquitatis urbis Patavii*. Basle: Nicolas Episcopus, 1560.

Schoolboys of Barbiana. *Letters to a Teacher*. New York: Random House, 1970.

Simoni, A. *Storia di Padova*. Padua: Randi, 1968.

Stern, Alan. "Political Legitimacy in Local Politics: The Italian Communist Party in the Northeast." In *Communism in Italy and France,* edited by S. Tarrow and D. M. Blackmer. Princeton: Princeton University Press, 1976.

Susmel, L., and Famiglietti, A. *Condizioni ecologiche ed attitudini colturali dei Colli Euganei*. Padua: Consorzio per la Valorizzazione dei Colli Euganei, 1965.

Tommaseo, N. *Bellezza e civiltà, o delle arte del bello sensibile*. Florence: Le Monnier, 1857.

Wilkins, Ernest H. *Petrarch's Later Years*. Cambridge: Medieval Academy of America, 1959.

Wylie, Laurence. *Chanzeaux, A Village in Anjou*. Cambridge: Harvard University Press, 1966.

_________ . *Village in the Vaucluse*. Cambridge: Harvard University Press, 1957.

Zanotto, Sandro, ed. *Proverbi Pavani*. Milan: Scheiwiler, 1967.

Articles

Agger, Robert E., and Goldrich, Daniel. "Community Power Structures and Partisanship." *American Sociological Review* 23 (August 1958).

"The Agricultural Economy of the Italian Regions." *Italy: Notes and Documents* 15, no. 3 (May-June 1966).

Alfonsi, A. "Scoperte accidentali sulle rive del laghetto della Costa." *Notizie degli Scavi*. Padua, Fasc. 10 (1906).

Almond, Gabriel. "Determinancy-Choice, Stability, Change: Some Thoughts on a Contemporary Polemic in Political Theory." *Government and Opposition* 5, no. 1 (Winter 1969-70).

"Analisi del voto del 28 Aprile." *Tempi Moderni* 6, no. 13 (April 1963).

Anderson, Gallatin. "Il Comparaggio: The Italian God-Parent Complex." *Southwestern Journal of Anthropology* 13 (1957), pp. 32-33.

Balladoro, Arrigo. "Giuochi infantili veronesi." *Folklore Italino* 3, no. 2 (1928).

Bologna, Fernando. "Contributo allo studio della pittura Veneziana del trecento." *Arte Veneta*, vol. 5, fasc. 17-20 (1951).

Bonjean, Charles, and Carter, Lewis. "Legitimacy and Visibility: Leadership Structures Related to Four Community Systems." *Pacific Sociological Review* 8 (Spring 1965).

Briguglio, Letterio. "Gli internazionalisti di Monselice e di Padova." *Movimento Operaio* 7, no. 5 (1955).

Burchardt, D. E. "The Urban Aesthetic." *Annals of the American Academy of Political and Social Science*, vol. 314 (November 1957).

Burgalassi, Silvano. "Metodologia statisticia per indagine di pratica religiosa." *Orientamenti Sociali*, vol. 10 (August 1954).

Callegari, Adolfo. "Santa Maria." *Rassegna Studi Francesi*. Bari, 1934.

_________ . "Usi e costumi degli Euganei." *Atti,* IV Congresso Arti e Tradizione Popolare, vol. 1. Rome, 1942.

Cappelletti, Luigi. "Local Government in Italy." *Public Administration* 41 (Fall 1963).

"Un Comune Veneto." *Comunità*, no. 29 (February 1955).

Corrain, Cleto. "Costumanze nuziale venete." *Rivista di Etnologia,* 1964.

_________ . "Leggende delle macchie lunari." *Sociologia Religiosa*, vol. 2 (1958).

Foster, George M. "Peasant Society and the Image of Limited Good." *American Anthropologist* 67 (April 1965).

"Gli Euganei nelle testimonianze classiche." *Studi Trentini di Scienze Storiche*, vol. 35, Fasc. 1-2 (1955).

Honigmann, John J. "Dynamics of Drinking in an Austrian Village." *Ethnology* 2, no. 2 (1963).

Manzini, Giorgio M. "Tradizione e innovazione in alcune forme di religiosità della famiglia rurale Veronese." *Sociologia Religiosa*, no. 9-10 (1963).

Marcuzzi, G., and Camuffo, A. "Prima applicazione della teoria dell'informazione allo studio dell'ecologia umana." *Rivista di Biologia* 61, no. 5 (April-September 1968).

Miotti, Lia. "La Resistenza nel Veneto." *Civitàs* 16, no. 12 (1965).

Nuñez, Theron A. "Tourism, Tradition and Acculturation: Weekendismo in a Mexican Village." *Ethnology* 2, no. 3 (July 1963).

Photiadis, John D. "The Position of the Coffee House in the Social Structure of the Greek Village." *Sociologia Ruralis* 5, no. 1 (1965)

Pin, Emile. "Les motivations des conduites religieuses et le passage d'une civilisation pré-technique à une civilisation technique." *Social Compass* 13, no. 1 (1966).

Pitkin, Donald S. "Marital Property Considerations Among Peasants: An Italian Example." *Anthropological Quarterly* 33, no. 1 (1960).

Pizzorno, Alessandro. "Amoral Familism and Historical Marginality." *International Review of Community Development* 15 (1966).

Powell, John Duncan. "Peasant Societies and Clientelistic Policies." *American Political Science Review* 64 (June 1970).

"Santa Maria." *Nuova Illustrazione Italiana*, vol. 1-2 (1874).

Newspapers

For the period 1945 onward we consulted *Il Gazzettino* (Venice) and *Il Resto del Carlino* (Bologna), which have special editions covering the Euganean Region, as well as *Corriere della Sera* (Milan) and the weekly *L'Espresso* (Rome).

Unpublished Material

Unless otherwise indicated this material is available at the Archivio di Stato in Padua.

Acquaviva, Sabino S. *Bozze del terzo capitolo del rapporto sulle aspirazioni delle categorie agricole nel Veneto*. Venice: IRSEV, 1966.
Archivio Municipale. 1945-1972.
Brunacci, G. *Storia Ecclesiastica Padovana*. Manuscript, Padua Municipal Library. 1755.
Estimi, 1418, vol. 307.
Gabinetto Prefetto, Ufficio Politico, 1922-1944. These yearly files have not yet been classified.
Kesselman, Mark. "Over-institutionalization and Political Constraint: the Case of France." APSA, 1969.
Miscellanea, 1789.
Miscellanea, Busta 124.
Ordini per li Mag. li Sindici ala Sp. Vicaria e Comune di Santa Maria, 1672.
Reale Deputazione Provinciale, 1871-1913. The files are maintained by year but not classified beyond 1881.
Visitationem Diocesis, vol. 79 (July 1747). Padua: Museum.
Zuckerman, Alan. "On the Institutionalization of Political Clienteles: Party Factions and Cabinet Coalitions in Italy." APSA, 1973.

Index